MIGRANT DOMESTIC WORKERS IN EUROPE

This book explores the often neglected, but overwhelmingly common, everyday vulnerability of those who support the smooth functioning of contemporary societies: paid domestic workers.

With a focus on the multiple disadvantages these – often migrant – workers face when working and living in Europe, the book investigates the role of law in producing, reinforcing – or, alternatively, attenuating – vulnerability to exploitation. It departs from approaches that focus on extreme abuse such as 'modern' slavery or trafficking, to consider the much more widespread day-to-day vulnerabilities created at the intersection of different legal regimes. The book, therefore, examines issues such as low wages, unregulated working time, dismissals and the impact of migration status on enforcing rights at work.

The complex legal regimes regulating migrant domestic labour in Europe include migration and labour law sources at different levels: international, national and, as this book demonstrates, also EU. With an innovative lens that combines national, comparative, and multilevel analysis, this book opens up space for transformative legal change for migrant domestic workers in Europe and beyond.

Migrant Domestic Workers in Europe

Law and the Construction of Vulnerability

Vera Pavlou

·HART·
OXFORD · LONDON · NEW YORK · NEW DELHI · SYDNEY

HART PUBLISHING

Bloomsbury Publishing Plc

Kemp House, Chawley Park, Cumnor Hill, Oxford, OX2 9PH, UK

1385 Broadway, New York, NY 10018, USA

29 Earlsfort Terrace, Dublin 2, Ireland

HART PUBLISHING, the Hart/Stag logo, BLOOMSBURY and the Diana logo are trademarks of Bloomsbury Publishing Plc

First published in Great Britain 2021

First published in hardback, 2021

Paperback edition, 2023

Copyright © Vera Pavlou, 2021

Vera Pavlou has asserted her right under the Copyright, Designs and Patents Act 1988 to be identified as Author of this work.

All rights reserved. No part of this publication may be reproduced or transmitted in any form or by any means, electronic or mechanical, including photocopying, recording, or any information storage or retrieval system, without prior permission in writing from the publishers.

While every care has been taken to ensure the accuracy of this work, no responsibility for loss or damage occasioned to any person acting or refraining from action as a result of any statement in it can be accepted by the authors, editors or publishers.

All UK Government legislation and other public sector information used in the work is Crown Copyright ©. All House of Lords and House of Commons information used in the work is Parliamentary Copyright ©. This information is reused under the terms of the Open Government Licence v3.0 (http://www.nationalarchives.gov.uk/doc/open-government-licence/version/3) except where otherwise stated.

All Eur-lex material used in the work is © European Union, http://eur-lex.europa.eu/, 1998–2023.

A catalogue record for this book is available from the British Library.

Library of Congress Cataloging-in-Publication data

Names: Pavlou, Vera, author.

Title: Migrant domestic workers in Europe : law and the construction of vulnerability / Vera Pavlou.

Description: Oxford, UK ; New York, NY : Hart Publishing, 2021. | Based on author's thesis (doctoral - European University Institute, 2016) issued under title: Migrant domestic workers in the European Union : the role of law in constructing vulnerability. | Includes bibliographical references and index.

Identifiers: LCCN 2021035357 (print) | LCCN 2021035358 (ebook) | ISBN 9781509942374 (hardback) | ISBN 9781509942411 (paperback) | ISBN 9781509942398 (pdf) | ISBN 9781509942381 (Epub)

Subjects: LCSH: Household employees—Legal status, laws, etc.—European Union countries. | Foreign workers—Legal status, laws, etc.—European Union countries. | Migrant labor—Legal status, laws, etc.—European Union countries.

Classification: LCC KJE3192.H68 P38 2021 (print) | LCC KJE3192.H68 (ebook) | DDC 344.401/62—dc23

LC record available at https://lccn.loc.gov/2021035357

LC ebook record available at https://lccn.loc.gov/2021035358

ISBN:	PB:	978-1-50994-241-1
	ePDF:	978-1-50994-239-8
	ePub:	978-1-50994-238-1

Typeset by Compuscript Ltd, Shannon

To find out more about our authors and books visit www.hartpublishing.co.uk. Here you will find extracts, author information, details of forthcoming events and the option to sign up for our newsletters.

FOREWORD

This brilliant book breaks new ground by offering a multiscalar and comparative analysis of how intersecting and overlapping legal regimes regulating migration and labour in Cyprus, Spain, Sweden, and the UK both contribute to the exploitation of migrant domestic workers and provide spaces for resistance. In *Migrant Domestic Workers in Europe*, Vera Pavlou eschews the dominant framing of the exploitation of migrant domestic workers as a form of modern slavery and human trafficking that is best tackled by invoking transnational human rights, such as the prohibition against forced labour in Article 4 of the *European Convention of Human Rights*. While she acknowledges that extreme forms of abuse occur, she argues that the anti-slavery and human rights approaches, by focusing on egregious cases, tend to obscure potentially more transformative framings. For this reason, Vera Pavlou explores the capacity of labour law to address everyday, 'mundane' forms of exploitation, such as low wages, wage deductions, long hours of work and instant dismissals, created by the combined operation of migration law and labour law. Persuasively challenging the accepted wisdom that European Union (EU) labour law does not apply to domestic workers, *Migrant Domestic Workers in Europe* provides a sophisticated and lucid assessment of the extent to which the labour laws of the four countries match the level of protection stipulated in EU law. Drawing on attempts by different social actors in the four countries to represent the interests of migrant domestic workers and to advocate for legal and policy changes to reduce their vulnerability, Vera Pavlou illustrates the significance of the national regulatory and institutional contexts when it comes to devising a strategy that can begin to transform exploitative working conditions.

Engagingly written, *Migrant Domestic Workers in Europe* offers a fresh perspective on the constitutive and transformative potential of law when it comes to the exploitation of migrant domestic workers. Vera Pavlou deftly situates her contribution within the broader literature on migrant workers who cross national borders in order simultaneously to cater to the social reproductive needs of households in the Global North for domestic labour and to meet the need for remittances to sustain their households and communities in less developed countries, many of which are in the Global South. She is also sensitive to how domestic workers occupy a stigmatised social position shaped by an understanding of domestic work as 'merely' women's 'natural' work and, depending upon the specific context, by processes of racialisation and the legacies of colonialism and slavery. What this book offers is an account of how state law also constitutes migrant domestic workers' subordinate status.

A huge strength of Vera Pavlou's approach is her sensitivity to how the law is used by states to construct different structures and degrees of vulnerability to exploitation. She unpacks what it means to be a migrant domestic worker by comparing and juxtaposing national migration regimes, and, in doing so, she develops an extremely helpful four-fold typology of migration law regimes in Europe based on how they regulate the entry and stay conditions of migrant domestic workers. This typology clearly establishes that specific migration regimes construct different forms and degrees of migrant domestic workers' vulnerability to exploitation. By layering this typology on the labour law treatment of domestic workers in the four countries, Vera Pavlou demonstrates not only how law contributes to making migrant domestic workers vulnerable to exploitation, but also how it can be used to alleviate it. Her nuanced comparative analysis of different legal statuses created by EU migration law identifies the migration rules that particularly disadvantage migrant domestic workers.

This book offers practical strategies for challenging migrant domestic workers' vulnerability to exploitation that are sensitive to national contexts. Vera Pavlou treats the International Labour Organization's ground-breaking 2011 Domestic Workers Convention (C 189) as an inspiration for countries to reconsider their approach to regulating domestic work and as a model for such regulation, one which combines a sectoral approach to domestic work with the goal of providing equality of employment protection and rights for domestic workers. She provides a careful and thorough consideration of strategies that use national and EU laws to challenge legally constructed vulnerabilities. This contribution is both humble and inspiring; she does not pretend to know all the answers, yet she provides a framework for analysing how law creates vulnerabilities and examples of successful strategies of how to transform it. *Migrant Domestic Workers in Europe* exemplifies the benefits of rigorous comparative and multiscalar socio-legal analysis for understanding how law can both constitute and transform structures of vulnerability. It will inspire researchers and activists to continue to find ways to achieve decent work for migrant domestic workers.

Judy Fudge
LIUNA Enrico Henry Mancinelli Professor in Global Labour Issues
McMaster University

ACKNOWLEDGEMENTS

Completing this book has been made possible thanks to the support and encouragement of several people. I will always be grateful to Claire Kilpatrick for being such an inspiring, supportive and reliable mentor from the very beginning of my research endeavours. Judy Fudge has also given me generous support and advice at different stages of my academic career. My doctoral project, which provided the starting point for this book, benefitted from helpful discussion and feedback from Bruno de Witte, Petra Herzfeld Olsson, Catharina Calleman, Mark Bell, Antonio Baylos and Luz Rodríguez. When I joined the University of Glasgow in 2018, I found myself surrounded by many supportive colleagues. I would like to thank especially Ruth Dukes, Gregoris Ioannou, Eleonor Kirk, Alessio Bertolini and Ou Lin for welcoming me into the Work on Demand research group. I am also grateful to Nicole Busby and Sarah Graig for reading and commenting on parts of the manuscript and to Muireann McDermott for excellent research assistance. Many good friends made writing a book during successive lockdowns bearable and even fun at times. Thanks are due to Meha, Toni and their boys, Guillem, Aphroditi, Vincent and little Danae. My parents, Zoe and Andreas, as well as, Persa gave me unconditional love and support.

Finally, and above all, I am grateful to my partner Antonio for lifting me up whenever I needed it. This book is dedicated to him.

CONTENTS

Foreword .... *v*
Acknowledgements .... *vii*
Table of Cases .... *xi*

Introduction 1
    Globalisation and Migrant Domestic Labour 2
    Migrating for Domestic Work and Vulnerability to Exploitation 4
    Framing and Contesting the Role of Law in Structuring
        Migrant Domestic Workers' Vulnerability 6
    The ILO Instruments: Potential and Limitations 9
    Migrant Domestic Labour in Europe 13
    Aims and Approach 15
    Chapter Overview 16
    Data Collection 20

1. **Domestic Workers under National Migration Regimes** 22
    Introduction 22
    Migration Regime Features as Vulnerability Vectors 24
    A Typology of European Migration Regimes on Domestic Workers ... 30
    Comparing the Construction of Vulnerabilities under European
        Migration Regimes 43
    Conclusion 45

2. **Labour Law Regimes and Vulnerability** 46
    Introduction 46
    Labour Law Regulation of Domestic Work in the UK, Cyprus,
        Sweden and Spain 47
    Approaches to Illegally Employed Migrant Domestic Workers 65
    Illegality Doctrines and Migrant Workers' Rights under Labour Law .. 67
    Conclusion 75

3. **Migrant Domestic Workers under EU Migration Law:**
    Fragmentation and the Value of Work 77
    Introduction 77
    EU Sources on the Movement of EU and Non-EU Workers 80

Fragmentation, Different Hierarchies and the Value of Work:
  Implications for Migrant Domestic Workers..92
Domestic Workers under EU Law Sources on the Integration of
  Non-EU Migrants..95
EU Migration Law Norms on Illegally Resident Domestic Workers............100
Conclusion...103

4. **Using EU Labour Law Sources to Challenge Domestic Workers' Vulnerability** **105**
Introduction..105
Domestic Work and the Personal Scope of EU Labour Law Sources...........107
Substantive Rights in Selected Areas..117
How Does National Law Fare?..124
Conclusion...130

5. **Challenging Vulnerability** **131**
Introduction..131
Organising Migrant Domestic Workers 132
Processes of Reform and Avenues to Challenge
  Domestic Workers' Vulnerability..135
Conclusion...148

Conclusion.. **151**

Bibliography..*155*
Index *163*

TABLE OF CASES

CJEU

Allonby v Accrington & Rossendale College, Education Lecturing Services, trading as Protocol Professional and Secretary of State for Education and Employment (Case C-256/01) EU:C:2004:18 108
Athanasios Vatsouras (C-22/08) and Josif Koupatantze (C-23/08) v Arbeitsgemeinschaft (ARGE) Nürnberg 900 (Vatsouras) (Case C-22/08) EU:C:2009:34. 108
Betriebsrat der Ruhrlandklinik gGmbH v Ruhrlandklinik gGmbH (Ruhrlandklinik) (Case C-216/15) EU:C:2016:883. 113
Dermod Patrick O'Brien v Ministry of Justice, formerly Department for Constitutional Affairs (O'Brien) (Case C-393/10) EU:C:2012:110. 113
El-Yassini v Secretary of State for Home Department (Case C-416/96) EU:C:1999:107. 86
Federación de Servicios de Comisiones Obreras (CCOO) v Deutsche Bank SAE (Case C-55/18) EU:C:2019:402 .... 54, 121, 124
George Lawrence Webb v Lawrence Desmond Webb (Webb) (Case C-294/92) EU:C:1994:193. 119
Gérard Fenoll v Centre d'aide par le travail "La Jouvene" and Association de parents et d'amis de personnes handicapées mentales (APEI) d'Avignon (Fenoll) (Case C-316/13) EU:C:2015:200. 112
Jessica Porras Guisado v Bankia SA and Others (Porras Guisado) (Case C-103/16) EU:C:2018:99. .... 120, 126
Landeshauptstadt Kiel v Norbert Jaeger (Jaeger) (Case C-151/02) EU:C:2003:437. 123
Lawrie-Blum v Land Baden-Württemberg (Case C-66/85) EU:C:1986:284 108
Maria Luisa Jiménez Melgar v Ayuntamiento de Los Barrios (Melgar) (Case C-438/99) EU:C:2001:509. 119–20
María Paz Merino Gómez v Continental Industrias del Caucho SA (Merino Gómez) (Case C-342/01) EU:C:2004:160 122
SIMAP v Conselleria de Sanidad y Consumo de la Generalidad Valenciana (SIMAP) (Case C-303/98) EU:C:2000:528. 123
Staatssecretaris van Justitie v Mangat Singh (Singh) (Case C-502/10) EU:C:2012:636 97–98
Stringer and Others v Her Majesty's Revenue and Customs (Stringer) (Case C-350/06) EU:2009:18 122

Tele Danmark A/S v Handels- og Kontorfunktionærernes Forbund i Danmark (HK) (Tele Danmark) (Case C-109/00) EU:C:2001:513. 119
The Queen v Immigration Appeal Tribunal, ex parte Gustaff Desiderius Antonissen (Antonissen) (Case C-292/89) EU:C:1991:80. 80
The Queen v Secretary of State for Trade and Industry, ex parte Broadcasting, Entertainment, Cinematographic and Theatre Union (BECTU) (Case C-173/99) EU:C:2001:356. 122
Tümer v Raad van bestuur van het Uitvoeringsinstituut werknemersverzekeringen (Tümer) (Case C-311/13) EU:C:2014:2337 .... 106, 116
Union Syndicale Solidaires Isère v Premier Ministre and others (Isère) (Case C-428/09) EU:C:2010:612. 112
United Kingdom of Great Britain and Northern Ireland v Council of the European Union. Council Directive 93/104/EC Concerning Certain Aspects of the Organization of Working Time – Action for annulment (UK v Council) (Case C-84/94) EU:C:1996:431 109
Ville de Nivelles v Rudy Matzak (Matzak), (Case C-518/15) EU:C:2018:82. .... 112, 123
Wolfgang Lange v Georg Schünemann GmbH (Lange) (Case C-350/99) EU:C:2001:84. 118

Cyprus

Astynomikos Diefthintis Lemesou v Yorgos Xistouris and others, Case number 6757/09. 66
Astynomikos Diefthintis Lemesou v Siful Molla and others, Case number 5926/08. 66
Cresencia Cabotaje Motilla v The Republic of Cyprus, (2008) 3 Supreme Court Judgment 29. .... 34, 98
General Attorney of the Republic v Aristou Evagorou, (2001) 2 Supreme Court Judgment 285. 66
Lin Qinlong v The Police, (2006) 2 Supreme Court Judgment 501. 66

Spain

STSJ EXT 581/2019, ES:TSJEXT:2019:581. 119
STS 591/2020, ES:TS:2020:591 119
STC 259/2007, ECLI:ES:TC:2007:259. 69
STC 236/2007, ECLI:ES:TC:2007:236. 69
STS 5439/2011, Sala de lo Social, ECLI:ES:TS:2011:5439. 70
STS 3940/2003, Sala de lo Social, ECLI:ES:TS:2003:3940. 70
STSJ CAT 533/2013, Sala de lo Social, ECLI:ES:TSJCAT:2013:533. 64

UK

Allen v Hounga and another [2011] UKEAT/0326/10/LA 73
Hall v Woolston Hall Leisure and Vakante v Governing Body of
    Addey and Stanhope School [2001] 1 WLR 225 71–73
Hounga v Allen and another [2014] UKSC 47; [2012] EWCA Civ 609 73–74
IWUGB v SSWP and Others [2020] EWHC 3050 (Admin) 110
Jose v Julio [2011] ICR 487 UKEAT 49–50
Okedina v Chikale [2019] EWCA Civ 1393 74–75
Vakante v Addey and Stanhope School [2004] EWCA Civ 1065 .... 71–72, 74
Zarkasi v Anindita and another [2012] ICR 788 UKEAT 72–74

Sweden

Labour Court Judgment AD 2/13 of 16 January 2013
    (Application No B 65/12). 60

Introduction

Despite predictions that modernity and technological advances would make paid domestic work obsolete, during the last three decades we have clearly been witnessing its resurgence, especially across the Western world.[1] The visual evidence is all around us. Passing by a nursery or school around the end of the school day in, for instance, Paris, Brooklyn or Madrid, one would invariably see non-Western women picking up white children whose parents are still in the middle of their workday. In Rome, Athens or Vienna, Eastern European women helping elderly locals take their afternoon walk is a common sight. As is that of Filipino, Sri Lankan or Nepalese women gathering on their free day in the parks of Tel Aviv, Nicosia or Singapore. What connects the lives of these women coming from and finding themselves in such diverse parts of the world is the experience of migrating to work in someone else's household which often involves taking care of someone else's child or elderly parent. They are part of – the driving force in fact – of what sociologists and economists characterise as the feminisation of migration, that is, the increase since the 1980s in the numbers of women embarking on international migration projects.[2] Tellingly, from the mid-1990s to 2010 the number of domestic workers, a large share of whom are migrants, increased by at least 19 million across the world.[3]

Today, in many countries across the world, migrant domestic workers play a key role in the sustainability of families, communities and economies. Their strenuous and often invisible work allows others to turn up to work every day, to spend 'quality' time with their children and ensures a dignified standard of life for the elderly and the disabled. Yet, despite this important societal and economic role, paid domestic work is one of the least valued and protected jobs, often carried out by exploited ethnic minority and migrant women.

By focusing on migrants in Europe, this book explores the role of law in domestic workers' vulnerability to everyday exploitation. I start this introductory chapter by discussing a series of interconnected reasons on the growth of migrant domestic labour, to then turn to literature on the roots of their vulnerability; I argue that

---

[1] R Sarti, 'Historians, Social Scientists, Servants and Domestic Workers: Fifty Years of Research on Domestic and Care Work' in D Hoerder, E van Nederveen Meerkerk and S Neusinger (eds) *Towards a Global History of Domestic and Caregiving Workers* (Leiden: Brill, 2015) 25–60.

[2] L Benería, CD Deree and N Kabeer, 'Gender and International Migration: Globalization, Development and Governance' (2012) 18(2) *Feminist Economics*, 1–33.

[3] ILO, 'Domestic Workers across the World: Global and Regional Statistics and the Extent of Legal Protection' (Geneva: 2013).

law has an important role in producing and reinforcing this vulnerability. Once a neglected theme for legal scholars, in the last decade or so, the vulnerability of migrant domestic workers has received increased attention in Europe. This increased research interest is thanks to the engagement of gender and human rights legal scholars with migrant domestic labour and, of course, to the adoption of ILO C.189 on decent work for domestic workers in 2011. An important line of European legal scholarship has therefore focused on the potential of European and international human rights instruments – including ILO C.189 – to remedy vulnerability. I look at the strengths and limits of basing reform projects on human rights instruments and argue of the need to broaden our scope of analysis by including discussion of national, as well as EU, migration and labour law regimes. Before explaining this book's approach and outlining the different chapters, I present ILO statistics on migrant domestic workers, which I place in a European context.

Globalisation and Migrant Domestic Labour

What accounts for the persistently growing numbers of migrant domestic workers? The demand for and supply of migrant domestic labour is attributed to a series of interconnected reasons. Feminist scholars have used the notions of 'global care chains' and 'care resource extraction' to highlight the interconnectedness of the phenomena fueling domestic workers' transnational migration.[4] These notions are useful in illustrating the unequal distribution of resources globally and how this inequality impacts on women's lives both in the Global South and the Global North and perpetuates the gendered division of labour.[5] Importantly, by placing the emphasis on the interconnectedness of the factors shaping demand for and supply of migrant domestic labour, the lens of global value chains illuminates the role of state policies in both sending and receiving countries.

In the relatively affluent societies of the Global North, low natality rates and increased life expectancy have created a demand for extra helping hands to care for the ever-increasing ageing population.[6] Related to the increasing needs for

---

[4] The term 'global care chains' was coined by sociologist Arlie Hochschild to denote 'a series of personal links between people across the world based on the paid or unpaid work of caring'. See, A Russel Hochschild, 'Global Care Chains and Emotional Surplus Value' in W Hutton and A Giddens (eds) *On the Edge: Living with Global Capitalism* (London: Jonathan Cape, 2000) 130–46, 131. Sociologist Rachel Parreñas used the term 'care resource extraction' to reflect the phenomenon whereby affluent societies in the Global North rely on temporary migrant workers from the Global South to allow them to combine paid with unpaid work. The emigration of care workers, often educated in their countries of origin, drains countries in the Global South of their resources both at an economic and emotional level. See, R Parreñas, *Children of Global Migration* (Stanford: Stanford University Press, 2005).

[5] J Fudge, 'Global Care Chains: Transnational Migrant Care Workers' (2012) 28(1) *International Journal of Comparative Labour Law and Industrial Relations* 63–69.

[6] According to Eurostat data, in 2008 the number of people over 65 in the EU27 was 84.6 million; this figure is expected to steadily rise reaching 151.5 million by 2060. Moreover, the old-age-dependency

paid domestic workers is also the preference to keep care services home based as a means of providing more autonomy and dignity to disabled and elderly individuals.[7] There is a societal expectation for care to be personalised, while care workers are more likely to work in private households instead of institutionalised settings such as care homes. Over the past decades, the participation of women in the labour market has increased in unprecedented numbers. Yet, as more women find paid work, there are increased pressures to replace their unpaid work at home. As feminist scholars have highlighted, women's inclusion in the labour market has been incomplete in the sense that much of their unpaid reproductive work is not equally shared by men nor shouldered by the state in a sustainable way.[8] At the same time, working patterns and expectations in the workplace demand a flexible workforce that is available and free of care and domestic responsibilities.[9]

Following the neoliberal ideological paradigm that dictates the shrinking of the welfare state, the state has withdrawn from the provision of care services, transferring these responsibilities to the market. The phenomenon of marketisation or commercialisation of care, that is 'the shift of care work from unpaid care work by women in the home into paid care work, performed predominantly by women in the home or other institutions'[10] is taking place across different welfare systems, intensifying the inequalities among those households who can and those that cannot afford to pay for care.

Thus, in the Global North, recruiting migrant labour who can provide affordable care, often live-in and working on a full-time basis, is currently an essential strategy in managing the social reproduction crisis.[11] The experience of the 2008 economic crisis and austerity policies tells us that the decline in wages and the deterioration of working conditions in many European countries, far from reducing the demand for paid domestic work, has increased the pressure to keep it low cost.[12] As states will seek to recover from the socio-economic impacts of

---

ratio is projected to double, reaching 53.5% by 2060. This means that while currently there are four people working for every person over 65, by 2060 this share will only be two to one, thus elderly care needs will increase. See, Eurostat (2008), Ageing characterises the demographic perspectives of the European societies, *Statistics in Focus* 72/2008.

[7] LJB Hayes, *Stories of Care: A Labour of Law* (London: Palgrave, 2017); K Andersson, and E Kvist, 'The Neoliberal Turn and the Marketization of Care: The Transformation of Eldercare in Sweden' (2015) 22(3) *European Journal of Women's Studies* 274–87.

[8] J Fudge, 'Feminist Reflections on the Scope of Labour Law: Domestic Work, Social Reproduction and Jurisdiction' (2014) 22 *Feminist Legal Studies* 1–23; N Busby, *A Right to Care? Unpaid Work in European Employment Law* (Oxford: Oxford University Press, 2011).

[9] J Fudge, 'A New Gender Contract? Work/Life Balance and Working-Time Flexibility' in J Conaghan and K Rittich (eds), *Labour Law, Work, and Family: Critical and Comparative Perspectives* (New York: Oxford University Press, 2005), 261–88; A Zbyszewska, *Gendering European Working Time Regimes: The Working Time Directive and the Case of Poland* (Cambridge: Cambridge University Press, 2016).

[10] J Fudge, 'Blurring Legal Boundaries: Regulating for Decent Work' in J Fudge, S McCrystal and K Sankaran (eds) *Challenging the Legal Boundaries of Work Regulation* (Oxford: Hart, 2012) 1–26, 10.

[11] N Fraser, 'Contradictions of Capital and Care' 100 *New Left Review* (July–August, 2016) 99–117.

[12] Z Ibáñez and M León, 'Resisting Crisis at What Cost? Migrant Care Workers in Private Households' in B Anderson and I Shutes (eds) *Migration and Care Labour* (London: Palgrave Macmillan, 2014).

the current COVID-19 pandemic, it is important to keep in mind that the need for care work will not automatically disappear because of households' reduced purchasing power. What is more likely to happen is that, where domestic work has been privatised, there will be more pressure to lower domestic workers' wages and make their working conditions more flexible.

On the supply side, global inequalities, that is a widening gap between low- and high-income parts of the world, have not only intensified migration flows, but have also compelled more women from the Global South to look for work in the Global North. Global inequalities are, in other words, at the heart of the feminisation of migration. Global inequalities, driven by structural adjustments and neoliberal transformations in many countries, unemployment and instability due to recurring economic crises, prompt people to cross borders in search of work and better life opportunities.[13] In developing economies, the use of remittances as a development strategy – within a neoliberal paradigm – shapes emigration policies that encourage people, especially women, to look for work in the Global North. Because of the crisis of social reproduction and the legal restrictions receiving states impose on the kind of work migrants can do and under what conditions, migrant women are more likely to find work in care and other domestic services.

Migrating for Domestic Work and Vulnerability to Exploitation

Domestic workers are confronted with multiple forms of disadvantage that range from informal work arrangements, notoriously low wages, long and unregulated working hours, instant dismissals, to increased risk of harassment at work. They face additional disadvantages related to their migration status, whether temporary or undocumented, such as deportability, dependence on their employer, restricted access to social services and adequate social security, lack of paths to permanent residence and family reunification. Language and cultural barriers can often make accessing rights and protections challenging, if not impossible. As is often the case, migrant domestic workers lack the collective voice and trade union representation that could help mitigate aspects of their vulnerability.

Throughout this book, I use the notion of vulnerability to exploitation to describe the different risks and disadvantages migrant domestic workers encounter when crossing borders to work in and for private households.[14] For this purpose,

---

[13] L Benería, 'The Crisis of Care, International Migration and Public Policy' (2008) 14(3) *Feminist Economics* 1–21; J Misra, J Woodring and S Merz, 'The Globalization of Care Work: Neoliberal Economic Restructuring and Migration Policy' (2006) 3(3) *Globalizations* 317–32.

[14] My understanding of domestic work follows the ILO definition under Article 1(a), ILO Convention 189: 'the term *domestic work* means work performed in or for a household or households'. I therefore use the term 'domestic work' in a broad sense as encompassing both care as well as other household work such as cleaning and cooking. That is why I also use the terms care work(er) and

I use vulnerability as a broader term than 'precarity' – a term often used in labour law scholarship – to encompass disadvantage created by migration law and the experience of migrating for work more generally. By talking about vulnerability, I certainly do not mean that migrant domestic workers lack power or agency. While we are all vulnerable in one way or another, there are different degrees of vulnerability and these degrees do matter. My focus is, therefore, not so much on how individual domestic workers experience and navigate their vulnerability to workplace exploitation, but rather on the law's role in structuring and alleviating vulnerability.

Before inquiring about the role of law, it is important to acknowledge that migrant domestic workers' vulnerability to exploitation is a complex social reality. The roots of this vulnerability are often attributed to intersections of race, gender and class prejudice.[15] The philosopher Marta Nussbaum writes of the 'social stigma' associated with paid domestic labour as work carried out predominantly by poor, working-class and often racialised women.[16] The association of domestic work with slavery and colonialism has contributed greatly to the production of this social stigma, framing work within the private household as undesirable.[17] The location where the work takes place, the private household, is another crucial factor contributing to domestic workers' disadvantage. Ideas of family privacy and the protection of the private sphere are typically invoked to shield the private household from the law's reach. The public/private divide in law – while ideological[18] – works as a convenient justification for the non-enforcement of labour standards to those who work in other people's households. Work carried out within the confines of the private household – predominantly by women and on an unpaid basis – has been historically and ideologically conceptualised as unproductive as opposed to productive, remunerated work carried out by men on the labour market. Traditional sexist ideas around household and care work being part of women's duties, natural inclinations and moral obligation as mothers, wives or daughters have contributed to the undervaluation of domestic work and of those who perform it. Drawing, for example, on the UK context, Lydia Hayes reveals the sexist and class biases permeating the contemporary laws governing paid care workers.[19] Hayes' work makes evident that the ideological construction of domestic work as a set of unproductive activities that require no skill and yield no economic value persists even when performed on a remunerated basis by professional care workers.

---

domestic work(er) interchangeably. See, also, A Blackett, 'Introduction: Regulating Decent Work for Domestic Workers' (2011) 23 *Canadian Journal of Women and the Law* 1–46.

[15] B Anderson, *Doing the Dirty Work? The Global Politics of Domestic Labour* (London: Zed Books, 2000).

[16] M Nussbaum, *Sex and Social Justice* (New York/Oxford: OUP, 1999).

[17] ILO 'Decent Work for Domestic Workers Report No IV(1) at the International Labour Conference 99th Session' (Geneva: ILO, 2009).

[18] K Klare, 'The Public/Private Distinction in Labor Law' (1983) 130(6) *University of Pennsylvania Law Review* 1358–1422.

[19] See Hayes (n 7) above.

The work of the gender and race legal scholar Dorothy Roberts emphasises an additional 'ideological split' that characterises work within the private household. On the one hand, there is what she refers to as 'spiritual work', that is, work related to child rearing and sustaining the family unit. Spiritual work is associated with motherhood and, as such, is valued even if provided on an unpaid basis;[20] this dimension of work within the household is reserved for white, affluent women. On the other hand, 'menial work' departs from values associated with motherhood and, even if remunerated, is considered less valuable and thought to require little or no skill. As Roberts explains, it is the undervalued, stigmatised and stigmatising menial work that is typically assigned to migrant, minority and working-class women. While the distinction is ideological and socially constructed, it serves to attach less value to the work delegated to migrant domestic workers from poorer countries.[21]

Framing and Contesting the Role of Law in Structuring Migrant Domestic Workers' Vulnerability

Yet, law not only reflects ideological biases around migrant domestic labour but also has an important constitutive role; law both produces and sustains different aspects of migrant domestic workers' vulnerability to exploitation. Through their migration laws, states may restrict entry to migrant domestic workers while leaving the crisis of social reproduction unaddressed, thus paving the way to more precarious forms of work and shaping a migrant workforce who works without a secure residence right. On the other hand, migration laws may facilitate the entry of migrant domestic workers through temporary schemes only to impose restrictions on their freedom to sell their labour power or on their chances of integrating in the host state. At the same time, labour law regimes might exclude or only partially include paid domestic work from the personal scope of protections and rights at work. It is the contention of this book that the two systems – migration and labour law – work in synergy to produce migrant domestic workers' vulnerability to exploitation. This book sets out to examine law's constitutive role by focusing on European migration and labour law regimes.

To be sure, I do not argue that state-designed legal regimes are the only sources of domestic workers' vulnerability. In 2019, Adelle Blackett, a leading labour law scholar and the legal architect behind the ILO Convention 189 on decent work for domestic workers, published a very insightful book discussing what she refers to as 'the asymmetrical, unequal and largely invisible law of the household workplace'.[22]

---

[20] See also, M Fineman, 'The Neutered Mother' (1992) 46 *University of Miami Law Review* 653.
[21] DE Roberts, 'Spiritual and Menial Housework' (1997) 9 *Yale Journal of Law and Feminism* 51–80.
[22] A Blackett, *Everyday Transgressions: Domestic Workers' Transnational Challenge to International Labor Law* (New York: Cornell University Press, 2019) 13. Adelle Blackett is the author of the ILO's

Starting from the idea that state law fails to disrupt domestic workers' disadvantage, Blackett sets out to examine alternative sources beyond the state governing the domestic work relationship. By drawing on a number of ethnographic studies on domestic workers in different countries and her own research of historical cookbooks, Blackett gives visibility to those non-state norms, expectations and practices that have shaped the law of the household workplace. In Blackett's account, the law of the household workplace is largely similar across the world.

My focus in this book is different as I examine how different legal regimes intersect in the production of different degrees of vulnerability. By focusing on state law, I do not ignore the myriad other ways by which non-state norms structure and perpetuate domestic workers' exploitation. Rather, my aim is to show how state law shapes, reinforces and perpetuates what Blackett calls the law of the household workplace. By doing so, I wish to explore using the law to challenge domestic workers' vulnerability to exploitation. While Blackett understandably places much of her hope in ILO Convention 189, I argue that, for the European context, it is useful to engage comparative legal material and EU legal sources.

The role of the migration and labour law nexus in producing migrant domestic workers' vulnerability has received increased scholarly attention in the last decade or so. In European legal scholarship, it was human rights and gender scholars, especially those focusing on the European Convention of Human Rights (ECHR), who first became interested in the legal treatment of migrant domestic workers. Driven by case law of the European Court of Human Rights (ECtHR) concerning cases of migrant women's severe abuse under Article 4 ECHR, an important line of scholarship framed migrant domestic workers' vulnerability as a problem of 'modern' slavery and human trafficking. Gender and human rights scholars, therefore, turned to relevant prohibitions in international and European human rights law in search of transformative solutions.[23]

The engagement of gender and human rights scholars with migrant domestic labour made important and valuable contributions. Scholarship in this area draws attention to severe abuses suffered by migrant women and shows how these might be addressed by resorting to international and European human rights law instruments. Activists for migrant workers' rights have also drawn extensively on anti-slavery arguments to challenge legal regimes and campaign for expanded rights and protections. Scholars and activists alike, have invoked the language of

---

Law and Practice Report which led to the adoption of Convention 189 on decent work for domestic workers. Apart from being a leading legal expert on domestic work, Blackett has a very intimate understanding of the issue because, as she explains in her book, her mother migrated from Barbados to Canada to work as a domestic worker.

[23] See, for example, V Mantouvalou, 'Servitude and Forced Labour in the 21st Century: The Human Rights of Domestic Workers' (2006) 35(4) *Industrial Law Journal* 395–414; C Murphy, 'The Enduring Vulnerability of Migrant Domestic Workers in Europe' (2013) 62 *International Comparative Law Quarterly* 599–627; S Mullally, 'Migration, Gender and the Limits of Rights' in R Rubio Marín (ed), *Human Rights and Immigration* (Oxford: OUP, 2014); V Mantouvalou, '"Am I Free Now?" Overseas Domestic Workers in Slavery' (2015) 42(3) *Journal of Law and Society* 329–57.

slavery to 'engage a powerful legal obligation',[24] but also as a strategy to inspire solidarity, to show the urgency of the matter and shame unscrupulous employers. For migrants' rights advocates, framing exploitation at work as modern slavery is often the only available strategy to gain public resonance and support for migrant workers' rights.[25]

Focusing on modern slavery and trafficking, however, has a number of downsides. First, once the focus is placed on modern slavery and trafficking, the language of extreme abuse becomes dominant and shapes the debate in ways that obscure the structural causes of migrant domestic workers' vulnerability. Second, the focus on identifying 'victims and villains', which goes hand-in-hand with modern slavery and trafficking frameworks, tends to put the blame on individual employers and to downplay – even if unintentionally – the role of the state in creating the background conditions that conduce exploitation and abuse. Also, by placing the focus on extreme abuse, we run the risk of making less likely other, potentially more transformative, framings. For the language of extreme abuse focuses on a minority of cases which, while grave, or precisely because they are so grave, tend to downplay the much more widespread, daily instances of exploitation. The synergies of migration and labour law not only expose individuals to conditions of extreme exploitation but the intersections of migration and labour law are also implicated in the production of day-to-day instances of abuse and exploitation which, while less extreme, are much more widespread.[26]

Crucially, different framings of the problem point to fundamentally different solutions. Thus, while exploitation as a form of modern slavery and trafficking dictates safeguarding borders, prosecuting perpetrators and protecting victims, exploitation as a labour issue points to responses that are grounded in labour law's protective and enabling dimensions. This book therefore advocates the need to 'shift the scholarly focus from the extraordinary to the ordinary'[27] and examine the role of law in the construction of day-to-day vulnerability, as well as considering the ways to turn this role around. To be sure, I am not denying that extreme abuse and exploitation is part of migrant workers' lived experience in Europe; there is no shortage of sorrowful stories.[28] By choosing not to focus on these, however,

---

[24] J Fudge and K Strauss, 'Migrants, Unfree Labour and the Legal Construction of Domestic Servitude. Migrant Domestic Workers in the UK' in C Costello and M Freedland (eds), *Migrants at Work. Immigration and Vulnerability in Labour Law* (Oxford: OUP, 2014). Fudge and Strauss are critical of the modern slavery framing.

[25] B Anderson, 'Migrant Domestic Workers: Good Workers, Poor Slaves, New Connections' (2015) 22(4) *Social Politics* 636–52.

[26] I have developed the argument against the modern slavery framing in V Pavlou, 'Where to Look for Change? A Critique of the Use of Modern Slavery and Trafficking Frameworks in the Fight against Migrant Domestic Workers' Vulnerability' (2018) 20(1) European Journal of Migration and Law 83–107.

[27] S Halliday and B Morgan, 'I Fought the Law and the Law Won? Legal Consciousness and the Critical Imagination' (2013) 66 *Current Legal Problems* 1–33 at 2.

[28] Fundamental Rights Agency, *Severe Labour Exploitation: Workers Moving Within or into the European Union* (Luxembourg: Publications Office of the European Union, 2015).

I am not denying them, nor downplaying their significance. The stories of extreme abuse that make it to the news and occasionally to the courts assisted by well-intended lawyers are only a small part of the story of migrant domestic workers' vulnerability in Europe. There exists a broader and more common story which needs an alternative framing and response; this is the story this book wishes to tell. I focus on everyday exploitation, that, because it is so mundane, has become normalised – it is this normalisation of migrant domestic workers' exploitation that I wish to challenge.

The ILO Instruments: Potential and Limitations

The adoption in 2011 by the ILO's International Labour Conference of Convention 189 and its supplementing Recommendation 201 on decent work for domestic workers created a much-needed impetus to rethink and review domestic workers' treatment under national legal regimes.[29] The first international legal instruments dedicated exclusively to domestic work have been another important focus of the growing body of legal scholarship on migrant domestic workers.[30]

ILO C.189 entered into force on 5 September 2013, a year after being ratified by two ILO Member States.[31] Ratifying states commit to incorporate all provisions into their domestic legal order and to report regularly to the ILO on the measures they take for implementation.[32] Unlike the Convention, Recommendation 201 is not open to ratification and it can thus be characterised as a 'soft law' instrument. Its purpose is twofold: to supplement the Convention's provisions and to give practical guidance as regards implementation.[33] Despite their non-legally binding nature, the Recommendation's provisions must therefore be considered along with those of the Convention.[34]

At the ILO, the first signs of a debate on domestic labour can be traced back to the years after the end of the Second World War. Against the commonly held belief of the time that paid domestic work would disappear, in 1948 the ILO adopted

---

[29] See ILO (n 17) above.
[30] See, eg, S Fredman, 'Home from Home: Migrant Domestic Workers and the International Labour Organization Convention on Domestic Workers' in C Costello and M Freedland (eds) *Migrants at Work: Immigration and Vulnerability in Labour Law* (Oxford: Oxford University Press, 2014) 399–421; E Albin and V Mantouvalou, 'The ILO Convention on Domestic Workers: From the Shadows to the Light' (2012) 41(1) *Industrial Law Journal* 67–78; M Oelz, 'The ILO's Domestic Workers Convention and Recommendation: A Window of Opportunity for Social Justice' (2014) 153(1) *International Labour Review* 143–172.
[31] ILO C.189, art 21(1).
[32] Ibid, art 22. States enjoy flexibility as to how they will fulfil their obligations; implementation can be done by adopting new laws, by amending existing legislation, through collective agreements, or with any other measure. See Ibid, art 18.
[33] Recommendation 201, Preamble and Art 1.
[34] Ibid, recital 1.

a Resolution on the conditions of employment in domestic work, followed by a second Resolution in 1965.[35] Yet it took several decades until a legally binding international instrument was finally adopted.[36] More than a decade before the adoption of C.189, Adelle Blackett argued that domestic workers were, to a large extent, already included in the personal scope of most ILO Conventions; the only limited exceptions are when an instrument explicitly excludes domestic workers or when a ratifying state exempted them on the basis of general flexibility clauses.[37] In the debates prior to the adoption of C.189, the ILO reiterated that domestic workers are, to a large extent, covered by most of its Conventions.[38] If this is so, what, then, is the added value of a Convention dedicated to domestic workers?

One of C.189's strengths is the combination of a sectoral approach with one that is based on equality of treatment. When considering the appropriate regulatory response to domestic workers' disadvantage, an academic debate that often emerges is whether domestic work should be regulated as 'work like any other' or 'work like no other'. In other words, are domestic workers better protected if they are included in the personal scope of generally applicable labour legislation or under legislation that is designed and enacted specifically for them?[39] Both perspectives put forward valid arguments. Regulation that embraces the 'work like any other' approach will emphasise domestic workers' equality to other workers by challenging any substandard norms that apply exclusively to domestic work. Those favouring a 'work like no other' approach argue, instead, that only specifically tailored instruments can meaningfully address disadvantage. C.189 embraces a combined approach that acknowledges domestic work as both 'work like any other' and 'work like no other'. By focusing on the specificities of domestic work in certain areas, the Convention gives visibility and challenges those vulnerabilities that are unique to this type of work – what has been described as the 'sectoral disadvantage' of domestic work.[40] However, by prescribing at the same time equality of treatment, C.189 seeks to ensure that specificities will not be used to perpetuate disadvantage.

C.189 makes ample textual and implied references to the specificities of domestic work. For example, under Article 9 the Convention contains three provisions that

---

[35] See ILO (n 17) above.

[36] Historians Eileen Boris and Jennifer Fish provide a fascinating account of why it has proved so difficult for domestic workers to achieve international labour standards. See E Boris and JN Fish, '"Slaves No More": Making Global Labor Standards for Domestic Workers' (2014) 40(2) *Feminist Studies* 411–43.

[37] A Blackett, 'Making Domestic Work Visible: The Case for Specific Regulation' (Geneva: ILO, Labour Law and Labour Relations Programme Working Paper 2, 1998).

[38] See ILO (n 17) above.

[39] For the 'work like no other' argument see, E Albin, 'From Domestic Servant" to "Domestic Worker"' in J Fudge, S McCrystal and K Sankaran (eds), *Challenging the Legal Boundaries of Work Regulation* (Oxford: Hart Oñati International Series in Law and Society, 2012), 231–51; See Albin and Mantouvalou (n 30) at 67–78. For the 'work like any other' approach see, G Mundlak and H Shamir, 'Bringing Together or Drifting Apart? Targeting Domestic Work as "Work Like No Other"' (2011) 23 *Canadian Journal of Women and the Law* 289.

[40] See Albin and Mantouvalou (n 30) at 41, 67, 78.

are crucial in safeguarding autonomy and ensuring the exercise of domestic workers' agency. Paragraph (a) challenges national rules that oblige domestic workers to live-in and states that decisions on accommodation arrangements should be taken freely between the parties; Recommendation 201 complements this provision by setting an extensive list of quality standards on living conditions for live-in domestic workers.[41] Paragraph (b) seeks to strengthen autonomy by stipulating domestic workers' freedom to spend their free time as they see fit and, most importantly, away from the employer. This provision fights against common paternalistic practices that oblige live-in domestic workers to spend their weekly or annual leave with the employer or remain in the household after finishing their normal working day. The last paragraph of Article 9 requires ratifying states to ensure that migrant domestic workers are entitled to keep in their possession their travel and identification documents; it seeks to protect those domestic workers who cross national borders from the not-so-uncommon practice of employers confiscating their personal documents. While such provisions might be unnecessary and would even seem bizarre for the regulation of any other employment relationship, to domestic workers they are of utmost importance. Another important example is Article 13 on health and safety; it challenges the classic exclusion of domestic workers from the personal scope of health and safety laws and requires states to take measures adapted to the specificities of working in a household to ensure a safe and healthy working environment for domestic workers.

When it comes to equal treatment, C.189 contains several provisions that challenge many of the assumptions that have traditionally been used to justify domestic workers' exclusion from entitlements and protections available to other workers. One such provision is Article 10 which goes against the idea that work within the private household is unmeasurable by entitling domestic workers to equal treatment in relation to normal hours of work, overtime and rest periods. Importantly, the same article requires the remuneration of domestic workers' on-call hours. Similarly, on remuneration, Articles 11 and 12 state that domestic workers should be treated equally to other workers in relation to entitlements to the minimum wage, where these exist, and to payments in kind. Article 14 finally stipulates equality of treatment in matters of social security.

Another strength of C.189 is that it couples protections and entitlements with a worker-enabling approach, centred on the importance of workers' agency that they should be able to exercise collectively. Ratifying states are expected to go beyond lifting prohibitions to domestic workers' freedom of association and 'respect, promote and realise fundamental principles and rights at work, including a) freedom of association and the effective recognition of the right to collective bargaining [...].[42] The Convention therefore does not envision domestic workers as mere subjects in need of protection, but as agents who will collectively shape the

---

[41] Recommendation 201, recital 17.
[42] ILO Convention C.189, art 3(2).

rules governing their working lives. A worker-enabling approach further implies that the state's role is not limited to the provision of protection – which would imply a paternalistic understanding of the state's role – but extends to the creation of conditions conducive to domestic workers' development of collective voice and agency.

While the value of ILO C.189 as a resource for domestic workers is undeniable, the question remains as to how to turn these provisions into tangible improvements. As with any international law instrument, the Convention's effectiveness in transforming people's lived experience depends largely on state ratification and compliance with adverse findings. Until early 2021, only eight European states had ratified C.189: Belgium, Finland, Germany, Italy, Ireland, Portugal, Switzerland and Sweden.[43] The UK and Czech Republic were two of the eight countries to abstain in the vote for the Convention's adoption and are therefore unlikely to ratify in the foreseeable future. A low ratification rate does not mean that the instrument is not useful – the Convention is being used as a mobilisation and law-reform tool even in countries that have not ratified.[44] The fact, however, that ratification is still an important first step for most national contexts and that the ILO has no means to compel states to ratify points to the need to identify additional legal sources with a transformative potential.

Even in those states that have ratified, does ratification translate to transformative legal change? Comparative studies suggest that this is not necessarily the case. In their study on the ratification of C.189 in four countries – Colombia, Italy, the Philippines and Taiwan – Cherubini, Garofalo Geymonat and Marchetti find that ratification is more likely to be transformative when a number of conditions are met. First, ratification is not a top-down process but the product of synergies between state and civil society actors. Second, a large share of domestic workers are nationals of the ratifying state. Third, the project of improving domestic workers' rights is embedded in pre-existing local struggles and larger political projects with egalitarian and social justice purposes.[45] As their case studies show, when these conditions are absent, ratification can have unintended chilling effects. Reflecting specifically on Italy's ratification story, they note:

> 'Not only did the C189 ratification fail to inspire change, it can also be seen as positively contributing to that lack of change in the sense that its particle implementation contributed to the legitimation of a situation where adherence to an international convention covers up exclusion from rights at the local level.'[46]

---

[43] For a list of ratifications, see www.ilo.org/dyn/normlex/en/f?p=NORMLEXPUB:11300:0::NO::P11300_INSTRUMENT_ID:2551460.
[44] I discuss this point in ch 5.
[45] D Cherubini, G Garofalo Geymonat and S Marchetti, 'Global Rights and Local Struggles: The Case of the ILO Convention N.189 on Domestic Work' (2018) 11(3) *The Open Journal of Sociopolitical Studies* 717–42.
[46] Ibid, 728.

On the other hand, they found that in Colombia, where the struggle for domestic workers' rights forms part of a broader social justice project, actors were successful in using the societal value of care work as a framing device. The fact that many domestic workers in Colombia are nationals meant that their claims had more public resonance compared to countries that rely heavily on migrant domestic labour.

These findings do not suggest that ratifying C.189 is not a useful strategy to improve domestic workers' rights. The message is rather that it is promising to consider the potential of other strategies to challenge vulnerability. In this book, I argue that comparatively analysing national material and looking into EU law sources can be usefully used for this purpose.

Migrant Domestic Labour in Europe

Gathering accurate data on the numbers and profile of domestic workers is not an easy task. Controversies around the very definition of domestic work and on who qualifies as a domestic worker – are au pairs included for instance? – but also the lack of adequate national data in many countries are the most common obstacles. The ILO has made significant efforts to gather comprehensive information to capture the real dimensions of the world of paid domestic work and its evolution; such efforts are part and parcel of the ILO's broader strategy of promoting decent work for domestic workers. The ILO's compilation of global and regional statistics and estimates offers a valuable starting point when trying to make sense of migrant domestic workers' profile. Still, in the European context, these data should be read with some caveats in mind, to which I turn to below.

In 2013 the ILO published a report titled 'Domestic workers across the world: Global and regional statistics and the extent of legal protection' which, taking 2010 as the reference year, estimated that there were 52.6 million domestic workers in the world.[47] Unsurprisingly, the report confirmed the highly feminised character of domestic work; globally, women make up 83 per cent of all domestic workers and outnumber men domestic workers in all countries. The report identifies Spain, France and Italy as the largest employers of domestic workers and highlights that, in Western Europe, the largest share of domestic workers are migrants. In 2015 the ILO produced updated and more detailed information on domestic workers with 2013 as the reference year. Using a new methodology that considered unemployed domestic workers, and thus involved a reduced risk of underestimating the sector's real dimensions, the ILO raised its global estimate of domestic workers to 67.1 million. Women's overrepresentation persists: 53.8 million of the world's domestic workers are female. Most domestic workers are citizens of the country where they work since migrant domestic workers count approximately

---

[47] See ILO (n 3) above.

11.5 million. High-income countries attract, however, most of those domestic workers who are migrants, that is, approximately 80 per cent. About 20 per cent of the world's migrant domestic workers – or 2.29 million – live and work in European countries; this makes Europe the second largest regional destination for migrant domestic workers after South-Eastern Asia and the Pacific. The 2015 report usefully distinguishes between two broad European sub regions: Northern, Southern and Western Europe on the one hand and Eastern Europe on the other hand. Northern, Southern and Western European countries are quantitatively much more important destinations for migrant domestic workers than countries in Eastern Europe; there are 2.21 million migrant domestic workers in Northern, Southern and Western Europe as opposed to 0.08 million in Eastern Europe. Migrants make up more than half of the domestic work sector in Northern, Southern and Western Europe (54.6 per cent), while in Eastern Europe their share is 25 per cent. The share of female migrants in domestic work is even higher in Northern, Southern and Western Europe making up 65.8 per cent of the sector.[48]

It is clear from the picture the ILO statistics paint that migrants, especially migrant women, predominate in domestic work at least in a considerable number of European countries. There is also a general convergence in the view that migrant workers are often more vulnerable to exploitation than national workers. I do not contest this view. However, the unified notion of migrant worker used in the ILO statistics is too broad to capture the legal complexities we encounter once in an EU context. In the EU, migrants move and work on a variety of legal statuses: EU migrant, transitional EU migrant, family member of an EU migrant, third-country national, asylum seeker, refugee and so on. EU law and, as a result, national law, grants each of these categories very distinctive sets of rights and protections.

EU migrant workers, for example, move and work under an EU legal framework that reduces the vulnerabilities typically associated with the migration experience. A migrant domestic worker in Italy can be a Polish citizen making use of her EU free movement rights. She can enter Italy without having to apply for a visa, go to the Italian city of her choice – where she has heard there are plenty of domestic work opportunities with good pay – meet potential employers and may even get a few offers to choose from. Once on the job, she is entitled to the same rights and protections as an Italian domestic worker. If the job does not meet her expectations, she might consider looking for another opportunity as a domestic worker, or even take an offer to work in something completely different. In case of unemployment, she does not have to worry that she might get immediately sent back to Poland if she does not find new employment. In fact, her chances of being returned to Poland against her will are very limited. She can even choose to go back and forth between Italy and Poland or decide to move to another EU Member State in search of new employment opportunities. She can bring her family with

---

[48] ILO, 'ILO global estimates on migrant workers. Special focus on migrant domestic workers' (Geneva, 2015).

her and, as an EU citizen, she may even have a more straightforward access to citizenship compared to non-EU migrants.

Now, when we think of the likely fate of a non-EU national who seeks entry to work as a domestic worker the picture is very different. Both are migrant workers, but their vulnerability is sharply different. As she has no independent EU law right to go to the host state of her choice, it is national states' diverse labour migration rules that will shape a non-EU national's decision and determine the destination. She will most probably go to a state that grants entry easily; easy access, however, will not necessarily guarantee the best treatment once in the country. A non-EU domestic worker will need to secure an employment offer from a specific employer before entry; to get such offer, she will almost certainly have to resort to an agency in her current country of origin or residence. Often, her work permit will tie her to a named employer, at least temporarily, with limited possibilities to even change to a different type of job. Losing a job jeopardises residence stability as the right to stay is often linked to continuous employment. For a non-EU national, bringing family members or accessing permanent residence are not straightforward rights at all and the possibility to exercise them will largely depend on the national rules of the destination state.

And yet the differences in legal treatment do not stop at the distinction between EU and non-EU migrant domestic workers. EU law treats non-EU migrants differently depending on whether the EU and its Member States have signed an Association and Cooperation Agreement with their country of origin; crucially, the type of Agreement shapes very distinct legal statuses. For instance, the legal status of a Swiss or a Norwegian national in an EU state – think of a young person on an au pair placement – is akin to that of an EU citizen and cannot be considered equally legally vulnerable as an au pair from the Philippines. Similarly, Turkish and Maghreb workers have a different set of rights under EU law – albeit certainly not as robust as EU nationals – that place them in a legally different position and reduce some of the vulnerability risks associated with the migration experience.

Thus, in the European context, the notion of 'migrant worker' is deceptively homogeneous. We need a nuanced account of the variety of legal statuses migrant domestic workers hold and how these statuses shape disadvantage or create opportunities to challenge disadvantage. This is a necessary first step in identifying the legal sources available to challenge vulnerability in each case. This book sheds light on these complexities.

Aims and Approach

Starting from the premise that law has a constitutive role in the construction of vulnerability, this book has two central aims: first, to show how law contributes to the creation of day-to-day vulnerabilities for migrant domestic workers and second, to identify legal sources and strategies that can best remedy such vulnerabilities. The limitations discussed above urge a broadening of perspective away from international and European human rights law instruments but without denying their utility. This book offers an alternative framing for the analysis of migrant domestic workers' vulnerability. Instead of adopting a human rights lens and focusing exclusively on egregious human rights abuses, the book examines law's constitutive role in the day-to-day construction of vulnerability and identifies those legal sources and strategies that carry most transformative potential. The analysis focuses on national migration and labour laws, which I then set in an EU law context, because these are the legal sources that directly impact and shape migrant domestic workers lived experience in Europe.

My approach is comparative because by comparing and contrasting national migration and labour law regimes, I wish to illuminate avenues for legal change that are not captured by the human rights lens; such avenues place labour law at the centre of gravity. I bring into the discussion the neglected EU law dimension of migration and labour law regimes to inform and complement the analysis of law's constitutive role and transformative potential. Contrary to what has been normally assumed in the existing literature on domestic work in Europe, I demonstrate that most EU labour law sources apply fully to migrant domestic workers including those who lack legal residence. Asserting the applicability of EU labour law to migrant domestic labour, opens up the potential to use a whole set of currently underutilised legal sources, to challenge important dimensions of vulnerability, such as exclusions from working time law. By focusing on Europe as a regional case study on the regulation of migrant domestic labour, the book shows that EU integration has been paramount is shaping the law in many, but clearly not all, areas of life. The book's comparative lens shows how national divergences on entry, stay and working conditions can have qualitatively very different impact on structuring domestic workers' vulnerability. The UK's exit from the EU, far from challenging, seems to confirm a very fragmented picture.

Chapter Overview

Chapter 1 examines the role of national migration law in creating vulnerability. The discussion begins by identifying key features of national migration regimes that make domestic workers vulnerable to exploitation such as deportability, or restrictions on their right to change employers. I then use these migration regime features as vulnerability indicators to evaluate the treatment of non-EU national domestic workers under the migration law regimes of a range of European states. I develop a four-fold typology of migration law regimes in Europe based on how they regulate the entry and stay conditions of migrant domestic workers: *Regulated Entry/Liberal Treatment*, *Open Entry/Restrictive Treatment*, *Employer-led/Mixed Treatment* and *Restrictive*. This mapping exercise and typology are important in demonstrating the range of migration law regimes on the regulation of domestic labour that exist in Europe. They provide an important corrective to the view that might be assumed if vulnerability is examined only through a human rights lens, that is, that all migration regimes are equally problematic.

Chapter 2 builds upon the migration regime typology by layering it on the labour law treatment of migrant domestic workers. I select four European states – representative of the fourfold typology developed in Chapter 1– and compare their labour law regulation of domestic work. I focus on Spain, Sweden, Cyprus and the UK and locate any norms of specific importance to migrant domestic workers. The four countries represent an interesting matrix of differences and similarities of welfare, immigration and labour law regimes which make them apt for a comparative study that is at the same time rich in analytical detail and representative of different European tendencies.

To different degrees, all four countries are important destinations for migrant domestic workers. *Spain* is consistently one of the three countries with the largest share of migrant domestic workers in Europe.[49] There are two sets of data that give an indication of the volume of paid domestic work in the country: social security statistics and the labour force survey. Social security statistics are detailed but only capture the number of domestic workers officially registered with social security. In 2020, a total of 381,170 domestic workers were registered with social security; about half of these were Spanish nationals.[50] Among migrants, the majority were non-EU nationals – the most representative countries of origin were Bolivia, Ukraine and Morocco. However, a significant number of migrants were EU nationals (about 40,000), the majority of whom were from Romania (about 30,000).[51] On the other hand, the labour force survey is broader and, when compared to social security statistics, can provide an estimation of informality.[52] According to the labour force survey in the last trimester of 2020, there were 563,100 domestic workers which indicates that a large number were working informally.[53]

In *Sweden*, the majority of those employed by private companies providing cleaning, childcare and housekeeping services are migrants.[54] Migrants also make up a large share of those working as personal care assistants for the elderly and the disabled.[55] Women from neighbouring Baltic EU Member States and Poland have a strong presence in both the cleaning and care sectors. Sweden's decision to fully open its labour market to new EU citizens in 2004 was one of the reasons that triggered the boom of private cleaning companies.[56] Similarly, the liberalisation

---

[49] Along with Italy and France. See, ILO ibid.
[50] Statistics on affiliations are published every three months; here, I provide the median for the full calendar year.
[51] Social Security Statistics.
[52] It captures the number of private households with activity as employers of domestic workers.
[53] Instituto Nacional de Estadística, Encuesta de Población Activa (EPA 37043).
[54] Interview with Kommunal officers, 20 September 2013, Stockholm; Interview with Kommunal officers, 6 September 2018, Stockholm.
[55] In Sweden, personal care services are provided via a mix of settings: direct employment, cooperatives, municipalities and private companies. Collective agreements exist in all these settings, except where someone is directly employed by a private person (direct employment).
[56] Interview with Kommunal officers, 20 September 2013, Stockholm; Interview with Kommunal officers, 6 September 2018, Stockholm. See discussion in ch 1.

of immigration rules in 2008, resulted in comparatively large numbers of non-EU nationals entering Sweden to work in cleaning, babysitting and housekeeping; their countries of origin are very diverse and include Ukraine, Mongolia, Bangladesh, Albania, Thailand and Iraq. For instance, in 2019 Sweden granted 734 new work permits just for cleaners. In 2020, amidst the pandemic, 628 new permits were granted for the same category.[57] Sweden is also an important destination for au pairs, both within and from outside the EU.[58]

Cyprus, despite being a small and peripheral country, is an important destination for migrant domestic workers in the region. Today, domestic work in private households is the type of work that attracts by far the majority of migrant workers – EU and non-EU nationals. According to Ministry of Labour statistics, in 2020 there were 23,107 migrant domestic workers, which represents a share of 36 per cent of all migrant workers in Cyprus; construction, the second sector attracted only 8.4 per cent of migrants.[59] The majority of migrant domestic workers in Cyprus are non-EU nationals, originating mainly from the Philippines, Sri Lanka, Nepal, India and Vietnam.[60]

In the *UK*, the Home Office grants between 17,000 and 21,000 temporary visas for overseas domestic workers every year.[61] Similar to Sweden, the UK's decision in 2014 to open its labour market to new EU citizens in 2004 without transitional restrictions attracted many new EU citizens who found work as temporary agency workers providing care services and as au pairs.[62] While it is impossible to give exact figures, Rosie Cox and Nicole Busch, experts on au pair migration to the UK, estimate that there are about 90,000 au pairs at any given time in Britain.[63]

Chapter 2 also examines the four countries' different approaches to the work of migrant domestic workers who are illegal residents. The strength of the comparative approach is that it provides for a much more nuanced analysis of the role of law in constructing vulnerability than a mono-state study which would typically find domestic workers to be at a disadvantage when compared with other workers.

---

[57] Swedish Migration Agency Statistics, Work permits granted to non-EU nationals (2019 and 2020).
[58] T Anving and S Eldén (2016) 'Precarious Care Labor: Contradictory Work Regulations and Practices for Au Pairs in Sweden' (2016) 6(4) *Nordic Journal of Working Life Studies* 29–48.
[59] Ministry of Labour Statistics, Total Aliens and Europeans Data, 2020.
[60] The Migration Department of the Ministry of Interior is the state authority responsible for publishing data on the number of migrant domestic worker visas it grants every year to non-EU nationals and the countries of origin. The latest publicly available data (July 2016) reports 18,844 non-EU domestic workers, but without any disaggregating data on countries of origin. More recent secondary sources report that in 2019, 98% of all migrant domestic workers originated from these five countries. See N Hadjigeorgiou, Commissioner for the Administration and the Protection of Human Rights, 'Report on the Status of Foreign Domestic Workers in Cyprus' (Nicosia, 18 December 2020).
[61] The majority of visas outside the Points-Based System are granted to domestic workers. See, D Kierans and m Sumption (2020) 'Work Visas and Migrant Workers in the UK', Migration Observatory briefing' (COMPAS, University of Oxford).
[62] B Anderson, M Ruhs, B Rogaly and S Spencer, 'Fair Enough? Central and East European Migrants in Low-wage Employment in the UK' (York, Joseph Rowntree Foundation, 2006).
[63] R Cox and N Busch, *Au Pairing after the Au Pair Scheme? New Migration Rules and Childcare in Private Homes in the UK* (London: University of London, 2014).

While this is of course true, comparing and contrasting labour law norms in different countries sheds light on the different ways in which law structures, but may also contribute in reducing vulnerability to, exploitation.

The place of domestic work in the EU migration law framework is the focus of *Chapter 3*. I provide a detailed and nuanced analysis of the various EU migration law sources to examine whether they apply to migrant domestic workers and to what extent they contribute to the creation of vulnerability. This is an important part of the book which clarifies some typical misunderstandings in the existing literature on migrant domestic workers in Europe. While there is abundant scholarship on EU migration law, this literature tends to pay little attention to migrant domestic workers. On the other hand, most scholars interested in the position of migrant domestic workers seem to assume that domestic workers are typically non-EU nationals who in addition lack legal residence. Yet, migrant domestic workers include EU nationals as well as various categories of non-EU nationals. Thus, through a nuanced comparative analysis of the different migrant statuses and rights EU migration law creates, this chapter shows which migration rules make the difference in creating disadvantage. The analysis reveals that while there are some sources in EU migration law which could challenge vulnerability, these are largely unavailable to domestic workers. The chapter finally provides some reflections on why this is so.

Chapter 4 draws on a previous analysis concerning the inclusion of paid domestic workers in EU labour law sources. I have argued that the position of domestic workers in the personal scope of EU labour law was largely misunderstood – or neglected – in scholarly analyses and that, in fact, certain EU labour law sources apply to domestic workers and challenge aspects of their vulnerability, such as their exclusion from the working time regulation.[64] After briefly presenting the rights and protections domestic workers can derive from EU labour law, I analyse the extent to which the national regimes of Spain, Cyprus, Sweden and the UK comply with EU law requirements in specific areas, such as, pregnancy discrimination, working time and the right to receive information on terms and conditions of work. The analysis identifies country-specific mismatches between the level of protection stipulated in EU law and what national law delivers. From this follows a broader conclusion that invoking compliance with EU law is a useful strategy to boost rights and protections at work for migrant domestic workers.

Chapter 5 examines different processes – or lack thereof – of challenging vulnerability which have taken place in Spain, Sweden, Cyprus and the UK to draw broader lessons on the collective organisation and legal mobilisation of migrant domestic workers in Europe. I also consider the role of the ILO C.189 as a mobilisation tool used by local actors in framing claims against vulnerability. Out of

---

[64] V Pavlou, 'Domestic Work in EU Law the Relevance of EU Employment Law in Challenging Domestic Workers' Vulnerability' (2016) 41(3) *European Law Review* 379–98.

20   *Introduction*

the four selected states only Sweden has ratified the Convention. It is therefore important to ask whether C.189 has had any other direct or less direct impact on national discussions concerning the improvement of domestic workers' rights at work.

The conclusions use the insights from the different chapters to reflect on and formulate recommendations for the improvement of migrant domestic workers' legal treatment in Europe. A promising, but still underexplored strategy in Europe, would be to turn migration controls around and use them to enforce labour rights for non-EU domestic workers rather than simply to produce precariousness. Other strategies include advocating for the professionalisation of domestic work service while being attentive to the specificities of national settings.

Data Collection

The book draws on documentary and doctrinal analysis supplemented with key informant interviews. Because of the specificities of domestic work some kinds of legal sources are scarce. Apart from labour and migration legislation there is, for instance, very limited case law on domestic workers in general and on migrant domestic workers in particular. The UK is exceptional in this respect; recently, there has been a growing number of litigation cases by migrant domestic workers in UK Employment Tribunals and Courts; I analyse this case law extensively. For Cyprus, Sweden and Spain, where case law on migrant domestic workers is scarce to non-existent, I rely on alternative sources to analyse the legal and institutional context of migrant domestic labour. In relation to Cyprus, I use the reports of the Equality Body, an Institution that has received numerous claims by non-EU domestic workers. To complement the information on the law and policy context in the Spanish and Swedish cases, I conducted a series of interviews with trade union representatives (Sweden and Spain) and a domestic workers' association (Spain).

The interviewees were selected because of their expertise on the situation of migrants in the domestic work sectors in their respective national contexts. In Sweden, I interviewed representatives of Kommunal, the largest trade union in Sweden, because it organises service workers, including caretakers for the elderly and children. In addition, I conducted an interview with the legal advisor of the Swedish Confederation of Professional Employees (TCO). In Spain, the interviewees were representatives of two major trade unions, *Comisiones Obreras* (CC.OO) and *Unión General de Trabajadores* (UGT), because they organise service workers and have been involved in the labour law reform of the Spanish regime on domestic work. The interviews with CC.OO and UGT revealed that, even though trade unions take part in the debates concerning the regulation of domestic work, domestic workers themselves, especially migrants, rarely become union members. Migrant domestic workers in Spain have instead formed alternative groups and associations. In order to complement the information, I interviewed the representatives of one such association, *Servicio Doméstico Activo* (SEDOAC), whose members are mainly domestic workers from Latin America.[65] I used semi-structured interviews with open-ended questions that allowed for a focused but flexible communication.

---

[65] SEDOAC, despite being a small association, was a key informant on the Spanish domestic work sector for a study prepared by the EU Fundamental Rights Agency 'Fundamental Rights Agency, Migrants in an Irregular Situation Employed in Domestic Work: Fundamental Rights Challenges For The European Union and its Member States' (Luxembourg: EU Publications Office, 2011).

1
Domestic Workers under National Migration Regimes

Introduction

During the last decade a growing body of socio-legal scholarship has examined the numerous ways in which migration and migration law impact on work relations. An important insight from this line of research is that the legal regulation of migration is a key vector of migrant workers' vulnerability. Migration rules and controls do much more than decide who gets in and who stays out; formal rules in their interaction with informal actors and practices increase migrant workers' likelihood of experiencing workplace exploitation in the host state, while effectively limiting their access to redress mechanisms.[1] In relation to migrant domestic workers, legal scholars, especially those employing a human rights lens to study exploitation at work, have demonstrated migration law's key contribution in structuring vulnerability to severe forms of exploitation such as human trafficking and modern slavery.[2] Yet, how is migration law implicated in the production of everyday vulnerability? Importantly, are all migration regimes governing migrant domestic labour equally problematic?

Building on the important work that has already examined the migration and labour nexus, this chapter examines the role of migration law as a source of vulnerability for migrant domestic workers in Europe. The aim of my analysis is twofold. First, to show that the role of migration law in structuring vulnerability

---

[1] B Anderson, 'Migration, Immigration Controls and the Fashioning of Precarious Workers' (2010) 24(2) *Work Employment and Society* 300–17; J Fudge, 'Precarious Migrant Status and Precarious Employment: The Paradox of International Rights for Migrant Worker' (2012) 34(1) *Comparative Labor Law and Policy Journal* 95–132; C Costello and M Freedland, 'Migrants at Work and the Division of Labour Law' in Costello and Freedland (eds) *Migrants at Work: Immigration and Vulnerability in Labour Law* (Oxford: Oxford University Press 2014); J Howe and R Owens, 'Temporary Labour Migration in the Global Era: The Regulatory Challenges' in Howe and Owens (eds) *Temporary Labour Migration in the Global Era* (Oxford, Hart Publishing, 2016); L Berg, *Migrant Rights at Work: Law's Precariousness at the Intersection of Migration and Labour* (Abingdon, Routledge, 2016).

[2] V Mantouvalou, 'Servitude and Forced Labour in the 21st Century: The Human Rights of Domestic Workers' (2006) 35(4) *Industrial Law Journal* 395–414; S Mullally, 'Migration, Gender and the Limits of Rights' in R Rubio Marín (ed) *Human Rights and Immigration* (Oxford: Oxford University Press, 2014); C Murphy, 'The Enduring Vulnerability of Migrant Domestic Workers in Europe' (2013) 62 *International and Comparative Law Quarterly* 599–627.

is functional to the policy aim of facilitating access to low-cost domestic labour for the host state's population. And second, to demonstrate the important national variations in the role of migration law in structuring vulnerability. By examining variations in national migration regimes, this chapter provides a corrective to the view one might assume if they examine the role of migration law through the lens of international human rights law, that is, that all migration regimes are equally problematic. What a focus on European national migration regimes shows is that while states share a common policy of creating a supply of low-cost domestic labour, this aim is pursued under different migration law regimes. These important regime variations have a decisively differentiated impact on the fate of domestic workers embarking on migration projects with a European state as the destination.

Europe provides a useful case to examine migration law regime variations. While many rules have been adopted at the EU level to regulate migration from outside the EU,[3] admission conditions are still very much a national law issue. When a prospective non-EU migrant seeks to enter an EU Member State independently for the purpose of work, she must primarily rely on national migration rules and procedures.[4] We can therefore expect to find divergences in the way states, through their migration law regimes, regulate the entry and stay conditions of non-EU domestic workers. This chapter sets out to map these divergences and to evaluate the extent to which different regimes create conditions that can accentuate, or alternatively, attenuate vulnerability to workplace exploitation.

I structure the discussion as follows. Section 2 identifies key features of migration regimes and discusses their role as vectors of migrant domestic workers' vulnerability to exploitation at work. I examine the following issues: migrant illegality and deportability, restrictions on the right to change employers, restrictions on sectoral mobility, reliance on intermediaries, live-in work and the place of the au pair scheme in migration regimes. Section 3 develops a typology of European migration regimes based on how they regulate migrant domestic labour. The typology is attentive to both admission conditions and what happens to the migrant worker post entry. As Northern, Western and Southern European states are quantitatively more important destinations for migrant domestic workers, my focus is on countries from these regions instead of Eastern Europe.[5] The typology is useful in showing the commonalities between different European migration regimes and most importantly, their differences. What this chapter illustrates is that there is a range of regime choices available to states; such regime choices shape

---

[3] See discussion in ch 3.
[4] EU nationals and some categories of non-EU nationals, such as the family members of EU nationals, can rely on harmonised EU free movement rules which are examined in ch 3.
[5] My linguistic skills determined and limited my choice of countries as well. Thus, I have selected states with a broad range of sources available in Greek, English, Spanish and Italian. This meant not considering, for instance, France despite that country being a major destination for migrant domestic workers.

vulnerability to exploitation and any opportunities to challenge it differently. In section 4, I use the vulnerability vectors identified earlier to comparatively examine the construction of migrant domestic workers in the different regime types. Section 5 concludes the chapter.

Migration Regime Features as Vulnerability Vectors

This section identifies and discusses six common features of migration regimes and their impact on migrant domestic workers' vulnerability. While having access to a legal status under migration law is a key protection, often the conditions upon which the right to stay is granted are equally important in structuring vulnerability to exploitation. Features such as restrictions on labour market mobility, ie permits tied to a named employer or no right to change sectors, living in the employer's household, or reliance on intermediaries shape a cheap and amenable workforce that is vulnerable to exploitation.

Migrant Illegality and Deportability

In the public imagination, migrant illegality is associated with migrants crossing borders smuggled in an overcrowded, rickety boat or at the bottom of a truck. Juxtaposed to this image is often that of the lawful migrant, someone who acquires all the necessary permits before embarking on a planned migration journey. In such constructions, migration status is understood as a binary; one is either a 'legal' or an 'illegal' migrant. The reality, however, is much messier.

There is a broad range of situations falling under the notion of 'illegality' in migration law terms, while the very boundaries between legality and illegality are not always clearly defined. One might enter a state without the necessary permit, enter with a permit and then overstay its duration, or contravene the permit's rules in many different ways. For instance, one might take up work while on a tourist visa or, work for more hours than a student visa allows. One might be deemed lawfully resident during a certain period and then fall into a situation of illegality because she lost her job when being employed is a requirement for lawful stay. Social science research in the area of migration studies demonstrates that conceptualising migration status as a binary between legality and illegality is artificial and does not reflect many migrants' reality on the ground; illegality under migration law is therefore best understood as a spectrum.[6]

No matter where one falls along the spectrum, illegality under migration law inevitably impacts upon the employment relationship as any form of illegality

---

[6] A Kubal, 'Conceptualizing Semi-Legality in Migration Research' (2013) 47(3) *Law & Society Review* 555–87.

increases the likelihood of experiencing exploitation at work. In the hands of an abusive employer, the worker's illegal migration status can become a tool of coercion and intimidation. While this is, of course, true for all illegal migrant workers, for domestic workers the implications are even more acute because of the very intimate nature of their employment relationship.[7] The higher-than-normal levels of intimacy entailed in the relationship between domestic worker and employer and the dependence on the employer, not just for work but often for accommodation as well, exacerbates illegally resident domestic workers' vulnerability to abuse.

Importantly, despite high risks of exploitation, illegal migrants are less likely to access redress mechanisms normally available to other workers.[8] This is one of the major consequences of their deportability. While any non-citizen is, in principle, deportable, those with a migration status on the illegality spectrum face an enhanced danger. In the context of the EU, migrant deportability is reinforced through common EU rules requiring Member States to remove illegal residents.[9] For any illegally resident migrant worker, the stakes of coming forward to file a complaint are simply too high. Additionally, the barriers are not only factual but also legal as illegality doctrines can sometimes bar illegally resident workers from enforcing their employment contracts.[10]

While deportation is a major danger for any illegally resident migrant, domestic workers are paradoxically somewhat shielded because they work in the isolation of private households. Police or labour inspection raids in private households in search of illegally resident migrants are highly unlikely. Yet deportability has many knock-on effects that affect domestic workers, too. Several studies examine how illegality and deportability impact on migrants' everyday life by pushing them into the margins of society and making them dependent on ethnic networks.[11] Gleeson's study shows the powerful ways in which illegality impacts on workers' understanding of their legal rights and the likelihood of enforcing them. By shaping 'a pragmatic and short-term understanding of their working life', illegality makes undocumented workers more likely to endure difficult working conditions and reluctant to seek enforcement even of those rights available to them.[12]

Migration policy is a factor contributing to illegality. While the stated aims of restrictive labour migration policies might be reducing irregular migration, protecting the national labour market or even protecting the migrants themselves,

---

[7] See the discussion of UK case law on illegally resident migrant domestic workers in ch 3.
[8] M Bell, 'Invisible Actors? Irregular Migrants and Discrimination' in B Bogusz et al (eds), *Irregular Migration and Human Rights: Theoretical, European and International Perspectives* (Leiden: Martinus Nijhoff Publishers, 2004), 345–62.
[9] Directive 2008/115/EC on common standards and procedures for returning illegally resident TCNs.
[10] See discussion in ch 2.
[11] N De Genova, 'Migrant "Illegality" and Deportability in Everyday Life' (2003) 31 *Annual Review of Anthropology* 419–44; S Nando, '"I Have Too Much Baggage": The Impacts of Legal Status on the Social Worlds of Irregular Migrants' (2012) 20(1) *Social Anthropology* 50–65.
[12] S Gleeson, 'Labor Rights for All? Undocumented Status and Worker Claims' (2010) 35(3) *Law and Social Inquiry* 561–602.

the actual effects are often contradictory. Restrictive migration laws and policies coupled with unmet needs for affordable care, potentially increase vulnerability to exploitation for migrant domestic workers by pushing them to illegality. Research has demonstrated that limited opportunities to enter a state and work legally increases irregular migration by making migrants overstay or contravene the terms of visas granted for non-work purposes and, to a lesser extent, seek unauthorised entry.[13]

As the analysis in this chapter shows, there are a surprisingly large number of European states, especially Northern and Western ones, who effectively limit the possibility for migrants to enter lawfully for the purpose of working in domestic work. Yet, even those migration regimes with generous first entry rules for labour migrants do not necessarily guarantee stable legal residence over time because of migration rules that make legal residence dependent upon continuous employment. In other words, in regimes where migrants' legal residence is linked to their employment, losing their job means they become illegally resident and deportable.

Restrictions on the Right to Change Employer

Making a legal stay conditional on continued employment with a named employer is a common feature of temporary labour migration schemes. Restrictions on the right to change employers can be temporary – during for instance the first months of residence – or throughout the duration of the migrant worker's permit. Sometimes migration law only allows a change of employer in very limited situations, typically in cases of extreme abuse, which requires the migrant to meet a high threshold before being able to walk away lawfully.

Restrictions of this sort sit very uneasily with one of the premises of modern labour law, that of the parties' contractual freedom. Without the right to change employers, migrant workers are not free to choose their employer, nor to walk away from an employment relationship simply because it does not meet their needs. Impermissible for national workers and, in the context of the EU, for EU migrants as well, restricting the right to change employers is one of the ways that migration law gives employers 'additional means of control over labour'.[14] Migration law therefore hands employers the additional power to extract more labour or to impose more onerous working conditions knowing that migrant workers will either have to endure or risk becoming illegal if they leave.

For domestic workers, the restriction of their right to change employers adds extra layers of vulnerability. Most migrants on employer-sponsorship-type permits normally arrive in the host state without any previous contact with their employer

---

[13] F Düvell, 'Paths into Irregularity: The Legal and Political Construction of Irregular Migration' (2011) 13 *European Journal of Migration and Law* 275–95.
[14] See Anderson (n 1) above at 300–17.

and workplace. Domestic workers, additionally, enter an employment relationship that is emotionally charged and entails very high levels of intimacy. They work – and sometimes live – in the isolation of the employer's private household and have limited opportunities to meet and engage with colleagues, or indeed anyone who is not linked to their employer. As I discuss in chapter 2, domestic work is often subject to differentiated dismissal rules that foster employer flexibility in terminating the employment relationship. Such dismissal rules, coupled with legal restrictions on the right to change employers, make domestic workers even more dependent on luck and the employer's good will in ways that profoundly frustrate the emancipatory promise of modern labour law.

Sectoral Mobility Restrictions

Migration law typically restricts, temporarily or permanently, migrant workers' sectoral mobility, that is, the possibility to take up employment in a different sector to the one for which entry was granted. Temporary migrants in sectors deemed low-skilled, such as domestic work, often receive entry and residence permits on the condition that they will only work in that specific sector. While sectoral mobility restrictions are not as restrictive of personal freedom as being tied to a named employer, they still negatively impact upon migrant workers' position in the labour market and their prospects of finding better employment opportunities. Channelling migrant workers into low-skilled, low-paid sectors, without career paths, and restricting their labour market mobility contributes to creating and sustaining migrant-dominated, precarious and undesirable types of jobs.[15] Sectoral mobility restrictions have, moreover, long-term effects for migrant workers in the sense that it becomes very difficult, if not impossible, to move into better jobs even when restrictions are lifted.[16]

Reliance on Intermediaries

Migrants make use of different networks to arrange their entry and work in the destination state. Such networks can be informal and often include family members already living in the destination country, or religious organisations.[17] When no social or family networks are available, prospective migrants may have

---

[15] J Andall, 'Hierarchy and Interdependence: The Emergence of a Service Caste in Europe' in J Andall (ed), *Gender and Ethnicity in Contemporary Europe* (Oxford: Berg, 2003).

[16] See generally, Fudge (n 1) above at 95–131; See Anderson (n 1) above.

[17] In Italy and Spain, for instance, organisations affiliated to the Catholic Church have been important actors in the transnational recruitment of migrant domestic workers. See F Scrinzi, 'Migrations and the Restructuring of the Welfare State in Italy: Change and Continuity in the Domestic Work Sector' in H Lutz (ed), *Migration and Domestic Work: A European Perspective on a Global Theme* (Aldershot: Ashgate, 2008) 29–42.

to rely on private recruitment and placement agencies who act as intermediaries. Transnational recruitment often involves a long line of intermediaries located in many different levels of jurisdiction which makes attributing responsibility, including duties under labour law, a particularly complex endeavour.[18] Due to the vast global inequalities, incurring debt to finance a migratory project is inevitable for any economic migrant; such debts with a range of intermediaries make migrants reluctant to walk away from unsatisfactory working and living conditions.

Intermediaries' exploitative practices are well documented in scholarship examining migrants' transnational recruitment. Problematic from a workers-rights perspective, practices include charging exorbitant fees for placement and travelling arrangements, lowering labour standards and giving false information as regards the type and conditions of work.[19] Particularly in the case of domestic workers, agencies have been identified as key actors in the perpetuation of racial and ethnic stereotypes in the sector.[20] When dependent on an agency, migrant domestic workers may be reluctant to claim rights out of fear of losing both their current job and the support of the agency in finding further work opportunities.

Migration law has an important role in shaping a migrant worker's dependency on intermediaries. This is evidently the case when migration law requires the use of a recruitment agency. While such provisions are not common in Europe, intermediaries are factually necessary in the recruitment of non-EU migrant workers because, typically, the migration laws of first entry require them to find work and submit permit applications in the country of origin. In the case of domestic workers from outside the EU, no European state grants them jobseeker visas which are normally reserved for migrants looking for work in highly skilled, highly paid sectors. Thus, a non-EU national seeking to come to Europe to work as a domestic worker – because she does not meet the requirement for other labour migration permits – must rely on a range of intermediaries in both the states of origin and destination.

Obligation to Live in the Employer's Household

Bridget Anderson's pioneering study of migrant domestic workers' conditions in Europe revealed the many vulnerabilities live-in employment entails: sharing the same living space with the employer exposes domestic workers to abuse

---

[18] J Fudge, 'Global Care Chains, Employment Agencies and the Conundrum of Jurisdiction: Decent Work for Domestic Workers in Canada' (2011) 23(1) *Canadian Journal of Women and the Law* 235–64; J Fudge and C Hobden, *Conceptualizing the Role of Intermediaries in Formalizing Domestic Work* (Geneva: International Labour Office, 2018).

[19] International Labour Organization, *Preventing Discrimination, Exploitation and Abuse of Migrant Workers: An Information Guide – Booklet 3: Recruitment and the Journey of Employment Abroad*, (Geneva, 2003); See Fudge, ibid.

[20] AB Bakan and DK Stasiulis, 'Making the Match: Domestic Placement Agencies and the Racialization of Women's Household Work' (1995) 20(2) *Signs* 303–35.

such as sexual harassment, physical and verbal violence, lack of privacy, excessive control, as well as isolation at the workplace.[21] In addition, live-in employment blurs the limits between working and free time and may result in the worker being constantly on call.[22] Live-in employment frames domestic work as more associated with women's unpaid work in the household than to that of an employment relationship.[23] This framing has served to further exclude domestic workers from statutory employment protections such as overtime pay or compensation for night work.[24] Also, the private household, normally out of reach for labour inspectorates, is not monitored for its suitability to accommodate a domestic worker nor for the conditions of work.

The migration law regimes of European states do not typically require migrant domestic workers to live in the employer's household.[25] There are, however, exceptions such as the au pair scheme which normally requires living in with the host family. The requirement to live in is another example of how migration law empowers employers to exercise extended control over migrant workers.[26] Yet, even when immigration law does not require domestic workers to live in, the particularly low wages states set for domestic work, give migrant workers practically no other option but to do so.[27] Many migrants, especially newcomers, may prefer to live in as a way to find immediate accommodation and minimise their expenses; for illegally resident domestic workers, the isolation of the employer's household also provides a shelter from law-enforcing authorities.[28]

The Place of the Au Pair Scheme in Labour Migration Policy

Au pair schemes officially aim to facilitate young people's mobility and cultural immersion in another country. Au pairing is supposed to offer the opportunity to live abroad and study a foreign language while helping with child-care and domestic work in exchange for accommodation and food. While formally

---

[21] B Anderson, *Doing the Dirty Work?: The Global Politics of Domestic Labour* (London: Zed Books, 2000).
[22] See Anderson (n 1) above at 300–17.
[23] R Cox, 'Gendered Work and Migration Regimes' in RA Sollund (ed), *Transnational Migration, Gender and Rights* (Bradford: Emerald Publishing, 2012) 33–52.
[24] G Mundlak, 'Gender, Migration and Class: Why are Live-in Domestic Workers not Compensated for Overtime?' in S Van Walsum and T Spijkerboer (eds), *Women and Immigration Law: New Variations on Classical Feminist Themes*, (London, Routledge-Cavendish 2007); G Mundlak and H Shamir, 'Bringing Together or Drifting Apart? Targeting Care Work as "Work Like No Other"' (2011) 23(1) *Canadian Journal of Women and the Law* 289–308.
[25] A contrasting example was the recently terminated Live-in Caregivers Programme (LCP) in Canada; migrants admitted under this scheme could apply for a permanent residence after completing two years of live-in employment as carers for children or the elderly. See Fudge (n 18) above.
[26] See Anderson (n 1) above at 300–17.
[27] For a discussion on wages in domestic work, see ch 2.
[28] See Anderson (n 21) above.

framed as cultural exchange, evidence from a number of countries suggests that the au pair scheme is increasingly used as a source of – even cheaper –domestic labour.[29] Living in with the host family is an intrinsic feature of the programme; this exposes au pairs to all the risks normally associated with live-in work. Often, au pair permits do not allow a change of host family. Yet, even when migration rules permit this, there can be important practical hurdles in exercising the right such as the permit's short duration, language barriers and lack of support from the agency. Importantly, framing the au pair scheme as cultural exchange instead of work might frustrate the application of labour law rights and protections. It is, thus, not uncommon for au pairs to be excluded from the personal scope of labour legislation, such as minimum wage laws.[30]

Most European countries allow the entry of non-EU nationals under au pair schemes.[31] But why is the au pair relevant and where does the scheme fit in the different migration law regimes regulating domestic labour? For those states that take a restrictive approach to the admission of non-EU domestic workers, the au pair scheme becomes an alternative – often the only – route for a prospective female migrant who might hope to use it as an entry point and a stepping-stone to a better future. To evaluate the construction of vulnerability under different regimes of domestic labour, it is therefore important to map the place and analyse the function of au pair schemes.

A Typology of European Migration Regimes on Domestic Workers

The national migration arrangements under which non-EU migrants can enter European states to work as domestic workers vary significantly. While all European states seek to have access to affordable domestic labour, they do so in distinct ways. I identify four different migration regime types governing the entry and stay conditions of non-EU domestic workers in Europe. Under the *Regulated Entry/Liberal Treatment* regime, domestic workers get straightforward but regulated access and a relatively good set of rights once they are in the country. The *Open Entry/Restrictive Treatment* type grants even easier access yet imposes restrictive conditions and treatment once the migrant domestic worker is in the country. The *Employer-Led/Mixed Treatment* migration regime type combines an open, employer-led entry with a post-entry treatment with both restrictive and liberal elements. The fourth type is the *Restrictive* regime; European states with

---

[29] H Stenum, *Abused Domestic Workers in Europe: The Case of Au Pairs* (Brussels: European Parliament, 2011); Chuang J (2013) 'The U.S. Au Pair Programme: Labor Exploitation and the Myth of Cultural Exchange' (2013) 36(2) *Harvard Journal of Law and Gender* 269–343.

[30] See, for example, reg 2(2) of the UK's National Minimum Wage Regulations 1999 discussed in ch 2.

[31] In 2016 the EU adopted Directive 2016/801 which sets common rules for the engagement of third-country nationals in different activities including au pairing.

this regime either grant no independent entry to non-EU migrant domestic workers or allow entry exclusively through the au pair scheme.

In this section, I discuss the features of these four distinct migration regimes by drawing on the examples of several European states. Two interrelated caveats are needed here. First, migration regimes are not necessarily stable over time. On the contrary, the examples discussed in this section demonstrate that migration regimes can change considerably as states shift from liberal to restrictive approaches and vice versa. Migration regimes are therefore not attached to each country in a permanent way. Second, my analysis does not aim to provide a comprehensive account of migration laws; it is not, in other words, a textbook analysis to assist the migration lawyer in navigating the migration rules of each state. My aim in this chapter is different. By comparing and juxtaposing national migration regimes, I wish to demonstrate the range of regime choices available to states and the differentiated impact these choices can have in structuring vulnerability to exploitation for migrant domestic workers.

Regulated Entry/Liberal Treatment

The *Regulated Entry/Liberal Treatment* regime is typically found in Southern European states.[32] The cluster of Southern European states has shared features of welfare, gender and care regimes.[33] One of the characteristics of the Southern European welfare regime is familialism, whereby the family, not the state, has had a traditionally central role in the provision of care.[34] Familialism further rests on the assumption of a male breadwinner/female care-giver gender regime where women typically shoulder most of the unpaid, reproductive work while having low levels of labour market participation.

During the last two to three decades, sociologists identify a shift from the 'family-model of care' where care is directly provided for by family members on an unpaid basis, to a 'migrant-in-the-family' model where the family employs a, usually live-in, domestic worker to provide paid care.[35]

---

[32] The cluster normally includes Spain, Portugal, Italy and Greece.

[33] F Bettio, A Simonazzi and P Villa, 'Change in Care Regimes and Female Migration: The "Care Drain" in the Mediterranean' (2006) 16(3) *Journal of European Social Policy* 271–85.

[34] G Esping-Andersen, *Social Foundations of Post-Industrial Economies* (Oxford, Oxford University Press, 1999).

[35] For studies documenting this shift in the context of Italy, see Bettio, Simonazzi and Villa (n 33) above. For Greece, see A Lyberaki, 'Dea ex Machina: Migrant Women, Care Work and Women's Employment in Greece' (London School of Economics, Hellenic Observatory Papers, 2008). For Spain see, M León, 'Migration and Care Work in Spain: The Domestic Sector Revisited' (2010) 9(3) *Social Policy and Society,* 409–18. To a certain extent, Portugal diverges from the migrant-in-the-family care model. Wall and Nunes observe that despite the increased entry of migrant women into Portugal, paid domestic work is still dominated by native Portuguese women as the employment of a migrant domestic worker is a viable solution only for high-income families. Diverse care arrangements have led to a mixed model which combines home-based care and institutionalisation, publicly subsidised and private services, both native and migrant workers. The authors report that, among the low-skilled

The shift did not occur in a vacuum. In attempts to increase women's labour market participation, Southern European states actively stimulated the marketisation of care through various cash-for-care and tax-reduction schemes.[36] In a context of ageing societies, the employment of a private caregiver who can provide home-based care services around the clock for an affordable price became the ideal alternative solution to the care provision gaps of the welfare state.[37] By hiring a domestic worker, families can keep care home-based, while native women are, to some extent, freed from unpaid reproductive work in the household and can engage in paid work in the labour market.[38]

Migration policy has also been used as a tool for promoting the marketisation of domestic work. A key dimension of the *Regulated Entry/Liberal Treatment* regime is that it facilitates the entry of non-EU nationals through regulated migration schemes to work exclusively in domestic work. Entry is regulated in the sense that states with this type of regime will, in principle, apply some form of labour market test before granting a permit to a non-EU migrant domestic worker. Local authorities will attest demand and grant a limited number of permits based on labour market needs not covered by the local workforce. States might use different administrative techniques which nonetheless have the same result – to facilitate the entry of non-EU national domestic workers. Italy, for instance, uses quotas for domestic work, ie a fixed number of permits are granted exclusively for non-EU national domestic workers. Other Southern European states such as Greece, Spain and Portugal occasionally include domestic work in lists of sectors with labour shortages which allow local employers to hire non-EU national workers.

At the same time, states with a *Regulated Entry/Liberal Treatment* regime encouraged the entry of new EU citizens for the purpose of working as domestic workers, especially in elderly care. Some states even facilitated the entry of domestic workers from new EU Member States while applying transitional restrictions to those migrants looking for other types of dependent employment. Italy, for instance, restricted labour market access for Central and Eastern European citizens during the first two years of their countries' accession to the EU in 2004 but set exceptional quotas for domestic and care workers.[39] In 2005, Italy granted 79,500 domestic work quotas for new EU nationals, followed by an impressive number of 170,000 quotas in 2006. In the 2007 EU Enlargement, even though

---

sectors in Portugal, domestic work is considered to be well-paid, with good working conditions, so it also attracts native workers. See, K Wall and C Nunes, 'Immigration, Welfare and Care in Portugal: Mapping the New Plurality of Female Migration Trajectories' (2010) 9(3) *Social Policy and Society* 397–408.

[36] J Misra, J Woodring and S Merz, 'The Globalization of Care Work: Neoliberal Economic Restructuring and Migration Policy' (2006) 3(3) *Globalizations* 317–32; A Anderson, 'Europe's Care Regimes and the Role of Migrant Care Workers Within Them' (2012) 5(2) *Population Ageing* 135–46.

[37] M Ambrosini, *Irregular Migration and the Invisible Welfare* (Palgrave Mcmillan, 2013); S Borelli, *Who cares? Il lavoro nell ambito ai servizi di cura alla persona* (Naples: Jovene Editore, 2020).

[38] G Barone and S Mocetti, 'With a Little Help from Abroad: The Effect of Low-skilled Immigration on the Female Labour Supply' (2011) 18(5) *Labour Economics* 664–75.

[39] For a discussion of transitional restrictions, see ch 3.

Italy enacted transitional arrangements for Bulgarians and Romanians, those willing to work as domestic workers were exceptionally granted access to the Italian labour market.[40]

The *Regulated Entry/Liberal Treatment* regime combines facilitated entry for migrant domestic workers with a relatively good set of rights post-entry. First, access to a legal route to enter and stay in the country independently for the purpose of working in domestic work reduces – without of course eliminating – the risk of irregularity and deportability. Second, states with this regime do not normally restrict domestic workers' right to change employers. Third, residence and work permits are normally separated, so that loss of employment does not lead to immediate termination of the residence permit. In Italy, for example, even if a migrant worker resigns from her job, the residence permit is not annulled; she can instead register in a jobseekers' list for the remaining period of her permit's validity.[41] Fourth, domestic workers normally have access to family reunification and permanent residence under the same conditions as other non-EU migrant workers.[42] Finally, states with a *Regulated Entry/Liberal Treatment* regime often use schemes that ease migrant workers' vulnerability structured in migration law by creating paths to a legal migration status even for those migrants already residing in the country irregularly. One such scheme is the regularisation of illegally resident migrants which most Southern European states have resorted to several times in the past; domestic workers were also included in regularisation programmes which allowed them to access a regular residence status.[43] In Spain, illegally resident migrants who have resided in the country for a period between two and three years can apply for a temporary but renewable residence and work permit which allows them to regularise their stay.[44]

In this regime, the main legal restriction imposed post-entry concerns sectoral mobility. Because the permits granted under the *Regulated Entry/Liberal Treatment* regime are sector specific, migrant domestic workers' right to change sectors is restricted at least temporarily.[45]

---

[40] Along with workers in a few other sectors: agriculture, construction, tourism and engineering.

[41] Article 18(11), Law No 189 of 30 July 2002, Changes in regulations on matters of immigration and asylum.

[42] Though factual barriers certainly do exist. In addition, as I discuss in ch 3, the requirement to prove stable financial means and adequate accommodation to qualify for family reunification is an important barrier for domestic workers.

[43] In fact, Italy has had regularisation programmes exclusively for domestic workers. For a discussion of regularisation programmes in Italy and Spain, see C Finotelli and J Arango, 'Regularisation of Unauthorised Immigrants in Italy and Spain: Determinants and Effects' (2011) 57(3) *Documents d'Anàlisi Geogràfica* 495–515.

[44] This type of regularisation is called '*arraigo*' in Spanish; essentially it means that an illegally resident migrant can access a regular status on the basis that they have developed roots in the country either through work, social integration or family ties. Royal Decree 557/2011, art 124.

[45] For instance, Spain restricts sectoral and geographical mobility during the first year; the migrant worker must remain in their geographical region and work in the sector for which the permit was granted. See, Organic Law 4/2000 of 11 January 2000, art 63(1) on the Rights and Freedoms of Aliens in Spain and their Social Integration. Similarly, Italian quotas do not allow a change of sector.

Open Entry/Restrictive Treatment

The *Open Entry/Restrictive Treatment* regime facilitates the entry of non-EU migrant domestic workers to a larger extent than the *Regulated Entry/Liberal Treatment* regime. Yet, much more onerous conditions are imposed once the migrant domestic worker is in the country. This migration regime is not common in Europe – currently only the small island state of Cyprus applies it. However, it is important to examine it not only because of the large number of non-EU migrant domestic workers it attracts, but also because it is the best example of a migration regime that combines very welcoming entry conditions with very restrictive treatment once the migrant domestic worker arrives in the country.

Since the early 1990s Cyprus has been recruiting migrants through a specific visa scheme for domestic workers which is unique in the EU.[46] The *Open Entry/ Restrictive* regime is essentially fully employer-led and open entry in the sense that visas are granted to as many non-EU domestic workers as local employers can sponsor. The only requirement is that a prospective employer advertises the post in a local newspaper; there is, in other words, no effective labour market test carried out by state authorities as in the *Regulated Entry/Liberal Treatment* regime. While the Cypriot migration regime is exceptionally open to domestic workers, it is traditionally very restrictive towards other types of labour migrants; a non-EU national has very limited options to enter the country independently for the purpose of work. Against this background, the domestic worker visa is often the only option a non-EU migrant worker has to enter the country lawfully.

Yet, while entry is relatively easy and straightforward, the conditions and restrictions attached to the domestic worker permit are particularly onerous for the migrant. The permit has a limited duration up to a maximum of six years and is in principle non-renewable.[47] While a six-year permit does, in principle, offer some residence stability, the right to reside as a migrant domestic worker is categorically temporary. Following a decision of the Supreme Court, migrants on a domestic worker visa are barred from accessing permanent residence. In *Motilla*, the Supreme Court held that a Filipino domestic worker – who had been legally and continuously residing in the country for nine years – was not eligible for long-term residence status.[48] This ruling was made despite the existence of EU legislation granting permanent residence rights to non-EU nationals residing for more than five years in a Member State.[49] The court based its reasoning on a broad

---

[46] The discussion of the Cypriot migration regime on domestic workers draws from and updates the discussion in V Pavlou, 'Migrant Domestic Workers, Vulnerability and the Law: Immigration and Employment Laws in Cyprus and Spain' (2016) 7(1) *Investigaciones Feministas* 149–68.

[47] There are exceptions for domestic workers employed to take care of disabled or permanently ill persons, elderly people over the age of 75 or employed by families with three or more children of which one is under 12 years old. In such cases, the permit can, in principle. be renewed beyond the six-year limit.

[48] *Cresencia Cabotaje Motilla v The Republic of Cyprus*, (2008) 3 Supreme Court Judgment 29.

[49] Council of the European Union Directive 2003/109/EC concerning the status of third-country nationals who are long-term residents [2004] OJ L16/44.

interpretation of an exemption in the personal scope of EU legislation in this area that allows Member States to exclude non-EU nationals 'whose residence permit has been formally limited'.[50] For the national court, the fact that migrant domestic worker permits are granted on a temporary basis – four years at a time – meant that they did not create an entitlement to permanent residence. Consequently, migrant domestic workers in Cyprus are also barred from family reunification because one of the requirements is that the applicant has reasonable prospects to acquire long-term residence.

Contrary to the *Regulated Entry/Liberal Treatment* regime, here residence is tied to continuous employment; if the migrant worker loses her job for any reason, she has a one-month time limit to find a new employer. If she fails to do so, the residence permit is annulled and the migrant domestic worker faces deportation. Migrant domestic workers are also tied to their employer; a change of employer is allowed only in exceptional circumstances following a formal complaint and the approval of migration authorities. Moreover, there can be only up to two changes of employer; no change is allowed if the migrant worker is on a domestic worker permit for more than six years.

Closely related to migrant domestic workers' tied status is the issue of the employer's guarantee. The employers of migrant domestic workers have to deposit a bank guarantee in favour of the state which makes them responsible for the non-EU migrant's conduct during her stay in Cyprus.[51] The guarantee is only returned when the migrant leaves the country or, in case of changing employers, when the new employer deposits the same sum.[52] Through this practice, the state is essentially transferring responsibility for migration control to the employer while, at the same time, enhancing employer control over the migrant worker. Clearly, the guarantee is very problematic as it encourages the exercise of excessive control over migrant domestic workers. In this context, withholding passports to ensure that the migrant will not 'run away' is a common, though illegal, practice.[53]

Even though there is no legal requirement to live in the employer's household, the permit for migrant domestic workers stipulates a wage – essentially set by the state – which is approximately 1/3 of the minimum wage in comparable professions and way lower than the median wage.[54] With such low remuneration, a migrant domestic worker has no other option but to live in. Living in the employer's household is, in fact, essential for the kind of work a migrant domestic worker is expected to provide – round-the-clock care. The low wage is therefore functional to guaranteeing this kind of work to local employers without the state having to legally impose a live-in arrangement.

---

[50] Directive 2003/109/EC, Article art 3, para 2 (e), Directive 2003/109/EC. For a detailed discussion and critique, see ch 3.
[51] The exact amount depends on the migrant worker's country of origin.
[52] The details in relation to the bank guarantee can be found on the website of the Migration Department.
[53] Office of the Ombudsman, 'Report of the Ombudsman as National Independent Human Rights Authority as regards the status of domestic workers in Cyprus' (Nicosia, 2 July 2013).
[54] See discussion on wages in ch 2.

While the *Open Entry/Restrictive Treatment* regime does not legally require the use of a recruitment intermediary, a complex chain of private intermediaries have de facto become key actors, monopolising the recruitment of migrant domestic workers. There are various reasons for this. To begin with, the receiving state has no public system in place to put prospective employers and migrant domestic workers in contact, thus fostering the creation of a market for private actors. Then, because recruitment is transnational and targets workers from very low-wage, distant countries,[55] it is almost impossible for an employer to find a domestic worker without the support of an agent and for the prospective migrant to apply for a visa without an agent in her country of origin. In 2013 the Office of the Ombudsman reported that, before arriving in Cyprus, migrant domestic workers become indebted to agents in the country of origin; they are then received by private brokers in Cyprus who often charge illegal fees and take advantage of their vulnerability and need to find immediate employment. National legislation on private recruitment agencies is largely not enforced which makes domestic workers practically dependent on luck and brokers' good will.[56] Even though several years have passed since the Ombudsman's findings there have been no serious attempts to address any of these concerns.

Employer-Led/Mixed Treatment

The *Employer-Led/Mixed Treatment* type of migration regime provides no specific visa scheme for non-EU domestic workers yet allows their entry through general labour migration rules. This regime differs from the *Regulated Entry/Liberal Treatment* regime of Southern European states because no labour market test is applied, while employers enjoy broad discretion over the migration process. Therefore, while entry is still regulated, such regulation rests primarily with individual employers instead of the state. In addition, in this regime, regulated entry is coupled with post-entry treatment that combines restrictive and liberal elements. I examine the *Employer-Led/Mixed Treatment* regime through the example of Sweden. In the last decade or so, Sweden shifted from a state regulated migration regime to a fully employer-led one; this shift makes Sweden a useful case study to examine the tensions between easier access and the protection of migrant workers' rights.

In 2008, with the stated aim of increasing global competitiveness, Swedish labour migration law and policy underwent a significant reform to attract migrant

---

[55] According to 2019 Migration Department data, 98% of migrant domestic workers in Cyprus come from the following five countries: Philippines, Sri Lanka, Nepal, India and Vietnam. The data is not publicly available but is cited in N Hadjigeorgiou, 'Report on the Status of Foreign Domestic Workers in Cyprus' (Office of the Ombudsman, 18 December 2020).

[56] See Office of the Ombudsman (n 53) above.

workers from outside the EU. The OECD has praised Sweden's transition from one of the most restrictive to one of the most liberal labour migration regimes in the world.[57] Political economist Lucie Cerna argues that the reform was pursued by employers' associations in collaboration with the pro-capital centre-right coalition government elected in 2006; for these actors, the liberalisation project was key in attracting workers of all skill levels from outside the EU to improve the competitiveness of Swedish firms on the global market.[58]

Prior to the 2008 reform, the Public Employment Service would carry out a labour market needs test and consult trade unions on the wage and working conditions offered before employers could recruit a migrant worker.[59] Employers were also responsible for arranging housing before the migrant's arrival in Sweden. By abolishing the labour market test, the 2008 reform also eliminated trade unions' involvement in the labour migration process.[60] Employers' obligation to arrange housing was also removed. Under the reformed migration rules, employers can recruit non-EU migrant workers for any position and at any skill level.[61] Migrant workers must hold an employment offer and apply for a work permit before entering Sweden;[62] domestic workers and au pairs can also apply under these rules.[63]

Compared to the situation prior to the 2008 reform, entry is now much easier for prospective migrant workers. Yet easier access comes with important trade-offs. First, the conditions attached to the permit restrict migrant workers' labour market freedom. Second, the liberalisation of labour migration rules has created important problems when it comes to enforcing labour standards in sectors where

---

[57] OECD, *Recruiting Immigrant Workers: Sweden 2011* (OECD Publishing).
[58] L Cerna, 'Changes in Swedish Labour Immigration Policy: A Slight Revolution?' (Working Paper No 10, Stockholm: Stockholm University, 2009).
[59] S Engblom, 'Reconciling Openness and High Labour Standards? Sweden's Attempts to Regulate Labour Migration and Trade in Services' in Costello and Freedland (eds) *Migrants at Work: Immigration and Vulnerability in Labour Law* 341–61.
[60] Interview with Samuel Engblom, representative of the Swedish confederation of trade unions for professionals, TCO, Stockholm, 18 September 2013.
[61] The Community Preference Rule still applies in principle; however, control is rather light touch. According to the Community Preference Rule, EU Member States must first offer any vacancy to nationals, EU nationals and legally resident non-EU nationals before recruiting any migrant worker from outside the EU. See, Council Resolution of 20 June 1994 on limitation on admission of third-country nationals to the territory of the Member States for employment [1996] OJ C274/3. There is, however, no obligation to recruit a specific individual and Member States apply this principle in divergent and rather different ways. For a discussion, see S Robin-Olivier, 'The Community Preference Principle in Labour Migration Policy in the European Union' *OECD Social, Employment and Migration Working Papers*, No 182 (OECD Publishing, Paris, 2016).
[62] Chapter 6, s 4 Aliens Act (2005:716) as amended by Government Bill 2007/08:147.
[63] For au pair permits, the applicant must be between 18 and 30 years old, have a demonstrated interest in the Swedish language, have been admitted to a language school and hold an invitation from the host family. The host family can engage the au pair for a maximum of 25 hours weekly to carry out light household and childcare tasks; in addition, the host family must offer accommodation and food, studies in the Swedish language and a stipend. The maximum duration of stay is one year. See, Swedish Migration Board, Special rules for certain occupations and citizens of certain countries: au pairs.

non-EU migrants predominantly work and has thus made migrant workers more precarious and vulnerable to exploitation.[64]

The permit is initially granted for two years during which time the migrant worker cannot change employer.[65] After two years, the permit can be renewed and the migrant worker may change employers as long as she remains in the same sector.[66] The work and residence permits are connected, thus in case of unemployment, the migrant worker must find a new employer within four months;[67] if she fails to do so, her residence permit might be revoked and she will be subject to deportation.[68] Migrant workers can, however, apply for family reunification and, after four years, for permanent residence.

Employers must commit to offering terms of employment equal to those of national workers and a set minimum monthly salary.[69] The problem, however, is that the offer of employment is not legally binding and is thus not legally enforceable against the employer. In reality, an employer may promise a certain level of pay and working conditions before entry and then provide lower standards post entry.[70] While on the one hand migration law stipulates no effective sanctions against employers who do not adhere to the terms of the employment offer; on the other hand, the Migration Board may withdraw the work permit of a migrant found working in conditions that undercut Swedish labour standards.[71] This incoherence exposes migrant workers to the risk of being deceived and even exploited by unscrupulous employers. What is more, instead of having access to a remedy, a deceived migrant worker risks expulsion.

In addition, the specificities of the Swedish industrial relations model create further grey areas for migrant workers. In Sweden, the monitoring and enforcement of labour standards in the workplace is, to a large extent, carried out by trade unions. High unionisation levels and the fact that workplaces are covered by collective agreement are prerequisites for the effective enforcement of labour rights and protections; basic rights, such as a minimum wage, are stipulated only in collective agreements.[72] Yet, some of the sectors where migrant workers have

---

[64] P Herzfeld Olsson, 'Empowering Temporary Migrant Workers in Sweden: A Call for Unequal Treatment' in J Howe and R Owens (eds), *Temporary Labour Migration in the Global Era* (Oxford: Hart Publishing, 2016), 203–22.

[65] Aliens Act, chapter 6, s 2a.

[66] Ibid.

[67] Ibid, chapter 7, s 3 as amended by Government Bill 2013/14:227.

[68] Ibid, chapter 7, s 16.

[69] Ibid, chapter 2, s 2. Currently, the minimum salary offered to a migrant worker is set at 13,000SEK – approximately €1,475. Normally, however, the full-time pay stipulated in collective agreements is much higher. See S Engblom, 'Reconciling Openness and High Labour Standards? Sweden's Attempts to Regulate Labour Migration and Trade in Services' in Costello and Freedland (eds) *Migrants at Work: Immigration and Vulnerability in Labour Law* 341–61.

[70] See Engblom, ibid.

[71] Interview with the legal officer of the trade union confederation TCO, Stockholm, 18 September 2013.

[72] I discuss the problems related to the lack of trade union representation for domestic workers directly employed by a household and the low unionisation in the private cleaning companies sector in ch 2.

been primarily recruited since the 2008 reform – agriculture, as well as household services and hospitality[73] – suffer from low union density.[74] According to Kommunal, the trade union organising service workers, the level of unionisation is as high as to 25 per cent in the sector of personal carers and as low as 10 per cent in the sector of cleaning and other household services.[75] Scholars have critiqued the Swedish liberal turn in labour migration law and policy for fostering the creation of a 'segmented labour market' whereby the lower end of this market is dominated by non-EU migrants who enter into precarious sectors, with restricted labour market mobility and with few possibilities to move into better jobs.[76]

Restrictive

Under the *Restrictive* migration regime, non-EU domestic workers have either no legal entry route or very limited options for lawful entry and stay such as short-term visas for less than a year or the au pair scheme. Despite unmet needs in care and other domestic services in most European states, the *Restrictive* migration regime is very common, especially in Northern European countries. My analysis of the *Restrictive* regime draws on six European states that give no legal entry route to migrant domestic workers: Ireland, Germany, Austria, the Netherlands, Denmark and the UK. As I explain below, while the UK does provide a visa for migrant domestic workers, its terms are such that the regime should be characterised as *Restrictive*.

This section identifies three common features of *Restrictive* regimes and discusses its implications for non-EU domestic workers: (i) selective migration policies and their impact on migrants classified as low-skilled, (ii) facilitated labour market access for transitional EU citizens and (iii) the use of the au pair scheme as the only available lawful entry route.

Selective Migration: Attracting the Highly Skilled at the Expense of Low-Skilled Migrant Workers?

Migration policies in high-income countries, such as those of Northern Europe, are generally more likely to target the admission of highly skilled migrants in

---

[73] The OECD, in its 2011 report on the Swedish migration law reform, noted that the three main sectors where non-EU workers were recruited post-2008 were agriculture (27%), IT services (18%) and domestic work and hospitality (18%). OECD, *Recruiting Immigrant Workers: Sweden*, 2011.
[74] CA Woolfson, J Fudge and C Thornqvist, 'Migrant Precarity and Future Challenges to Labour Standards in Sweden' (2013) *Economic and Industrial Democracy* 1–21.
[75] Interview with Kommunal officers, Stockholm, 1 October 2013; Interview with Kommunal officers, Stockholm, 6 September 2018.
[76] See Woolfson, Fudge and Thornqvist (n 74) above.

highly-paid jobs rather than low-skilled migrants who earn low wages.[77] Politically less controversial, migration policies based on discourses around attracting skill and global talent enjoy more support with the public and are thus easier to pursue than policies targeting migrant workers considered low-skilled.[78] As discussed in chapter 3 of this book, EU Member States are also bound by EU rules to encourage and facilitate the admission of highly skilled, highly paid migrant workers from outside the EU. In some European countries, policies to attract highly skilled migrants co-exist with entry routes for those considered low-skilled, such as domestic workers. In the *Restrictive* regimes discussed here, however, preference for highly skilled labour migration has been accompanied by closing or restricting legal entry routes for migrant workers likely to earn low wages.

In early 2020, and in preparation for Brexit, the UK Government announced its plan for a points-based migration system to replace EU free movement of workers which would allow admission only to those highly skilled migrants who already hold an employment offer.[79] Yet, prioritising highly skilled migrants at the expense of those framed as low-skilled is nothing but a new policy objective in the UK. It is in the context of selective immigration that, in April 2012, the UK amended the terms of the overseas domestic worker visa. Under the new rules, migrant domestic workers are granted a six-month non-renewable permit to accompany wealthy employers in the UK. During their employment, migrants on a domestic worker visa have no right to change employers, no path to permanent residence and no family reunification rights. Introduced in the late 1990s after a long process of mobilisation by domestic workers the visa scheme, which was in place until April 2012, was far from ideal.[80] As an entry route, the overseas domestic worker visa was already restrictive because it was open only to domestic workers with a pre-existing labour relationship, accompanying wealthy non-EU employers. The scheme was never designed to allow independent entry to domestic workers. Yet despite its limitations, the domestic worker visa was an important source of protection for thousands of migrant domestic workers in the UK; it granted a legal migration status independent of their employer, the right to change employers, to apply for family reunification and a path to permanent residence. The current visa represents a clear deterioration of migrant domestic workers' rights in the UK and has been criticised by academics and domestic workers' advocates alike.

---

[77] M Ruhs, *The Price of Rights: Regulating International Labour Migration* (Princeton NJ, Princeton University Press, 2013).

[78] M Helbling and H Kriesi, 'Why Citizens Prefer High- Over Low-Skilled Immigrants: Labor Market Competition, Welfare State, and Deservingness' (2014) 30(5) *European Sociological Review* 595–614; E Naumann, L Stoetzer and G Pietrantuono (2018) 'Attitudes Towards Highly Skilled and Low-skilled Immigration in Europe: A Survey Experiment in 15 European Countries' (2018) 57 *European Journal of Political Research* 1009–30.

[79] See the relevant policy statement, Secretary of State for the Home Department, *The UK's Points-Based Immigration System* (February 2020).

[80] B Anderson, 'Mobilising Migrants, Making Citizens: Migrant Domestic Workers as Political Agents' (2010) 33(1) *Journal of Ethnic and Racial Studies* 60–74.

Similarly, in the Netherlands, there are differentiated entry rules for highly skilled and low-skilled workers based on their prospective income.[81] Migrants meeting a high-income threshold are granted entry without having to apply for a work permit.[82] It is extremely unlikely that a private household could meet this requirement, so prospective employers must follow the procedure for acquiring a work permit which, in practice, excludes new entrants; the permit is issued only if no Dutch, EU-national or legally resident non-EU national available for the position.[83] As a result and, despite the fact that migration law does not explicitly exclude the recruitment of non-EU domestic workers, it renders it *de facto* impossible.

Priority for EU Citizens under Transitional Arrangements

Another common feature of the *Restrictive* regime is that of combining limited access for low-skilled non-EU migrant workers with facilitated access for new EU citizens to work as domestic workers in private households despite enacting transitional restrictions for other categories of workers.[84] Germany and Austria, for instance, restricted access to their labour markets for workers from new EU Member States in the 2004, 2007 and 2013 EU enlargements. Yet, they granted unrestricted access to nationals from those new EU Member States willing to work as live-in carers for the elderly.[85] Ireland, before opening its labour market to Bulgarian and Romanian nationals in January 2012, had in place specific arrangements to employ Bulgarians and Romanians as carers. Similarly, in the UK until January 2014, Bulgarian and Romanian nationals had to obtain a 'work authorisation' before they could take up employment; nonetheless, they could exceptionally work as domestic workers in private households without having to apply for a permit.

The exception granted to migrants from the new Member States to take up employment as domestic workers indicates that older EU Member States expected that low-skilled positions would be filled by the new EU nationals, thus non-EU workers would no longer be necessary. This could work to a certain extent; new EU migrants, especially those subjected to transitional arrangements, are easily

---

[81] S van Walsum, 'Regulating Migrant Domestic Work in the Netherlands: Opportunities and Pitfalls' (2011) 23(1) *Canadian Journal of Women and the Law* 141–65.
[82] Article 1(d), Wet Arbeid Vreemdelingen (Dutch law on foreign labour).
[83] Ibid, art 8, para 1(a). See van Walsum (n 81) above.
[84] For a discussion of the EU regime on transitional restrictions see ch 3.
[85] The German programme was introduced in 2002 as a partial response to political campaigning that demanded a legal route for the recruitment of care workers from Central and Eastern Europe. With the accession of Bulgaria and Romania in the EU in 2007, the programme was extended to cover Bulgarians and Romanians. See, generally, H Lutz, 'When Home Becomes a Workplace: Domestic Work as an Ordinary Job in Germany?' in H Lutz (ed), *Migration and Domestic Work: A European Perspective on a Global Theme* (Farnham, Ashgate 2008) 43–60; Fundamental Rights Agency of the EU, Migrants in an irregular situation employed in domestic work: Fundamental Rights Challenges for the European Union and its Member States (Luxembourg: EU Publications Office, 2011).

channelled to low-skilled and precarious jobs such as domestic work.[86] However, transitional citizens eventually become fully mobile on the labour market and are thus likely to move on to related sectors and types of work that are not as precarious and underpaid as domestic work in private households such as institutional-based care; being fully mobile, EU citizens can also benefit from intra-EU mobility and move to a different Member State.

The Au Pair Scheme as the Only Route

Interestingly, countries with a *Restrictive* migration regime on the entry of migrant domestic workers instead tend to facilitate entry through the au pair scheme. Austria, for example, allows an unlimited number of non-EU nationals to enter on au pair visas and subsidises the purchase of au pair services as a form of childcare.[87] Austria facilitates and encourages au pair migration as a way to balance the tensions arising from restrictive migration policies and the reduction of public social care services.[88] Scholars note that, as in the Southern states and Germany, in Austria care is traditionally family-based, thus a migrant live-in caregiver becomes the ideal alternative when families can no longer fully respond to care responsibilities.[89] The Netherlands allows non-EU nationals to enter as live-in au pairs; yet they are not covered by labour and social security laws.[90] Similarly, in Germany the only independent entry route for a non-EU national domestic worker is the au pair scheme; au pairs are again legally required to live-in, are tied to the host family and the relationship falls outside the scope of labour law.[91]

In Nordic countries the traditionally strong egalitarian and feminist traditions have shaped a negative ideological standpoint towards buying domestic work services, especially live-in. The au pair scheme on the other hand, because it is framed as cultural exchange, provides a less negatively charged alternative. For example, Sollund's research in Norway highlights the tensions of employing domestic help in a state with strong egalitarian traditions and discourse and explains how the au pair's intrinsically ambiguous character allows families to surpass their ideological constraints and access paid domestic work through the scheme.[92] Through the au pair, host families can claim that they are not really

---

[86] B Anderson, M Ruhs, B Rogaly and S Spencer, *Fair Enough? Central and East European Migrants in Low-wage Employment in the UK* (York: Joseph Rowntree Foundation, 2006).

[87] See Stenum (n 29) above.

[88] B Haidinger, 'Transnational Contingency: The Domestic Work of Migrant Women in Austria' in S van Walsum and T Spijkerboer (eds), *Women and Immigration Law: New Variations on Classical Feminist Themes* (New York: Routledge, 2007), 163–82.

[89] B Weicht, 'Embodying the Ideal Carer: The Austrian Discourse on Migrant Carers' (2010) 5(2) *International Journal of Ageing and Later Life* 17–52.

[90] See van Walsum (n 81) above.

[91] See Stenum (n 29) above.

[92] R Sollund, 'Regarding Au Pairs in the Norwegian Welfare State' (2010) 17(2) *European Journal of Women's Studies* 143–60.

outsourcing care, but are instead engaging in a family-based cultural exchange while offering 'aid at the micro level' to migrants from much poorer nations.[93]

Read through this lens, the Danish approach to au pair migration might be better understood. Denmark is another good example of a country where the absence of a migration route for non-EU domestic workers has resulted in extensive use of the au pair scheme. Denmark manages labour migration based on a list of occupations with labour shortages – the so-called 'positive' list. Non-EU nationals can only apply for a work permit for one of the posts in the positive list which does not include domestic work. One would expect that in Denmark, the Nordic welfare regime with high levels of public care provision would offset the demand for private domestic workers. Yet, the number of non-EU nationals entering Denmark on au pair permits has sharply increased in the last decades.[94] Clearly, the lack of alternative independent entry routes pushes young, non-EU women who do not qualify for a highly skilled visa to use the au pair route.

Comparing the Construction of Vulnerabilities under European Migration Regimes

All regimess, with the exception of the *Restrictive* type, provide paths to independent legal entry and stay for non-EU domestic workers. Access to a legal path is important because it eases the vulnerabilities associated with illegality and deportability. Even though domestic workers can legally enter European states under regimes that can be grouped into three types – *Regulated Entry/Liberal Treatment, Open Entry/Restrictive Treatment, Employer-Led/Mixed Treatment* – the conditions attached to entry differ significantly under each regime.

Under the *Regulated Entry/Liberal Treatment* regime, domestic workers can change employers, and can legally access long-term residence and family reunification. Because the state is to some extent involved in the recruitment process, it can exercise more effective regulation of private recruitment agencies. Importantly, migrant domestic workers have some security of residence in case of unemployment; residence security and the right to change employers equips them with important tools to challenge their employer and walk away from unsatisfactory working conditions. The legal restriction imposed on migrant domestic workers

---

[93] Sollund analyses various discourses employed by host families to legitimise their purchase of domestic and child-care services like the member-of-the-family discourse. See Sollund, ibid. Anna Gavanas reports similar strategies in the way Swedish families approach the au pair. See, A Gavanas, 'De onämnbara: jämlikhet, "svenskhet" och privata hushållstjänster i pigdebattens Sverige' in P de los Reyes (ed.) *Arbetslivets (o)synliga murar: rapport av Utredningen om makt, integration och strukturell diskriminering* (Stockholm, Fritzes, 2006) 305–48 cited in Sollund (2010).

[94] Helle Stenum reports that while in 1996 only 318 au pair permits were issued, by 2007 this number had increased to 2,207, of which 1,510 were granted to Filipino nationals. See H Stenum, 'Au pairs in Denmark: Cheap Labour or Cultural Exchange' (Copenhagen: FOA- Trade and Labour, 2008).

under the *Regulated Entry/Liberal Treatment* regime – ie temporal restrictions on the right to change sector – is, of course, important but not as restrictive of personal freedom as features that we find in the *Open Entry/Restrictive Treatment* and the *Employer-Led/Mixed Treatment* regimes.

In the *Open Entry/Restrictive Treatment* and the *Employer-Led/Mixed Treatment* regimes, entry for migrant domestic workers is relatively easy and straightforward. Here, the state exercises minimal control over transnational recruitment as it has delegated most of its authority over recruitment decisions to private employers who essentially determine the need for migrant domestic workers.

Additionally, in regimes where the state is minimally involved in regulating transnational recruitment, there is more scope for private brokers – often operating with no or lax regulation – to exacerbate domestic workers' vulnerability.

In terms of post-entry conditions, the *Open Entry/Restrictive Treatment* and the *Employer-Led/Mixed Treatment* regimes share some features. Apart from restrictions on the right to change sectors, they also restrict migrant domestic workers' right to change employers and link residence permits with employment so unemployment puts residence stability at risk. Restrictions on labour market mobility – no right to change sectors and employers – coupled with residence instability make migrant domestic workers highly dependent on employers and intermediaries; such structural dependence makes challenging exploitation more difficult. The *Employer-Led/Mixed Treatment* regime contains some more favourable elements such as legal access to permanent residence and family reunification schemes which can aid integration and improve labour market prospects in the long term but do not really mitigate any immediate risks a temporary migrant domestic worker may face. In contrast, the *Open Entry/Restrictive Treatment* regime contains elements that reinforce vulnerability, such as the very low wages attached to the permit which channels domestic workers to live-in employment.

In the *Restrictive* regime, migrant domestic workers' vulnerability to exploitation is structured in the absence, or excessive restrictiveness, of legal entry paths. The so-called selective immigration policies, which translate into almost closed borders for domestic workers, have contradictory effects. Unmet needs for paid domestic work – often because public provision is inadequate – coupled with a *Restrictive* migration regime create informal markets of care where migrant workers are more easily exploitable.[95] In the absence of legal entry paths for domestic work, migrant workers who do not qualify for preferential access as highly skilled are likely to use other routes such as taking up employment on a tourist visa or migrating under the ambiguous au pair scheme; it is no coincidence that the au pair scheme is more widely used in countries with a *Restrictive* regime. Here, migrant domestic workers are highly vulnerable to exploitation, yet their enhanced

---

[95] H Lutz, *The New Maids: Transnational Women and the Care Economy* (London: Zed Books 2011); H Shamir, 'What's the Border Got to Do With It? How Immigration Regimes affect Familial Care Provision – A Comparative Analysis' (2011) 19(2) *American University Journal of Gender Social Policy and Law* 601–69.

deportability makes it very difficult to challenge their conditions. Paradoxically, the *Restrictive* regime does little to curb migration flows but is more effective in creating semi-compliance practices and pushing migrant workers into informal and more exploitative working conditions.

Conclusion

This chapter set out to examine the role of European migration law regimes in structuring the vulnerability of non-EU domestic workers. The map of domestic workers' independent entry paths, as well as the conditions attached to these paths, reveal important variations. In one way or another, all countries examined here seek access to low-cost migrant domestic labour as a strategy of managing their social reproduction crisis. They do so either by targeting temporary domestic workers explicitly, by restricting access and then turning a blind eye to the presence or irregular migrants, or by making extensive use of the au pair scheme.

I have identified four different migration regime types: *Regulated Entry/Liberal Treatment* with relatively open entry and a good set of rights post entry, *Open Entry/Restrictive Treatment* with an even more liberal entry but more restrictive treatment post entry, *Employer-Led/Mixed Treatment* with a relatively easy entry but treatment that combines restrictive and liberal elements and a *Restrictive* regime that restricts access to migrant domestic workers. The typology shows that there is a range of different national migration regime possibilities and illustrates the different implications of each regime for migrant domestic workers' vulnerability. While none of the regimes examined here is ideal or even desirable, they clearly expose migrant domestic workers to different kinds of risks and sharply different degrees of vulnerability. In the *Regulated Entry/Liberal Treatment* regime, migration law impacts less on the employment relationship and has the potential to create less vulnerability because, apart from sectoral restrictions, it imposes no other constraints on the labour market mobility of migrant domestic workers. The analysis of the *Employer-Led/Mixed Treatment* and the *Open Entry/Restrictive Treatment* regimes illustrates that liberalising entry is no guarantee for migrant workers. Making migration employer-driven debilitates the role of the state and of collective labour institutions in the enforcement of labour rights. Crucially, open entry comes with an important trade-off: that of signing away crucial freedoms and protections. This inconsistency in migration law challenges the binary between vulnerable illegally resident and protected legally resident workers. To secure their right to stay as non-nationals, migrant domestic workers are expected to sign away important rights and freedoms as workers.

2

Labour Law Regimes and Vulnerability

Introduction

The previous chapter examined the role of different national European migration law regimes in constructing the vulnerability of non-EU migrant domestic workers. Beyond the diversity of national migration regimes on domestic labour, the analysis showed how different regimes construct different degrees of vulnerability to exploitation, depending on the kind of risks they entail and any opportunities to mitigate them.

Migration law, however, tells only part of the story. What happens once the migrant domestic worker is at the job? What kind of working conditions does she encounter and to what extent does labour law deliver its protective and emancipatory promise to those who make a living as domestic workers? To what extent does migration status impact on a migrant domestic workers' entitlement to labour rights and protections as well as the possibilities to access them? The discussion of these issues inevitably entails taking a closer look at how national labour law regimes regulate work that takes place within the private household. This is what Chapter 2 provides.

Over the last decade, many legal scholars have provided insightful and detailed analyses on domestic workers' treatment in labour law. Several of these analyses have focused on single-state studies to show how labour law creates conditions of vulnerability for domestic workers when compared to other workers. While that focus is, of course, valuable and provides important detail, examining the migration and labour nexus in a comparative perspective sheds helpful light onto how legal regimes not only construct, but may also reduce, domestic workers' vulnerability to exploitation at work. Comparing labour law norms supports the view that the state has an important role in structuring vulnerability and sheds new light on the European variations of this role. For migrant domestic workers, especially those who do not benefit from the EU's free movement of workers' regime, the discussion must also consider the extent to which the protective and enabling dimensions of labour laws mitigate risks related to migration law status and the migration experience more broadly.

After having identified, in chapter 1, four different migration regimes regulating migrant domestic labour in Europe – *Restrictive, Open Entry/Restrictive Treatment, Employer-Led/Mixed Treatment* and *Regulated Entry/Liberal Treatment* – I build upon this typology by layering on it the treatment of domestic work under labour law. I focus the analysis on one country from each of the four regime types: the UK, Cyprus, Sweden and Spain. The UK is a *Restrictive* regime as it allows very limited entry for non-EU domestic workers and with very restrictive conditions. Cyprus has an *Open Entry/Restrictive* regime because, while access is easily granted, very restrictive conditions are attached to migrant domestic workers' status once they are in the country. Sweden's regime is *Employer-Led/Mixed Treatment* in the sense that employers can freely recruit migrant domestic workers, while treatment after entry combines both liberal and restrictive elements. Spain's regime is one of *Regulated Entry/Liberal Treatment* as there is some state regulation on entry while still being open and it provides a relatively good set of rights after entry.

By paying close attention to the combination of migration and labour law elements, my analysis in this chapter aims to evaluate how each regime fares in relation to three overarching themes: (a) the substance of different rights and protections available to domestic workers; (b) the possibilities or obstacles to enforce rights and the related access to justice issues; and (c) the impact of migration status on all the above.

The comparative lens in this chapter also contributes to the debate on whether domestic work should be regulated as 'work like no other' or 'work like any other'.[1] The case studies selected demonstrate that it is important to move beyond focusing on regulatory models in favour of carefully scrutinising the substance of rights and protections and processes of their enforcement under each regime.

Labour Law Regulation of Domestic Work in the UK, Cyprus, Sweden and Spain

The UK, Cyprus, Sweden and Spain follow two divergent models concerning the labour law regulation of domestic work: a model of specific regulation, ie a special law to regulate domestic work, or inclusion in the personal scope of generally applicable labour legislation. Sweden and Spain have a special law regulating the employment relationship of domestic workers employed directly by a household, while domestic workers and the private household are exempted from generally applicable labour legislation. On the other hand, the UK and Cyprus have not enacted any specific legislative instrument and thus generally applicable labour legislation applies formally to domestic workers as well.

Irrespective of the model, the substance of labour law protections and entitlements varies significantly. This section identifies and discusses three different approaches: (i) the formally normal protection but with key exceptions in the UK; (ii) the less than normal protection approach in Cyprus and Sweden; and

---

[1] See Introduction.

(iii) the Spanish approach which is a special model adapted to deliver normal level of labour protection.

Formally Normal but with Key Exceptions: The UK

The UK has not enacted any specific instrument to regulate work in private households; the assumption, therefore, is that the working conditions of domestic workers would be governed by generally applicable labour legislation. Yet, closer scrutiny reveals that generally applicable legislation contains several key exceptions for domestic workers when directly employed by a private household. For instance, section 51 of the Health and Safety at Work Act 1974 introduces a blanket exclusion of domestic workers and their employers.[2] While excluding domestic work from the scope of workplace health and safety legislation might not be what we would normally consider conducive to workplace exploitation, it is nonetheless indicative of a certain regulatory approach and understanding of paid domestic labour. Instead of thinking carefully about how legal provisions could be adapted to deliver protection to all those who need it, the legislator here turns a blind eye to the needs of those working in a private household. Once this approach of neglect is entrenched, however, not only does it become very difficult to challenge, but it is also easily invoked to resist transformative change projects. The exclusion of domestic workers from health and safety at work is not, in other words, just a minor omission of little practical significance. The UK government has used the health and safety exclusion to justify it's decision to not ratify ILO Convention 189. In response to a European Commission query on the prospect of ratifying ILO Convention 189, the UK government stated that:

> Ratifying the convention would require changes to health and safety legislation and impose unnecessarily onerous obligations on, for example, people employing home helps or personal carers, and would be neither practical nor proportionate.[3]

When it comes to provisions on working time, regulation 19 of the 1998 Working Time Regulations introduces several key exemptions for domestic workers. In particular, domestic workers in private households are not entitled to the 48-hour weekly limit, limits to the length of night work, health and safety entitlements during night work and limits on patterns of work that can pose a risk to the health of employees.

It is no coincidence that all exemptions are in relation to limits to working time. The regulation of domestic workers' working time is a contentious issue all over the world because of prevalent societal ideas that view work within the home as having

---

[2] The Health and Safety at Work Act 1974, s 51 states: 'Nothing in this Part shall apply in relation to a person by reason only that he employs another, or is himself employed, as a domestic servant in a private household.'
[3] European Commission and European Migration Network, 'Ad-Hoc query on ratification of ILO Domestic Workers Convention concerning irregular migrant domestic workers' 8/09/2015.

no boundaries or at least not the same boundaries as other types of work.[4] In the case of the UK, working time legislation fails to challenge societal expectations on domestic workers to be constantly available. By framing domestic work as exceptional, where the law cannot interfere to impose limits, working time legislation, in fact reinforces the idea of 'boundariless time' in the domestic work relationship.[5]

Apart from explicit exclusions for domestic workers in the areas of occupational health and safety and working time, UK tribunals and courts construed an, already ambiguously wide, exception in the minimum wage legislation in a way that practically excludes domestic workers when they live in the employer's household. Regulation 2(2) of the 1999 National Minimum Wage Regulations stipulates that domestic workers are not entitled to the national minimum wage if they live in the employer's household and, even though they are not family members, are treated 'as such'.[6] The exemption was inserted in the legislation following the successful lobbying of au pair agencies who wanted to make sure that their clients, the host families, would not be bound by the obligation to pay the minimum wage.[7] Initially, employment tribunals were careful not to apply the exemption to cases involving exploitation.[8] Yet, since 2012, the ambiguous framing of regulation 2(2) gave rise to judicial interpretations that have widened the exemption's scope. As it stands today, practically any live-in domestic worker runs the risk of being considered to be treated 'as a member of the family' for minimum wage purposes even if their working conditions are clearly exploitative.[9]

In *Jose v Julio* the Employment Appeal Tribunal (EAT) examined three jointly appealed decisions of employment tribunals (ETs).[10] All three cases concern non-EU migrant domestic workers who brought several claims, including claims for non-payment of the national minimum wage. The way the ETs and the EAT read the relationship between the migrant domestic workers and their employers is

---

[4] A Blackett, *Everyday Transgressions. Domestic Workers' Transnational Challenge to International Labor Law* (Cornell University Press, 2019).

[5] Ibid, 61.

[6] Regulation 2(2) states:

'work' does not include work (of whatever description) relating to the employer's family household done by a worker where the conditions in sub-paragraphs (a) or (b) are satisfied.

(a) The conditions to be satisfied under this sub-paragraph are–

  (i) that the worker resides in the family home of the employer for whom he works, that the worker is not a member of the family but is treated as such in particular as regards to the provision of accommodation and meals and the sharing of tasks and leisure activities; [...].

[7] A Bridget, 'Who Needs Them? Care Work, Migration and Public Policy' (2012) 30(1) *Cuadernos de Relaciones Laborales* 45–61.

[8] See, for instance, the case *G Sujatha v A Manwaring* 2202606/2002 [ET] 17/7/03, cited and discussed in E Albin, 'From "Domestic Servant" to "Domestic Worker"' in F Fudge, S McCrystal and K Sankaran, *Challenging the Legal Boundaries of Work Regulation* (Oxford: Hart, Oñati International Series in Law and Society: 2012) 231–51.

[9] It must be noted, however, that the wording of reg 2(2) does not indicate that the exemption applies only to au pairs; the provision is ambiguously wide. See, also, B Simpson, 'Implementing the National Minimum Wage – The 1999 Regulations' (1999) 28 *Industrial Law Journal* 171–82.

[10] *Jose v Julio* [2012] ICR 487 UKEAT.

telling of a systemic failure to acknowledge and challenge structural vulnerabilities in paid domestic work. The EAT endorsed previous ET findings that none of the three live-in domestic workers was entitled to the national minimum wage; they were treated as members of the family and, as such, they fell within the exemption under regulation 2(2).

Paradoxically, this finding was despite the tribunals' acknowledgement that the employers took advantage of their workers' vulnerable position as temporary migrants with limited English language skills and little knowledge of their rights in the UK.[11] The employers had systematically exploited the claimants and had, at times, denied them suitable accommodation. However, for the EAT, exploitation and ill-treatment do not necessarily rule out the possibility that the claimants were treated as members of the employer's family. What is instead needed to decide whether a worker is integrated into the family so as to be disqualified from the minimum wage is what the EAT refers to as a 'holistic approach'. This entails, for the EAT, considering different aspects of the relationship between domestic workers and their employers. For instance, in the case of Ms Jose, spending holidays with the employer was an indication of a close relationship. Not complaining about the fact that the employer failed to pay her the contractually agreed wage raised suspicion;[12] it suggests that Ms Jose was not as unhappy with her working conditions as she had claimed. Sharing meals with the family and then cleaning up was a sign of integration into the family. So was joining the family for social activities and showing affection to the employer's children, the children whose care Ms Jose was entrusted with.

The exemption and its judicial interpretation are highly problematic. The only clear-cut criterion regulation 2(2) sets is the live-in requirement. All other aspects which must be assessed – to what extent the claimant was treated on a par with the rest of the family regarding accommodation and daily activities – are so broad that it is difficult to imagine a situation where a domestic worker would not fall under the exemption. Domestic workers are employed precisely to care for family members and to support the day-to-day running of a household. Will they not be spending a substantial amount of time with the family? Will they not share certain daily activities and tasks such as eating, clearing up or even some free time with the people they not only work for but also live with? The indications tribunals use to determine integration are integral aspects of the day-to-day life of a live-in domestic worker.

Essentially, any live-in domestic worker whose accommodation is not appallingly inadequate could fall under the exemption. Such a broad reading of the exemption, however, fails to consider the imbalance of power which is inherent in any employment relationship and even more pronounced in the case of migrant

---

[11] Ibid, para 19.

[12] To support the argument that Ms Jose was treated as a member of the employer's family, the EAT said: 'Even after the claimant must have become aware that she was not receiving what had been agreed she did not complain and only did so after she had left the respondent's employment' *Jose v Julio* [2012] ICR 487 UKEAT, para 50.

live-in domestic workers. The interpretation, for instance, of not complaining against ill-treatment as an indication of integration in the family is a clear failure to acknowledge the structural dependence on the employer to provide a job, a residence permit and a roof. This structural dependence, apart from rendering it particularly difficult for the domestic worker to challenge her employer, further questions the assumption that she could ever be treated 'as a member of the family'.

There are wider societal assumptions underpinning domestic workers' exclusion from the personal scope of minimum wage laws. The exclusion illustrates well how types of work that resemble intimate, domestic life, tend to fall outside the scope of protective labour legislation.[13] In essence, the exclusion of paid domestic workers from minimum wage legislation when they are supposedly treated as members of the employer's family results in imposing on domestic workers societal expectations and responsibilities that are normally shared among family members. The domestic worker is expected, in other words, to behave in the same way as family members who may have mutual moral duties to love and even a legal obligation to take care of each other. However, a domestic worker is never a member of the employer's family and can be dismissed at any moment. By treating the relationship between employer and domestic worker as one between family members distorts its nature as an employment relationship, a relationship of subordination which should trigger the application of rules designed to protect the subordinated party. As the case law discussed here illustrates, courts can play an important role in upholding and reinforcing these societal expectations.

Importantly, the exclusion of domestic workers from labour legislation operates in a regulatory context where the enforcement of workers' rights takes place predominantly through individual civil ligation with all the difficulties this entails. It is telling that none of the national minimum wage cases discussed here were brought by the migrant domestic workers themselves. As with most low-paid migrant workers, the claimants lacked knowledge of their rights under UK law and the necessary resources to pursue their claims; the claimants were assisted by charities. Because regulation 2(2) was judicially construed in a way that results in the exclusion of live-in domestic workers from the minimum wage as a group, this case law has a chilling effect on other live-in domestic workers bringing claims to challenge their wages. The exemption should therefore be reformed through legislative intervention and in line with the purpose and spirit of the national minimum wage legislation. There should also be state involvement in the enforcement of domestic workers' entitlement to the minimum wage.

In the UK, domestic workers' inclusion into the generally applicable labour law regime is only formal. In practice, the regime is replete with provisions – introduced by the legislator and then judicially reinforced – that exclude domestic workers from key entitlements and protections at work. Migration and labour law regimes work in synergy here to frustrate the application of provisions whose very

---

[13] S Mullally and C Murphy, 'Migrant Domestic Workers in the UK: Enacting Exemptions, Exclusions, and Rights' (2014) 36 *Human Rights Quarterly* 397–429.

purpose is to guarantee non-exploitative conditions. Migration law creates a type of entry route which channels non-EU migrants classified as low-skilled to live-in domestic work. Then labour law layers another level of vulnerability by enacting exclusions that keep the cost of migrant domestic labour low; yet the price is paid by the worker's vulnerability to exploitation.

A Very Special Vulnerability: Cyprus

As in the UK, the labour law regime in Cyprus prima facie includes domestic workers; there is no special law to regulate household employment, while generally applicable labour legislation does not normally exclude domestic workers. Despite this apparent inclusion, the state has designed an employment regime with a very exclusive personal scope as it only applies to non-EU nationals on a domestic worker visa. The source of this regime is a model contract of employment designed and distributed by the Migration Department to migrants entering on a domestic worker visa and their employers.[14] As a source of employment regulation, the contract is atypical and problematic; it was drafted by migration authorities to regulate a private law relationship, while in many respects diverging from the generally applicable statutory legislation and collective agreements.

Cyprus' labour migration regime dates back to the early 1990s when the government adopted a policy decision setting the general framework for the entry and employment of migrants.[15] According to the policy decision, migrant workers are entitled to the same rights as national workers except for the right to change employer, place of work and sector. Also, migrant workers are expressly granted the freedom to join a trade union and are entitled to salaries and benefits equal to those set for nationals in collective agreements.[16] The authorities in charge of the implementation and supervision of the policy decision are the Labour Department, which is part of the Labour and Social Insurance Ministry and the Migration Department, which is part of the Home Affairs Ministry. The two governmental departments are expected to work in close cooperation; the Labour Department is responsible for examining whether the model contracts of employment which the Migration Department prepares and disseminates to migrant workers and their employers are in line with generally applicable employment legislation.

---

[14] In addition, a Ministerial Committee on the employment of third-country nationals composed of the Ministers of Interior, Labour and Social Insurance, Justice, Tourism and Trade, which designs and implements the national policy on migrant labour and issues, from time-to-time, decisions which are relevant to migrant domestic workers. The Committee's decisions are not open to parliamentary debate.

[15] Prior to this, Cyprus had an almost closed-door approach to labour migration and granted work visas only in very limited situations such as to exceptionally highly skilled technical or managerial staff in foreign companies. See, generally, N Trimikliniotis and C Demetriou, 'Labour Integration of Migrant Workers in Cyprus: A Critical Appraisal' in M Pajnik (ed) *Precarious Migrant Labour Across Europe* (Ljubljana: Mirovni Institut, 2011) 73–96.

[16] Council of Ministers decision of 6 December 1991.

While the cooperation between the two departments is a procedure that has been followed for all categories of labour migrants, the contract for migrant domestic workers has never received any input from the Labour Department. The Migration Department consistently rejects requests from the Labour Department to review the contract and ensure compliance with labour law. Migration is of the view that migrant domestic workers' employment has no effect on the national labour market, so the Labour Department need not be consulted.[17] This stance shows that paid domestic work, especially when done by migrants, is perceived as a type of work that is separate from the rest of the labour market; national workers do not compete with migrants for jobs and, as a result, there are no incentives or effective pressures to improve working conditions. In practice, the Migration Department became the sole authority regulating not only the rules on entry and stay, but also the working conditions of migrants on a domestic worker visa.

The Migration Department's exclusive competence over the working conditions of a group of migrant workers results in a highly restrictive and exclusive labour regime. Until May 2019, the Migration Department was distributing a contract replete with threatening references to migration law enforcement rules and procedures, explicitly emphasising the domestic worker's status as a migrant first and foremost. The contract contained, for instance, clauses prohibiting the change of employers,[18] threatening the migrant with deportation in case any contractual term was breached,[19] or limiting the worker's bargaining power by ruling out the right to negotiate salary increases.[20] The contract went as far as to include a clause restricting migrant domestic workers' right to freedom of association, an otherwise internationally and constitutionally protected freedom.[21]

This model contract of employment and the overall labour regime governing migrant domestic labour in Cyprus was highly criticised in several Ombudsman reports,[22] civil society briefs and academic scholarship.[23] In a 2005 report, the

---

[17] Office of the Ombudsman, Report of the Ombudsman as National Independent Human Rights Authority as regards the status of domestic workers in Cyprus (Nicosia, 2 July 2013).

[18] Clause 2(a) states: '[the Employee] shall not be allowed to change Employer and place of employment during the validity of this contract and his Temporary Residence/Work Permit'.

[19] Clause 5 (c) states: '... breach of any clause of the contract will automatically cause the termination of the contract as well as the validity of the Employment and Residence Permit'.

[20] Clause 2(g) states: 'the Employee shall not be entitled in any way and for any reason to any increase of his (sic) fixed salary [...]'.

[21] Clause 2(h) stated it included a clause stating that the employee 'shall not engage, contribute or in any way directly or indirectly take part in any action or activity during the course of his [sic] stay in Cyprus'.

[22] The Ombudsman is a publicly funded but independent body established in 1991. Today, its mandate is carried out by different departments and covers several areas including the protection of human rights – as Commissioner for the Administration and the Protection of Human rights – and non-discrimination on different grounds including sex and ethnicity – as Equality Body. In this book, I will use the umbrella term 'Ombudsman' to refer to this institution, but I will specify which department issued each report.

[23] See, for example, Office of the Ombudsman, (n 17) above; V Pavlou, 'Migrant Domestic Labour and Models of Immigration and Employment Law Regulation: A Comparative Perspective of Cyprus and Spain' (2016) 7(1) *Revista de Investigaciones Feministas* 149–68; KISA, *International Migrants' Day: KISA claims full respect for their rights* (Nicosia, 18 December 2017).

Ombudsman urged the Migration Department to remove the clause restricting associational rights and the Labour Department to review the contract to ensure equality of treatment between migrant domestic workers and other workers.[24] Despite these calls for reform, however, for several years nothing changed in the way the state treated migrant domestic workers in Cyprus.

The contract was finally reviewed under the pressure of a scandal that broke in April 2019 when it was revealed that a Cypriot man had murdered seven migrant women and girls over the course of three years. While the appalling crimes were not committed in the context of employment, they exposed the systemic failures of the state's migration regime which makes migrant women vulnerable to abuse. Most importantly, the crimes exposed police negligence; they had failed to promptly and thoroughly investigate complaints when the migrant women and their children had first disappeared.

Following local protests by migrant groups and supporters, as well as condemnation in international media,[25] the Migration Department hastily drafted a new model employment contract in May 2019. The new contract toned down the references to migration restrictions and removed the clause prohibiting political activity. In reality, however, nothing of substance has changed. The reform of the model contract seems to be more of an attempt to conceal what can be readily pinpointed as problematic rather than a meaningful effort to regulate migrant domestic workers' conditions in a way that reduces their vulnerability to exploitation at work. It is indicative of the general approach that contracts signed before the reformed model was released remain in force; state authorities have made no effort to revoke them. As I now discuss, there are still several problematic areas both in the model contract and in other aspects of the regime governing migrant domestic labour in Cyprus.

In relation to working time, even though the generally applicable legislation does not exclude domestic work, the contract stipulates a lower level of protection. While legislation should clearly prevail over the contract of employment, in the way the state has crafted the regulation of migrant domestic workers' working conditions the normal hierarchy of sources is simply disregarded. The contract, therefore, makes no provision for daily rest breaks, contains no guarantees for night work and no provision on maximum weekly hours or overtime hours and their remuneration.

The new model contract introduced an obligation for the employer to keep records of working time – a nod to recent jurisprudence in this area from the Court of Justice of the EU.[26] This is certainly an important provision which carries transformative potential not only for working time but also for wages; by measuring

---

[24] Office of the Ombudsman, ibid.
[25] BBC, 'Cyprus serial killer case exposes abuse of migrant women' (2 May 2019); The New York Times, 'Domestic workers are killed in Cyprus, and authorities face a reckoning (2 May 2019).
[26] *Federación de Servicios de Comisiones Obreras (CCOO) v Deutsche Bank SAE* (Case C-55/18) EU:C:2019:402.

the hours actually worked, the worker can substantiate a claim for overtime pay. Given that there is no labour inspection in private households, one would expect some further guidance from state authorities on how the provision should be implemented as well as information campaigns to raise awareness among employers and domestic workers on their obligations and rights under the new contract. However, there is no guidance or awareness campaigns to support the view that the contract's reform is not supported by a commitment to improve migrant domestic workers' conditions. This leads me to the next interrelated point which concerns enforcement; how can a migrant domestic worker enforce any of her available rights against the employer?

Non-EU workers and their employers must first try to settle any disputes through a special, non-judicial procedure before resorting to the courts. According to the procedure, the migrant must file her complaint with the police and then with the labour department. If the complainant is a domestic worker who has abandoned the workplace, she has a time-limit of 15 days to file a complaint; should she fail to do so, she is declared illegal and a deportation order is issued. The Labour Department then invites the two parties to a joint meeting to express their views and submit any relevant documentation. Both parties may be represented by a lawyer and/or have an interpreter. The Labour Department reports to the Labour Disputes Committee. This Committee was created in 2000 by the Council of Ministers to examine the complaints of migrant workers against their employers. It is constituted by representatives of the police and the Labour and Migration Departments. The Committee deliberates on the case and reports back to the Immigration Department which makes the final decision. If negotiations fail then, and only then, may the parties resort to an employment tribunal.

Between 2006 and 2009 the Office of the Ombudsman received 18 complaints from migrant workers, the majority of whom were domestic workers, concerning the procedure and practice of labour dispute settlement. The complaints concerned issues such as the length of time to deliver a decision, lack of interpreters during procedures, biased treatment of migrant workers and poor investigation of their complaints, as well as a general inefficiency of the system.[27] The Ombudsman's report analyses the many problematic aspects of the labour dispute settlement system in relation specifically to domestic workers.[28] The report identifies lack of clarity regarding the rules, rights and obligations of each party as well as the mandate of each authority. Lack of clarity has, on many occasions, led to arbitrary decisions against migrant workers. For example, in the case of two domestic workers who filed complaints against their employers for breach of contract, the authorities, instead of thoroughly examining the allegations, brought criminal charges against the migrants who were subsequently deported. The report highlights that, when a migrant worker files a complaint, it is a common practice for

---

[27] Office of the Ombusdsman (n 17) above.
[28] Ibid.

the employer to accuse her of committing a crime, usually theft. Instead of keeping the two procedures separate – labour dispute settlement and criminal – the authorities normally stop the labour dispute settlement procedure and deport the migrant as a response to the criminal charges.[29]

Secondly, the report highlights that the imbalance of power between worker and employer is rarely taken into account when complaints are examined. For instance, there have been many cases of domestic workers who complained that their employer, also required them to work for others. The migrant workers were considered equally liable for breach of work and residence permit – which are tied to a named employer – and were deported with absolutely no consideration given to their personal circumstances and vulnerability. Often, the authorities demonstrate bias against migrant domestic workers; employer claims are normally accepted in a straightforward way, while those of the worker are rejected without any serious efforts to investigate them further.[30] Thirdly, the report point outs that there is no effective and impartial enforcement of the decisions. For example, when a decision concludes that the migrant violated migration rules the authorities deport her with due diligence; however, if the employer has breached the contract and must, for example, pay overtime, there is no enforcement whatsoever.[31]

The linking of labour dispute settlement to migration law enforcement and especially the involvement of the Migration Department is highly problematic. The structure and way the procedure functions deters migrant workers from attempting labour dispute settlement in the first place and is factually inaccessible to illegally resident migrants who would face criminal charges and deportation.

Another highly problematic aspect of migrant domestic workers' employment regime in Cyprus is wage regulation. As there is no statutory national minimum wage, wages are set in collective agreements at the sectoral or enterprise level and in individual employment contracts. The state only intervenes annually to set minimum wages for certain low-paid, non-unionised jobs. The minimum wage applies, inter alia, to caretakers in elderly and nursing homes, private security guards and clerks. Domestic workers employed in private households are not covered, but the Migration Department sets a wage for migrants on a domestic worker visa. Just to illustrate, in 2020 the monthly net salary for migrant domestic workers was set at €309 which corresponds to less than €1.40 per hour provided that normal working hours are respected; in case of overtime, the hourly net rate would be even lower.[32] The two groups of workers covered by the statutory minimum wage and with tasks

---

[29] Ibid.
[30] Ibid.
[31] Ibid.
[32] The previous version of the model contract of employment categorically stated that the salary was 'fixed' and the employee was 'not be entitled in any way and for any reason to any increase of his fixed salary, unless it is provided under this contract or it is considered appropriate by the employer'. While that provision has now been eliminated in the new version, there is still no clause stating that the parties can negotiate a higher wage than that set by the Migration Department.

comparable to those of domestic workers in private households, are caretakers and cleaners. In 2020, the monthly minimum salary for caretakers in nursing homes was set at €870 rising to €920 after six consecutive months of employment with the same employer. For hourly-paid cleaners employed in business and corporate premises, the hourly minimum rate was set at E€4.55 rising to €4.86 after six months of continuous employment. The disparity between the remuneration of domestic workers in private households and that of workers with comparable tasks employed by businesses is obvious and highly problematic; such a vast discrepancy cannot be justified even if one considers deductions for accommodation and food in the case of live-in workers.

The regulation of domestic workers' wages in Cyprus illustrates well Adelle Blackett's observation on how 'work has been constructed around racialized, patriarchal norms attached to the bodies undertaking the work in someone else's home rather than to skill'.[33] The Ombudsman has considered that the wage disparity constitutes race discrimination given that most domestic workers in private households are racialised migrants. One can, of course, further argue that it also constitutes sex discrimination since domestic workers are predominantly women.[34] The exceptionally low wage the state sets for migrant domestic workers determines their accommodation options and explains why most of them have no other option but to live in the employer's household.

Domestic Workers in Private Households in Sweden: A Double Exclusion

In Sweden, the direct employment of a domestic worker by a natural person is governed by the provisions of a specific legislative instrument introduced in 1970, the Domestic Work Act which also applies to au pairs. Important pieces of labour legislation, such as the Working Hours Act on the organisation of working time and the Employment Protection Act which, inter alia, regulates dismissals and fixed-term contracts, exclude those directly employed by private households. While the Domestic Work Act is supposed to fill in the protective gaps created by the exclusion from other pieces of employment legislation, in reality, it provides a lower level of protection when compared to the one available under generally applicable legislation in several respects.

Under the Domestic Work Act, normal working hours are 40 per week which is in line with the statutory maximum for other workers. However, when domestic workers' tasks involve personal care, the normal working hours can be extended

---

[33] A Blackett, 'Introduction: Regulating Decent Work for Domestic Workers' (2011) 23(1) *Canadian Journal of Women and the Law* 1–45.
[34] Office of the Ombusdsman (n 17) above.

to up to 52 hours per week according to the employer's needs.[35] Domestic workers can also be required to complete up to 300 hours of overtime in a calendar year instead of 200 hours which is the statutory limit set for other workers.[36] Contrary to workers falling under the personal scope of the Employment Protection Act, domestic workers may be dismissed without just cause and on a shorter notice. In addition, the Domestic Work Act contains no provision on limits in relation to fixed-term contracts similar to the ones applicable to other workers. Finally, the Work Environment Authority, which carries out ex officio inspections at workplaces to ensure compliance with health and safety and working time regulations, can only exceptionally inspect a private household if one of the parties so demands, or for other 'special reasons'.[37] As one would expect, labour inspections in private households are extremely rare even if they are not completely ruled out in the legislation.

Apart from explicit exclusions and protective gaps structured in the legislation, in Sweden, domestic workers working directly for a private household face disadvantages also in relation to the social context of their work; essentially, they are, de facto, excluded from the Swedish model of industrial relations.[38] The Swedish model of industrial relations is voluntarist, characterised by self-regulation and the state's non-intervention.[39] Collective agreements are key instruments in the Swedish regulatory context as they set the most important terms and conditions governing employment relationships such as wages and working time. In Sweden, at least 80 per cent of all private sector jobs are covered by collective agreements.[40] In terms of working time, collective agreements will normally provide worker protections and entitlements that exceed the statutory minimum. Regarding wages, in the absence of a statutory minimum wage in Sweden, collective agreements have a crucial function in terms of guaranteeing workers a good level of pay; workers not covered by a collective agreement must practically negotiate their salary individually with their employer. Trade unions are very important actors in this context; they provide financial support to their members when they become unemployed, provide legal advice and support in the management of workplace conflicts, ensure workers' representation at the workplace and take industrial action when negotiations fail. Unionisation in Sweden is at 64 per cent which, while this has fallen in the last few years, it is still strong compared to other European states.[41] Crucially, trade unions supervise and guarantee the

---

[35] Domestic Work Act 1970, s 2.
[36] Ibid, s 3 and Working Hours Act, s 8.
[37] Domestic Work Act 1970, s 15.
[38] C Calleman, 'Domestic Services in a 'Land of Equality': The case of Sweden' (2011) 23(1) *Canadian Journal of Women and the Law* 121–39 at 132.
[39] M Rönnmar, 'Sweden' in M Freedland and J Prassl (eds) *Viking, Laval and Beyond* (Oxford: Hart Publishing, 2014) 241–61.
[40] A Kjellberg, 'Sweden: Collective Bargaining under the Industrial Norm' in T Müller, K Vandele and J Waddington, *Collective Bargaining in Europe: Towards an Endgame* (Brussels: European Trade Union Institute, 2019).
[41] Ibid.

enforcement of labour standards set in collective agreements.[42] High unionisation levels and coverage by a collective agreement are, therefore, prerequisites for workers to be able to benefit from the Swedish model of industrial relations which, for the most part, delivers a good set of rights at work and employment protection.

As I discussed in Chapter 1, the 2008 liberalisation of labour migration rules for non-EU nationals and the increased mobility of EU nationals since the first large-scale EU Enlargement in 2004 have contributed to the expansion of low-skilled service sectors in Sweden. Many migrant workers are now concentrated in sectors with low trade-union density and low coverage by collective agreements.[43] As a consequence, migrant workers – especially those in low-skilled jobs with less individual bargaining power – are often on their own when it comes to negotiating their working conditions in the first place and then enforcing any rights they have against their employer.[44] It is therefore clear that, against this background, the Swedish model fails to deliver its emancipatory promise to many migrant workers.

What, then, is the place of migrant domestic workers in this regulatory context? The extent to which the expansion of service sectors during the last decade has also led to more migrants working directly for private individuals as domestic workers is not clear; there is no available data as to how many people fall under the personal scope of the Domestic Work Act. There are, however, indications that the Domestic Work Act is now more relevant than ever not least because of the increase in au pair migration. Trade union representatives report that the lack of data on the number and profile of individuals falling under the personal scope of the Domestic Work Act is due to the invisibility of this type of work.[45]

Clearly, migrant domestic workers employed directly by a private individual are in an even more disadvantageous position than other migrant workers. Not only do they have no collective agreements, they have fewer statutory rights than other workers and have no trade union to rely on to enforce the most basic labour rights such as wages. If we also take into account the lack of effective labour inspection for those working in private households, it becomes evident that the migrant worker is charged with the responsibility not only of knowing her rights, but also of navigating a complex legal system and resorting to court if she wants to pursue a claim against the employer.

---

[42] See Rönnmar (n 39) above 241–61; P Herzfeld Olsson, 'Empowering Migrant Workers in Sweden: A Call for Unequal Treatment' in J Howe and R Owens (eds) *Temporary Labour Migration in the Global Era: The Regulatory Challenges* (Oxford: Hart, 2016) 203–22.

[43] E Samuel, 'Reconciling Openness and High Labour Standards? Sweden's Attempts to Regulate Labour Migration and Trade in Services' in C Costello and M Freedland *Migrants at Work: Immigration and Vulnerability in Labour Law* (Oxford: Hart, 2014) 341–61; CA Woolfson, J Fudge and C Thornqvist, 'Migrant Precarity and Future Challenges to Labour Standards in Sweden', *Economic and Industrial Democracy*, August 2013, 1–21.

[44] See Herzfeld Olsson, (n 42) above, 203–22.

[45] Interview with Kommunal officers, 1 October 2013, Stockholm; Interview with Kommunal officers, 6 September 2018.

Unsurprisingly, those falling under the Domestic Work Act have rarely litigated in court to enforce their rights.[46] One of those rare instances, however, helps to illustrate the disadvantages of those falling under the Domestic Work Act and litigation's lack of transformative potential when legal sources offer so little. In a 2013 Labour Tribunal case concerning protection against dismissal, the claimant, a caregiver for a disabled person, was directly employed by her employer and thus fell under the scope of the Domestic Work Act.[47] Following her unlawful dismissal, the claimant filed a claim for pecuniary damages. The tribunal held that personal damages in unlawful dismissal cases for workers under the scope of the Domestic Work Act are not comparable to the those under generally applicable labour law – the Employment Protection Act. As a result, the claimant's personal damage was calculated using a lower rate.

In addition, as they are not unionised, domestic workers in private households have no right to take industrial action and have no access to trade union support in case of unemployment or when settling disputes with their employer.[48] The lack of a statutory minimum wage – while emancipatory for other workers who can rely on their industrial strength to agree on much higher wages than a national minimum wage could ever provide – for non-unionised domestic workers it means there is no baseline to negotiate their pay nor any limits to deductions or payments in kind. Domestic workers in private households essentially fall outside the Swedish model of industrial relations and its key entitlements and protections.

In Sweden, migrant domestic workers' vulnerability stems from a double exclusion; they are *de facto* excluded from the Swedish model of industrial relations, while their entitlements and protections under the Domestic Work Act are significantly lower than those normally enjoyed by other workers in the Swedish labour market. These exclusions place domestic workers in private households in a uniquely vulnerable position.

Separate Regime, but Near-Normal Protection: Spain

Under Spanish law, working for a private household is an employment relationship of 'special character' and is thus regulated under a special legal instrument.[49] The special instrument applies exclusively to domestic workers and its provisions take precedence over generally applicable labour legislation, ie the Spanish Workers' Statute. The Workers' Statute applies to domestic work only exceptionally, when the matter in question is not dealt with in the special legal instrument.

---

[46] See Calleman (n 38) above, 121–39.
[47] Labour Court Judgment AD 2/13 on 16 January 2013 (Application No B 65/12). With thanks to Hanna Eklund for translating this decision from Swedish to English.
[48] See Calleman (n 38) above, 121–39.
[49] Spanish Workers' Statute, art 2.

Historically, the employment of domestic workers in Spain was conceived outside the scope of labour law as a contract for services and regulated under the corresponding Civil Code provisions.[50] The first piece of legislation to regulate paid domestic work as an employment relationship was introduced in 1985.[51] While that first instrument acknowledged the employment character of the relationship between a domestic worker and her employer, it was more orientated towards upholding the parties' autonomy than providing protection to the vulnerable party.[52] That legislation governed paid domestic labour in Spain for 26 years but the significantly low protection it offered did little to integrate domestic workers within the scope of labour law and attenuate their vulnerability to exploitation.

In 2011, Spain reformed its labour and social security legislation on domestic work responding to long-standing claims to improve the sector's conditions and end its marginalisation.[53] The aim of the reform was twofold; to progressively equalise the employment rights and social protections of domestic workers with those of other sectors and to put an end to the perennial problem of informality by facilitating domestic workers' affiliation to social security.[54] The new legislation, Royal Decree 1620/2011, introduced significant improvements for the sector's working conditions in several areas.[55] I now turn to discuss provisions in the following key areas: wages, working time issues and innovative provisions strengthening domestic workers' personal autonomy.

In relation to the statutory regulation of wages, domestic workers now have an enhanced protection when compared to the previous regime which is equal to that of other workers. Domestic workers' entitlement to the national minimum wage is reaffirmed with the qualification that this may not be subjected to reductions for payments in kind.[56] Payments in kind, normally granted in the form of nutrition and/or accommodation, are now subjected to a maximum limit of 30 per cent of the total salary; this is a significant improvement from the previous regime and brings domestic work to the same level as workers under the general regime in terms of payments in kind.[57] In contrast to Cyprus, Spanish legislation explicitly gives domestic workers the possibility to negotiate a raise from the minimum

---

[50] MC Cueva Puente, *La relación laboral de los empleados de hogar* (Valladolid: Lex Nova, 2005).
[51] Royal Decree 1424/1985.
[52] YM Miñarro, *El trabajo al servicio del hogar familiar: análisis de su nueva regulación* (Madrid: Editorial Reus, 2013).
[53] J López Gandía and GD Toscani, *El nuevo régimen laboral y de seguridad social de los trabajadores al servicio del hogar familiar* (Albacete:Bomarzo, 2012); YM Miñarro, 'La nueva regulación de la relación laboral de carácter especial del servicio de hogar familiar: una mejora mejorable I y II' (2012) 4 *Relaciones Laborales* 49–60.
[54] ML Fernández Rodríguez, 'Efectos de la crisis económica sobre el trabajo de las mujeres' (2014) 1 *Relaciones Laborales* 69–83.
[55] For a comprehensive comparison between the previous and current legislation see M León, 'A Real Job? Regulating Household Work: The Case of Spain' (2013) 20(2) *European Journal of Women's Studies*, 170–88.
[56] Royal Decree 1620/2011, art 8(2).
[57] The previous Decree allowed in-kind payments for up to 45% of the total salary while the National Minimum Wage was not guaranteed. The rate is adjusted annually; in 2020 it was set at €950 per month.

wage through a collective or private agreement which is important in fostering the idea that domestic workers are workers like any other.[58] The payment of two extraordinary monthly salaries per year, as for other categories of workers, is also guaranteed.[59]

In relation to working time, Royal Decree 1620/2011 establishes a maximum of 40 hours of work per week which is equal to the statutory maximum for other workers.[60] In addition to the normal working hours, the parties may also make arrangements for on-call hours. The notion of on-call hours refers to the time during which the worker, while not carrying out any tasks, is available to the employer. Contrary to the previous regime, which was silent on the issue of on-call hours, the new legislation sets standards to reduce domestic workers' risk of exploitation by being expected to be constantly available.[61] In particular, Royal Decree 1620/2011 sets a weekly limit of 20 on-call hours and requires the employer to remunerate them at the same rate as normal hours or, alternatively, compensate the worker with additional rest time.[62] Here, Spanish legislation addresses one of the most complex issues in the regulation of working time in general which could not be more relevant to domestic workers. On-call time, illustratively described by Alain Supiot as a 'third kind of time', blurs the boundaries between work and rest time and poses important regulatory challenges especially for those domestic workers living in the employer's household.[63] Having no regulation of on-call – as for instance in the case of Cyprus – is an important driver of vulnerability as live-in domestic workers often end up being constantly available to the employer without an entitlement to pay. By setting limits on domestic workers' constant availability and treating on-call hours as normal working time that must be paid for, the Spanish legislator here takes an important step to challenge one of the 'tough spots' as Adelle Blackett describes the most challenging areas in the regulation of domestic work.[64]

Royal Decree 1620/2011 further stipulates a minimum of 12 consecutive hours of rest between work shifts. There is, however, a degree of flexibility in relation to rest for live-in domestic workers; their daily rest can be reduced to ten consecutive hours and the remaining two hours may distributed over the course of four weeks.[65]

Regarding weekly rest, there is a provision of 36 consecutive hours and a specification that it is customary to enjoy these on a Saturday or Sunday evening or a

---

[58] Royal Decree 1620/2011, art 8(1).
[59] Ibid, art 8(4).
[60] Ibid, art 9(1) and Workers' Statute, art 34(1).
[61] See Yanini (n 53) above.
[62] Royal Decree 1620/2011, art 9(2).
[63] A Supiot, *Beyond Employment. Changes in Work and the Future of Labour Law in Europe*, (Oxford: Oxford University Press, 2001) 81.
[64] See Blackett (n 4) above, ch 5.
[65] This is an improvement from the previous regime which granted ten and eight hours of rest for live-out and live-in domestic workers respectively. I discuss the compatibility of the Spanish working time regulation with EU labour law in ch 4.

Monday morning. The claim to specify the days of weekly rest was successfully put forward by domestic workers' associations. Having a set day off during the week is particularly important for domestic workers who normally work in isolated workplaces without any peer support. Sunday as a full day off gives domestic workers the opportunity to meet and socialise with colleagues they would not be able to engage with otherwise; this is an essential condition for collective organisation and mobilising. The Decree also brings domestic workers' entitlement to paid annual leave to the same level as other workers, ie 30 days of paid annual leave of which at least 15 must be consecutive.[66]

When it comes to strengthening personal autonomy, the following two provisions address concerns specific to domestic workers. Article 9(1) stipulates that once the worker has completed the normal hours of work and the agreed standby time, she is not obliged to remain in the household. This is a good example of a provision aiming to protect the autonomy of workers who live in. The second provision is Article 9(7) which states that, during paid leave, the worker is not be obliged to reside in the household or to follow the family at their place of holiday. This is an innovative provision, introduced for the first time in Spanish legislation; even though still not ratified by Spain, the influence of ILO C.189 which contains a similar provision is evident.[67]

Overall, the reformed Spanish legislation introduced several important elements that approximate domestic workers' treatment to that available to other workers under generally applicable labour legislation.

There remain, however, certain areas where domestic workers' protections and entitlements are lower than those of other workers. One example are the rules on dismissal. In case of wrongful dismissal, ie termination by the employer without just cause or against procedural rules, the domestic worker is entitled to less compensation than other workers and has no right to be readmitted to work, which is one of the remedies contemplated for other workers.[68] The employer may also dismiss the domestic worker with a written declaration of withdrawal (*desistimiento*) and without just cause, which is a requirement in other employment relationships.[69] This form of dismissal, which gives important flexibility to the employer, is unique to domestic work.

The Decree does not contemplate any remedies for unfair dismissal – this is the case of dismissals against fundamental rights such as the dismissal of a pregnant worker or based on trade union activity. Under the generally applicable

---

[66] Royal Decree 1620/2011, art 9(7).
[67] See López Gandía and Toscani (n 53) above.
[68] Under generally applicable labour legislation – that is art 56 of the Workers' Statute – the wrongfully dismissed worker may be readmitted to work or receive compensation of 33 days' payment per year of employment for up to 24 months. Under art 11, para 2 of the Decree, domestic workers receive only 20 days of payment per year worked for up to 12 months and may not be readmitted to work.
[69] In this case, the employer must give 20 days' notice if the employment relationship lasted more than a year and seven days for shorter employment periods. In addition, the worker is entitled to compensation of 12 days' payment per year worked.

labour legislation, if the dismissal is deemed unfair, the employer must readmit the worker and pay any arrears.[70] The fact that the normal remedy against unfair dismissal is readmission to work instead of compensation reflects the idea that workers' fundamental rights – such as the right to be free from discrimination or freedom of association – cannot be monetarised; instead of compensation, fundamental rights must be safeguarded with effectively dissuasive remedies.[71] Spanish courts, however, have consistently held that unfairly dismissed domestic workers are not entitled to readmission. Readmission, they say, would constitute interference in the employer's private sphere; courts opt, instead, to treat the domestic worker's unfair dismissal as wrongful and grant compensation.[72]

The leveling down of domestic workers' protection against dismissal reflects persistent societal expectations for a higher level of trust and intimacy in the relationship between a domestic worker and her employer. To be sure, an element of mutual trust is an implied or even express expectation of any employment relationship. In the case of domestic workers, however, this expectation is one-sided, as it translates to greater flexibility and discretion for the employer only. Dismissal regulation is an instance of the so-called 'special character' of domestic work operating at the worker's disadvantage. The law here, far from challenging, endorses societal expectations that compromise domestic workers' rights at work.

Another example is domestic workers' exemption from the scope of occupational health and safety legislation.[73] This exemption, however, is not absolute as for instance in the UK but comes with an important caveat: employers have the obligation to ensure that their domestic workers carry out their tasks in adequate health and safety conditions.[74] This framing opens up the possibility to argue in favour of health and safety measures adapted to the context of the private household.

What we can see in the Spanish case is that while the regulation of domestic work is formally under a separate legislative instrument, the legislation is adapted to deliver nearly the same level of protection as for other workers. An added benefit of the sectoral approach is that it allows the introduction of provisions that address issues specific to domestic workers such as the explicit recognition of the right of those who live in to leave their workplace once they complete their work.

---

[70] Workers' Statute, art 55, para 6.
[71] A Baylos and J Pérez Rey, *El despido o la violencia del poder privado*, (Madrid, Trotta, 2009).
[72] See, for example, STSJ CAT 533/2013, Sala de lo Social, ECLI:ES:TSJCAT:2013:533.
[73] Law 31/1995, art 3(4), 8 November, on the prevention of risks at the workplace [Ley 31/1995, de 8 de noviembre, de prevención de Riesgos Laborales].
[74] Spanish law on health and safety may be juxtaposed to the EU Framework Directive on Health and Safety 89/391/EEC which introduces an absolute exemption of domestic workers from personal scope. See, Framework Directive 89/391/EEC on the introduction of measures to encourage improvements in the health and safety of workers at work, [1989], OJ L183/1, art 3(a).

Approaches to Illegally Employed Migrant Domestic Workers

In this section I turn to examine the legal regimes that regulate the work of migrants without the right to work under migration law. This is an important area of law for domestic workers who, as highlighted in Chapter 1, often fall into illegality regimes due to the lack of legal migration paths and restrictions on the right to change employers. Working in breach of migration law is rarely the fault of migrants themselves, yet, it is an important driver of their vulnerability to exploitation.

Migrants working in breach of migration rules face numerous practical obstacles in seeking redress for breach of contract or breaches of labour legislation providing rights and protections. Such obstacles are strongly related to the sanctioning and criminalisation of working without a permit. A bottom-up study conducted by the EU Fundamental Rights Agency on irregular migrant domestic workers in nine EU Member States identifies the fear of expulsion and residence insecurity during procedures as two of the most common obstacles in filing claims and accessing justice.[75] Beyond criminal liability and obstacles to file a claim, a further issue concerns the treatment of irregular migrants under labour law. Are migrants who have no right to work under migration law entitled to the same rights and protections under labour law as those – migrants and citizens – with an unrestricted right to work? Can they enforce their employment contracts and seek, for instance, redress in case of unlawful wage deductions or dismissal? To what extent are migrants without the right to work entitled to fundamental rights such as protection against discrimination or associational rights?

I start with an overview of the sanctions' regimes against employers and migrant workers and then examine the different approaches to the work of illegally resident migrants in Sweden, Spain, Cyprus and the UK. To discuss the inclusion of illegally resident migrants into labour law, I look at two different approaches: the overriding principle of worker's protection in civil law systems – Sweden and Spain – and the common law doctrine of illegality – Cyprus and the UK.

Criminal Liability and Sanctions Against Employers and Workers

In the UK, criminal law has been historically the main tool used to respond to the phenomenon of migrant workers' unauthorised employment. Even though migration law has contained several criminal offences against workers since 1971,

---

[75] EU Agency for Fundamental Rights, 'Migrants in an Irregular Situation employed in Domestic Work: Fundamental Rights Challenges for the European Union and its Member States' (Luxembourg: EU Publications Office, 2011). For a follow up of this study see, A Triandafyllidou (ed), *Irregular Migrant Domestic Workers in Europe: Who cares?* (Burlington: Ashgate, 2013).

sanctions against employers were introduced for the first time only in 1996.[76] However, as that first regime on employers' sanctions was heavily focused on criminal law and required a high threshold of culpability, it was not effective in curbing the phenomenon of migrants' unauthorised work.[77] In 2008 a system of civil penalties (fines) for those employing migrant workers in violation of migration rules came into force.[78] Under this scheme, while employers could be held criminally liable if they knowingly employed a migrant in breach of migration rules, migrant workers found working without authorisation were subject to deportation but not imprisonment. The Immigration Act 2016, however, introduced a dual criminality that affects not only the employer but the worker as well. Section 34 states that migrants working in breach of immigration rules are liable to a fine and/or imprisonment of up to 51 weeks in England and Wales and imprisonment of up to six months or a fine in Scotland and Northern Ireland. Section 35 provisions up to five years' imprisonment for the employer. Importantly, employers may bring a defence against any sanctions if they prove that they had diligently checked the workers' status under migration law.

In Cyprus, the employment of an illegally resident migrant is a criminal offence punishable by up to three years' imprisonment and/or a fine for the employer.[79] Domestic courts have steadily sanctioned employers with imprisonment instead of a fine, thus underlining the gravity of the offence for the employer. Courts' reasoning is based explicitly on the acknowledgement that the weak party is the migrant worker whose irregular status implies an inherent risk of being exploited.[80] There is established Supreme Court jurisprudence in this area imposing imprisonment for employers instead of a fine because imprisonment is seen as the only deterrent penalty for employers.[81] Migrants taking up employment in violation of migration rules are liable to up to 12 months' imprisonment and/or a fine.[82] In its jurisprudence, the Supreme Court takes a different position depending on the migrant's legality of stay. If the migrant lacks a residence permit, the court adopts a stricter approach and opts for imprisonment, while if the migrant has a legal right to stay, but has no work permit or works in violation of the permit's terms, the preferred penalty is normally a fine.[83]

---

[76] B Ryan, 'The Evolving Legal Regime on Unauthorized Work by Migrants in Britain' (2005–6) 27 *Comparative Labor Law & Policy*, 27–58.

[77] B Ryan, 'Employer Checks of Immigration Status and Employment Law' in Costello and Freedland (eds) *Migrants at Work: Immigration and Vulnerability in Labour Law* (Oxford: Oxford University Press, 2014), 239–59.

[78] Immigration, Asylum and Nationality Act of 2006, s 15 and Immigration (Restrictions on Employment) Order 2007 SI 2007/3290.

[79] Aliens and Immigration Law, art 14B(1).

[80] See, for example, *Astynomikos Diefthintis Lemesou v Yorgos Xistouris and others*, Case number 6757/09; *Astynomikos Diefthintis Lemesou v Siful Molla and others*, Case number 5926/08.

[81] See, for example, Decision of the Supreme Court in *General Attorney of the Republic v Aristou Evagorou* (2001) 2 Supreme Court Judgment 285.

[82] Aliens and Immigration Law, art 19(1)(κ).

[83] See, for example, *Lin Qinlong v The Police*, (2006) 2 Supreme Court Judgment 501.

In Sweden, the recruitment of a migrant without a work permit constitutes a crime under the Aliens Act punishable with a fine and, in aggravating circumstances, with imprisonment of up to one year; a migrant who takes up employment without a work permit is sanctioned with a fine.[84]

Spanish migration law establishes three grades of offences: minor, grave and very serious. Employing an illegally resident migrant is classified as a very serious offence, punishable by a fine between €10,000 and €100,000.[85] Employing illegally resident workers under conditions which restrict their rights stipulated in law, collective agreements or contract, triggers a criminal offence punishable with two to five years' imprisonment.[86] Taking up employment while being illegally resident is classified as a grave offence and carries a fine between €500 and €10,000.

Criminalising the work of illegally resident migrants, especially when this is not accompanied by effective sanctions against employers who take advantage of their need to work, can do very little to eliminate the phenomenon of working in breach of migration rules. Research in this area illustrates that criminalising illegal migrant working is part of a broader political agenda that seeks to deregulate the labour market by removing labour rights and protections from all those who engage in paid work, including national workers. By engaging in a so-called 'fight against illegal migrant labour', governments with a deregulation agenda seek to divert attention and convince citizens that the root of their deteriorating material conditions is illegal migrant workers, not deregulation itself.[87]

Illegality Doctrines and Migrant Workers' Rights under Labour Law

The protection of the worker is an overriding principle in the legal order of the majority of European states.[88] In essence, this principle means that a migrant's lack of permit under immigration law should not impair her rights as a worker under labour law. The principle's starting point is the autonomy of labour law; it holds that as long as an individual is a worker for the purpose of a specific piece of labour legislation, she is entitled to all rights and protections therein. While the protection of the worker tends to be a consolidated principle in civil law systems,

---

[84] Aliens Act (2005:716) Chapter 20, ss 3 and 5.
[85] Law 4/2000 on the rights and freedoms of foreigners and their social integration, arts 54(d) and 55(c).
[86] Spanish Penal Code, art 312(2).
[87] J Fudge, 'Illegal Working, Migrants and Labour Exploitation in the UK' (2018) 38(3) *Oxford Journal of Legal Studies* 557–84.
[88] For an overview of the legislation on criminal sanctions in the EU27 see Fundamental Rights Agency, Fundamental Rights of Migrants in an Irregular Situation in the European Union. Comparative Report (Luxembourg: EU Publications Office, 2011).

this is not the case in countries with a common law tradition where the private law doctrine of illegality bars irregular migrant workers from accessing otherwise legitimate labour law rights and protections.[89]

The Principle of Worker's Protection: Sweden and Spain

In Sweden there is very limited case law concerning the labour law rights of those who work in breach of immigration rules; the discussion is still at a somewhat theoretical level. The implementation of the EU Directive on Employers' Sanctions gave rise to a legal debate concerning the labour law rights of irregular migrant workers;[90] this was mainly because of Article 6 of the Sanctions Directive on the employers' obligation to pay back payments to workers they employed in breach of immigration law.[91] Overall, the application of labour law to irregular migrant workers is not disputed in Sweden, the only exception being protection against dismissal.[92]

The starting point in Swedish legal scholarship concerning the labour rights of illegally resident migrants was a general principle of contract law, *pactum turpe*, or the 'immoral contract' concept.[93] When applied in an employment law context, the *pactum turpe* principle holds that an employment contract which is prohibited by law – in the case of illegally employed migrants by migration and criminal law – is illegal. Being illegal, the contract produces no legal effects and may not be enforced by the courts.[94] On the assumption that the contract is illegal, scholars have argued in favour of a more flexible application of the *pactum turpe* principle. According to this view, the contract must not be considered entirely void, but instead should be considered 'partly valid' and allow irregular migrants to derive 'a hard core of labour rights'.[95] In that case, 'core labour rights' would include rights to wages, working time and paid leave, protection against discrimination and health and

---

[89] See Ryan (n 76) above, 27–58. For a comparative analysis of the illegality doctrine in an employment context between civil and common law systems see M Freedland and N Kountouris, *The Legal Construction of Personal Work Relations* (Oxford: Oxford University Press, 2011) 147–52.

[90] Directive 2009/52/EC of the European Parliament and of the Council providing for minimum standards on sanctions and measures against employers of illegally staying third-country nationals [2009] OJ L 168/24. I provide a full analysis of the Directive's provisions in ch 3.

[91] Interview with Samuel Engblom, legal officer for the trade union TCO, Stockholm, 18 September 2013.

[92] Ibid.

[93] The theoretical foundations and application of *pactum turpe* are similar to those of the common law illegality doctrine discussed next.

[94] N Selberg, 'The Laws of "Illegal" Work and Dilemmas in Interest Representation on Segmented Labor Markets: À propos irregular migrants in Sweden' (2014) 35 *Comparative Labor Law & Policy Journal* 247–88.

[95] A Inghammar, 'The Employment Contract Revisited. Undocumented Migrant Workers and the Intersection between International Standards, Immigration Policy and Employment Law' (2010) 12 *European Journal of Migration and the Law* 193–214.

safety at the workplace, but would exclude protection from dismissal.[96] According to this line of scholarship, protection from dismissal may not be granted to those who lack a work permit because requiring the employer to continue an employment relationship against the law would constitute a 'legal paradox'.[97]

In their limited case law in this area Swedish courts follow the same stance. A 1979 case concerned a migrant worker employed under a fixed-term work permit. When the Migration Board rejected his application for renewal of his work permit, the employer dismissed him on the grounds that he was no longer authorised to work in Sweden. As he was dismissed without due notice, the worker claimed damages for wrongful dismissal. In its assessment, the court held that the Employment Protection Act, which lays down dismissal rules, did not apply in this case as the employer could not be legally required to maintain an employment contract that was in breach of immigration rules.[98]

However, another line of scholarship makes the case for the complete separation of migration and labour law. Instead of assuming that contracts are illegal and unenforceable, this line of scholarship relies on the lesser importance Swedish law normally attaches to the employment contract and the need to safeguard the autonomy of labour law to argue in favour of the disapplication of *pactum turpe* rules for those who work in breach of immigration rules. Thus, illegally resident migrant workers would be able to enforce all rights flowing from their status as workers under labour law, including protection from dismissal.[99]

In the Spanish legal order, the entitlement of irregular migrant workers to fundamental rights at work is not challenged. According to Constitutional Court jurisprudence concerning associational rights, migrant workers, regardless of their migration law status, are entitled to the same collective labour rights as Spanish workers.[100] This case law led to an amendment of the Spanish Immigration Law, which previously restricted irregular migrants' right to join a trade union; freedom of association and the right to strike for all migrant workers are now consolidated in Article 11.

Regarding the enforceability of contracts, Article 36(5) of the Spanish Immigration Law states that 'the lack of residence and work permit [...] does not nullify the employment contract in relation to the rights of the migrant worker'.[101] The explicit recognition of irregular migrant workers' contracts was included for the first time in the Spanish legal order with the enactment of the Immigration Law in 2000. Prior to this, Employment Tribunals considered such contracts illegal and void of legal effects, but recognised migrants' right to pay for work already

---

[96] Ibid.
[97] Ibid.
[98] The facts and the court's reasoning are discussed in Selberg (n 95) above, 247–88.
[99] Ibid.
[100] STC 259/2007, ECLI:ES:TC:2007:259; STC 236/2007, ECLI:ES:TC:2007:236.
[101] Law 4/2000, art 36(5).

carried out to avoid the unjust enrichment of the employer.[102] Since the legislative amendment, courts have reiterated the legal validity and enforceability of the contracts of irregular migrant workers.[103]

As in the case of Sweden, dismissal is the area of law that poses most conceptual and practical problems. Under general Spanish labour law, the remedy contemplated in case of unlawful dismissal is readmission to work. Illegally resident migrants cannot be readmitted on the basis that readmission would imply the regularisation of the migrant; readmission to work of someone who did not have the right to work in the first place would constitute, according to this view, interference with labour law in the terrain of migration law. Courts have consistently held that there can be no readmission to work for a migrant who lacks a work permit; instead, they grant compensation.

As I discussed earlier, domestic workers are not entitled to readmission on the assumption that it would be an interference with the employer's private sphere; courts have instead held that a domestic workers' unfair dismissal should be treated under the rules of wrongful dismissal and grant compensation. Thus, if for instance a domestic worker who works in violation of immigration rules is dismissed while pregnant, she will not be able to return to work but will be entitled to damages instead.

Comparing the Swedish and Spanish approaches one can observe that both jurisdictions generally accept that illegally resident migrants are entitled to labour law protection – with the exception of readmission as a dismissal remedy – and may also enforce their employment contracts.

Labour Rights under the Illegality Doctrine: Cyprus and the UK

The illegality doctrine is premised on a principle of public policy prohibiting individuals to profit from their wrongdoing. It is normally invoked in court proceedings to bar the enforcement of a contract which derives from the parties' illegal conduct. Controversially, the application of the illegality doctrine in an employment context can bar access to otherwise legitimate labour law rights and protections for migrants working in breach of immigration rules.

In Cyprus, courts have not yet addressed the enforcement of employment contracts nor access to labour legislation by migrants employed in breach of migration law. It must be noted though that Cyprus uses common law principles in the interpretation of contracts; the Cypriot Contract Law explicitly states that it

---

[102] MT Aznart Díaz, 'El trabajador extranjero en situación administrative irregular' in JL Monereo Pérez (ed), *Protección jurídico-social de los trabajadores extranjeros* (Granada: Comares, 2010).
[103] STS 5439/2011, Sala de lo Social, ECLI:ES:TS:2011:5439; STS 3940/2003, Sala de lo Social, ECLI:ES:TS:2003:3940.

must be interpreted in accordance with English law.[104] In addition, Cypriot courts invoke relevant UK jurisprudence in the field of contract law.[105] Therefore, if such a case arises, Cypriot courts are most likely to follow the illegality doctrine path and hold contracts unenforceable. Cyprus has fully implemented the EU Employers Sanctions Directive provision on an employer's obligation to pay back payments to illegally employed non-EU nationals;[106] how this provision will be enforced remains unclear. Given that there has been no relevant litigation in Cyprus, the common law position can best be understood by examining a number of very interesting UK cases on this issue.

In the UK, the illegality doctrine operates differently in relation to contract and tort claims. Normally, illegality will be applied more harshly on claims based on contract because of judicial concerns that enforcing the contract will allow the claimant to profit from her own wrongdoing.[107] The leading authorities in this area have, until recently, been *Hall v Woolston Hall Leisure* and *Vakante v Governing Body of Addey and Stanhope School*.[108]

In *Hall*, the employer had arranged the applicant's terms of employment so as to avoid paying tax; the applicant was aware of the employer's fraud. When dismissed because of her pregnancy, Ms Hall brought a sex discrimination claim; the employer raised the illegality defence arguing that the claim should be barred because it was based on an illegal contract. The Court of Appeal rejected the employer's defence and accepted Ms Hall's sex discrimination claim. The case clarified the three instances when a contract is 'inextricably bound up' with illegality and thus rendered unenforceable. These are when: (a) the contract is entered into with the intention of permitting an illegal act; (b) the contract is expressly or impliedly prohibited by law; and (c) the contract was lawful when made but has been illegally performed and the party who seeks enforcement knowingly participated in the illegal performance.[109] In the first two instances the contract is unlawful from the outset and courts may not enforce it. In the third instance, however, the contract is unenforceable only if a test of knowledge and participation is applied; this test is met if the party who seeks enforcement was not only aware of the illegality, but also actively participated in the illegal conduct. Only if a test of knowledge and participation is fulfilled can a lawful contract be rendered unenforceable.

Hall confirms that a further requirement must be fulfilled before the illegality defence can bar a claim based on statutory tort such as that of sex discrimination;

---

[104] Cyprus Contract Law, Chapter 149, art 2(1).
[105] N Hatzimihail, 'Reconstructing Mixity: Sources of Law and Legal Method in Cyprus' in V Palmer, M Mattar and A Koppel (eds) *Mixed Legal Systems, East and West*, (Farnham: Ashgate, 2015) 75–99.
[106] Aliens and Immigration Law, art 18.
[107] A Bogg, 'Okedina v Chikale and Contract Illegality: New Dawn or False Dawn? (2020) 49(2) *Industrial Law Journal* 258–83.
[108] *Vakante v Addey and Stanhope School* [2004] EWCA Civ 1065.
[109] Judge Peter Gibson in *Hall v Woolston Hall*.

the claimant's illegal conduct and claim must be causally linked. In his analysis Justice Gibson states:

> ... the correct approach of the tribunal in a sex discrimination case should be to consider whether the applicant's claim arises out of or is so clearly connected with or inextricably bound up or linked with the illegal conduct of the applicant that the court could not permit the applicant to recover compensation without appearing to condone the conduct.[110]

In *Vakante*, a migrant who was lawfully resident in the UK but without permission to work took up employment after falsely stating to the employer that he did not need a work permit.[111] Following his dismissal on grounds unrelated to the lack of work permit, Mr Vakante brought a race discrimination claim. The Employment Tribunal and the Court of Appeal rejected his claim based on the illegality doctrine. Although, the Court of Appeal proposed directly applying the principles laid down in Hall, the strict causality Hall required between the illegal conduct and the claim that must be met to defeat a claim of tort was disregarded. The Court of Appeal concluded that the claim – race discrimination – was bound up with illegality even though it was unrelated to the claimant's unlawful conduct – working without a permit. Thus, *Vakante* widened the scope of the illegality doctrine by relaxing the causal link requirement; the judgment created negative legal precedent for the protection of irregular migrant workers' rights, including those who enjoy fundamental status such as protection against discrimination.[112]

Litigation by migrant domestic workers over the last decade makes evident that the illegality doctrine, when applied in an employment context, is a crucial vector of vulnerability for migrants working in breach of migration rules.

In *Zarkasi v Anindita*,[113] the claimant, an Indonesian national, was approached by the employers in her home country who offered her domestic work in the UK. The employers instructed Ms Zarkasi to make false statements to the UK immigration authorities regarding her identity in order to obtain a passport and a visa. During her employment, she took care of her employer's child and carried out domestic chores. She was a live-in domestic worker but had no room of her own and slept in the living room. Her payment was less than that the employers had promised and below the national minimum wage. After two years of employment, Ms Zarkasi, following a quarrel with her employers, left the household and brought claims for unfair dismissal and unlawful deductions from wages.

---

[110] *Hall*, para 42.

[111] This was before imposing a legal obligation on employers to check the immigration status of their prospective employees.

[112] See, also, A Bogg and T Novitz 'Race Discrimination and the Doctrine of Illegality' (2013) 129 *Law Quarterly Review* 12–17.

[113] *Zarkasi v Anindita and another* [2012] ICR 788 Employment Appeal Tribunal.

The Employment Tribunal acknowledged that the claimant was in a vulnerable position and exploited by the employers:

> There is no doubt from our findings that in general terms the claimant was exploited. She was young, relatively poorly educated and vulnerable in a foreign country in which she had no right to be, let alone to work.[114]

Yet, following a strict application of the illegality doctrine, both the Employment and Employment Appeal Tribunals rejected Zarkasi's claims based on the contract's illegality. The Employment Appeal Tribunal reiterated that the contract fell under the second category in the test set in *Hall* – a contract expressly prohibited by statute – and thus was unenforceable from the outset. While acknowledging that the strict application of illegality in *Zarkasi* constitutes 'injustice', the Employment Appeal Tribunal affirmed that illegality is a not a principle of justice but one of public policy which leaves 'no room for holding lawful a contract as a matter of discretion or interpretation'.[115]

The facts in *Hounga v Allen*[116] unfold in a very similar manner. Mary Hounga, a Nigerian national, illiterate and from a poor socioeconomic background, was approached in Nigeria by the Allens, a British-Nigerian couple, who offered her a job as a live-in domestic worker in the UK. She was promised £50 per month, free accommodation and food as well as the possibility to receive some education in the UK. On the employer's instructions, she made false statements regarding her identity and the purpose of her travel and obtained a six-month tourist visa but no work permit; Ms Hounga was a minor when she arrived in the UK. When her tourist visa expired, she continued working for the Allens as a domestic worker and caregiver for their three children. During her employment, Ms Hounga received no payment for her service and was repeatedly physically abused. After 18 months of employment, she was dismissed and expelled from the household.

Assisted by a charity organisation, Ms Hounga brought claims for breach of contract, unfair dismissal, unpaid wages and unpaid holiday pay and a tort claim for race discrimination. Following a strict application of the illegality doctrine, the Employment and Employment Appeal Tribunals rejected all the claims except for race discrimination which is legally characterised a tort claim. The Employment Appeal Tribunal considered that Ms Hounga was aware of and actively participated in the illegality; this was despite acknowledging that her employer's conduct was instrumental to the illegality of her migration status.[117] The argument that Ms Hounga's active participation could be questioned because she was a minor and in a vulnerable situation was rejected. In its reasoning, the Employment Appeal Tribunal reiterated that illegality is:

> not a principle of justice: it is a principle of policy whose application is indiscriminate and can lead to unfair consequences as between the parties' litigation. Moreover the

[114] Ibid, para 7 citing the Employment Tribunal.
[115] Ibid, paras 27 and 28.
[116] *Allen v Hounga* [2011] UKEAT/0326/10/LA.
[117] Ibid, para 36.

principle allows no room for the exercise of any discretion by the Courts in favour of one party or the other.[118]

Ms Hounga's race discrimination claim had a different fate. Initially accepted by the Employment and the Employment Appeal Tribunals – given that it flows from tort and does not depend on the existence of a valid contract – it was then struck down by the Court of Appeal. In a much-criticised judgment, the Court of Appeal held that Ms. Hounga's race discrimination claim was 'inextricably bound up' with her own illegal conduct and, as such, had to be rejected.[119] As was the case in *Vakante*, the Court of Appeal failed to establish a strict causal link between the appellant's illegal conduct and the harm she complained of, a requirement to defeat a claim in tort such as that of race discrimination.

The UK Supreme Court reversed the Court of Appeal judgment on the basis that there was 'insufficiently close connection between her immigration offences and her claims for the statutory tort of discrimination'.[120] The disapplication of illegality rules to afford protection against discrimination is certainly a positive development. It is, however, highly problematic that the UK Supreme Court was only willing to set aside the illegality doctrine because elements of trafficking and forced labour were detected in Ms Hounga's case.[121] In essence, what the Supreme Court held is that the public policy of illegality should give way to the public policy against trafficking.[122] It is thus still unclear what will be the fate of the statutory claims of a migrant working in breach of immigration rules but who, contrary to *Hounga*, is not legally characterised as trafficking victim.

It should also be pointed out that the disapplication of illegality rules in *Hounga* only concerned statutory claims – in this case, race discrimination. The barring of contractual claims by the illegality defence was not questioned. Importantly, several claims that are based on statute, such as unfair dismissal, working time breaches or unpaid holiday pay, are now legally characterised, following *Hounga*, as contractual claims. Given that the disapplication of illegality rules in favour of enforcing the labour law claims of migrant workers can only take place in the context of what are judicially considered statutory claims – ie non-discrimination – the scope of protection, even after the Supreme Court's judgment in *Hounga* remained very narrow.

The judgment in *Okedina v Chikale*, handed down by the Court of Appeal in 2019, is the most recent example concerning the illegality doctrine in the context of employment.[123] It is an important judgment because it revisited the issue of whether migrant workers without the right to work can enforce claims based on contract.

---

[118] Ibid citing *Tinsley v Milligan* [1994] 1 AC 340.
[119] *Hounga* [2012] EWCA Civ 609, para 61.
[120] *Hounga v Allen and another* [2014] UKSC, para 67.
[121] Similarly, in *Zarkasi*, the fact that the UK Border Agency had recognised Ms Zarkasi as a victim of trafficking was used to argue in favour of setting aside the illegality doctrine.
[122] *Hounga v Allen and another* [2014] UKSC, para 52.
[123] *Okedina v Chikale* [2019] EWCA Civ 1393.

The case concerned a migrant worker from Malawi who was brought to the UK by her employer, also a Malawian national, to work as a live-in domestic worker. The employer, by giving false information to UK authorities, arranged a six-month domestic worker visa for Ms Chikale. When her visa expired, the employer confiscated her passport and led her to believe that they were taking steps to regularise her status. Ms Chikale, unaware of the illegality of her stay, continued working for another year and a half. During the approximate two years of her employment, she worked very long hours, seven days per week and was only paid around £3,300 in total. When she asked for more money, she was dismissed on the spot.

Ms Chikale then brought several claims judicially characterised as contractual – unfair dismissal, unlawful deductions from the minimum wage, working time breaches – and the tortious claim of race discrimination. The employer brought the illegality defence which was rejected by both the Employment and Employment Appeal Tribunals. The Court of Appeal upheld the Tribunals' decisions on the basis that only the employer had acted unlawfully by employing a migrant worker who lacked the right to work because, when the facts of the case arose, only the act of employing an illegally resident migrant was a criminal offence.[124] Ms Chikale was therefore able to enforce her contractual claims.

While *Okedina* is a positive development in relation to the contract claims of migrants without the right to work, the entry into force of the Immigration Act 2016 is likely to curtail any protective potential. As explained earlier, the Immigration Act 2016, now criminalises not only employing an illegally resident migrant, but also working without a right to work, ie the migrant's conduct. The existence of a criminal offence directed at the workers creates a much wider scope to consider the contract prohibited, expressly or impliedly, from the outset and therefore, unenforceable.[125]

Conclusion

In this chapter I examined the labour law regimes of Cyprus, Spain, Sweden and the UK to identify norms that structure or may potentially reduce domestic workers' vulnerability. While all labour regimes contain norms that disadvantage those working in private households, there are crucial qualitative differences.

In the *UK*, the restrictive migration model is coupled with key exclusions for migrant domestic workers under the labour law regime. In *Cyprus*, easy access to a legal migration status creates conditions of special vulnerability for migrant domestic workers who are granted a migration status with a range of restrictions. The state then crafted a labour regime applied specifically to those under a migrant domestic worker status. The combination of these two regimes exposes domestic

---

[124] Under the Immigration, Asylum and Nationality Act 2006, ss 15 and 21.
[125] See Bogg (n 107) above, 258–83.

workers to many vulnerabilities; not only are they granted substandard rights and protections, but they also face acute obstacles in enforcing any rights available. In *Sweden*, the employer-led migration regime increases migrant domestic workers' chances to fall under the personal scope of the Domestic Work Act, a labour law instrument with exceptionally low protections and rights as per Swedish standards. In *Spain*, on the other hand – while the picture is certainly not ideal – the combination of a migration regime with some state regulation on entry conditions and of a labour law regime that affords protection which is near to the one afforded to other types of work, makes migrant domestic workers less vulnerable.

The comparison of the four labour regimes offers a corrective to any straightforward account of whether domestic work should be regulated as a 'work like any other' or a 'work like no other'. It follows that the divisive line between the two approaches is somewhat flawed because much of the debate focuses on models. We need to look beyond these and scrutinise the substance of employment law protections and entitlements in different national contexts. Spain has a separate instrument but grants substantially more labour protection to domestic workers than the UK which, while including domestic work in the personal scope of generally applicable legislation, enacts exclusions from crucial entitlements such as minimum wage and working time. On the other hand, in Sweden, despite special legislation being in place, domestic workers in private households face special vulnerabilities.

The impact of migration law upon the employment relationship is also a crucial vector which must be taken into account when assessing the construction of vulnerability under national regimes. In Cyprus, the state has created a special regime for migrant domestic workers which deviates substantially from generally applicable norms. This regime is not enacted to regulate a type of work, but to construct a specific category of temporary migrant worker, with limited opportunities to challenge her situation and whose function is to provide low-cost care. A similar pattern is also noted in the UK, where norms such the 'as a member of the family' exemption from the minimum wage, as well as the illegality doctrine are crucial sources of disadvantage for migrant domestic workers.

3

Migrant Domestic Workers under EU Migration Law: Fragmentation and the Value of Work

Introduction

While there is a rich legal scholarship examining different aspects of EU migration law, little attention has been paid to the position of migrant domestic workers under the different sources that make up the EU's regime on migration. In addition, most analyses of EU migration law tend to focus on the category of the non-EU, or third-country national (TCN), to use EU law terminology. However, migrant domestic workers in Europe include EU nationals as well as various categories of non-EU nationals. A wider and more nuanced analysis of the role of EU migration law in creating a variety of migrant worker statuses with differentiated rights attached to each status is required. This is what this chapter aims to provide and, while it contains material familiar to EU migration lawyers, my analysis aims to bring this material to the attention of those primarily focused on migrant domestic labour.

EU migration law includes a plethora of legal sources governing the conditions of entry, stay and movement of EU and non-EU workers. The position of migrant workers under this complex regime is far from homogeneous. As this chapter shows, the various primary and secondary EU migration law sources introduce not only very different conditions of admission but also different employment norms for each category of migrant worker. My purpose in this chapter is twofold: to locate norms relevant to migrant domestic workers in the EU's labour migration regime and to evaluate to what extent they create or, can potentially reduce, vulnerability to exploitation.

The first important set of legal sources to consider is the EU regime on the free movement of workers. This grants a comprehensive and robust set of rights to those who move within the EU for the purpose of work.[1] The most recent EU

---

[1] The free movement of workers has been an essential aspect of the European integration project since the Treaty of Rome. What was then art 48 was inserted into the Treaty of Rome due to pressure from Italy which was experiencing high unemployment rates and was seeking to export its low-skilled national workforce to the more industrialised markets of the other EEC partners: Belgium, the Netherlands, Luxembourg, France and Germany finally accepted the provision on the free movement

enlargements in 2004, 2007 and 2013 challenged, to some extent, the comprehensiveness of the regime. The imposition of transitional arrangements on the free movement of workers for the citizens of the acceding states introduced a new category of EU migrant worker – that of transitional citizen. While transitional restrictions no longer apply in the EU today – Croatian workers were granted fully EU mobility as of July 2020 – the discussion here is still relevant because the status of transitional citizen adds another layer of complexity and fragmentation to the EU's labour migration regime.

Another set of EU law sources on the status of migrant workers are the association and cooperation agreements the EU has signed with third countries for the establishment of bilateral relations. The EU has signed such agreements with many non-EU states: EEA states and Switzerland, Turkey, the states of Morocco, Algeria and Tunisia, as well as with African, Caribbean and Pacific States, Russia and most ex-Soviet states.[2] The agreements liberalise trade relations or prepare the partner country's future accession to the EU. In addition, they contain provisions on the rights of resident workers from the partner countries. These are typically clauses on equal treatment with nationals in relation to wages, working conditions and social security.[3] The extent of rights varies greatly under the different agreements and the status of non-EU nationals therein is highly fragmented.

Contrary to the solid foundations of the free movement of workers' regime, the EU had initially no competence to legislate on the treatment of non-EU workers. In 1993 the Treaty of Maastricht equipped the EU with some limited powers over immigration matters. In the period between the Maastricht and Amsterdam Treaties, the EU adopted some non-binding, soft law measures in the form of resolutions and recommendations on immigration law.[4] It was only in 1999 with the

---

of workers, notwithstanding their divergent national preferences over the mobility of labour, to ensure the success of the integration of the market project. See S Goedings, *Labor Migration in an Integrating Europe: National Migration Policies and the Free Movement of Workers, 1950–1968* (Hague: Sdu uitgevers, 2005). Yet, despite being initially a mere compromise between the founding members, the free movement of workers evolved into a staple feature of the internal market and, especially since the introduction of the citizenship of the Union concept, of the EU integration project as broadly conceived. Over the years, the Court's jurisprudence has been pivotal in giving content and strengthening the position of the EU citizen when she moves to work in a member state other than her own.

[2] S Peers, 'Towards Equality: Actual and Potential Rights of Third-Country Nationals in the European Union' (1996) 33 *Common Market Law Review* 7–50.

[3] These equal treatment provisions have been characterised as 'bargaining chips' in the context of trade and external relations. See, MH Robinson, 'An Overview of Recent Legal Developments at Community Level in relation to Third-Country Nationals Resident within the European Union, with Particular Reference to the Case Law of the European Court of Justice' (2001) 38 *Common Market Law Review* 525–86, 532. Less cynically, the insertion of equality clauses in the agreements with third countries is attributed to European trade unions' lobbying for better protection both to avoid TCNs' labour exploitation and to safeguard the domestic labour market from social dumping practices. See, KA Dahlber, 'The EEC Commission and the Politics of Free Movement of Labour' (1968) 6 *Journal of Common Market Studies* 330. Overall, while equality of treatment might have been one of the objectives – a rather marginal one – it is clearly not the underlying aim pursued under the different agreements especially those orientated towards cooperation rather than association.

[4] S Peers et al., *EU Immigration and Asylum Law* (Leiden: Nijhoff Publishers, 2012).

entry into force of the Treaty of Amsterdam that the EU acquired formal competence to legislate on immigration issues.[5]

Currently, Article 79 TFEU sets out the EU's legislative competence in the field of immigration law; this competence covers, inter alia, the conditions of entry, residence and intra-EU mobility of TCNs, the rights of legally resident TCNs, as well as illegal immigration and unauthorised residence. During the last decade, the EU has adopted several legislative instruments that concern legally and illegally resident migrant workers. These include several sectoral directives on the conditions of entry, stay and work by category of migrant worker, a directive on sanctions against the employers of illegally employed TCNs, a directive on the return of illegally resident TCNs, as well as directives on long-term residents and family reunification.[6] While generally these sources are aimed at "bridging the rights gap between EU nationals and TCNs" in practice they create separate employment regimes for non-EU workers on the basis of their perceived market value.

The discussion in this chapter is structured as follows. Section 2 starts by giving an overview of the different legal sources that make up the EU's labour migration regime and examines their relevance for migrant domestic workers. I first examine the rules on the free movement of EU workers and that of transitional citizens and then turn to the sources on TCN workers. As regards the status of TCN workers under agreements with third countries, I distinguish between four types. First, agreements that grant first entry rights along with a comprehensive set of citizenship-like entitlements; these are the EEA and Swiss agreements. Second, agreements with no first entry rights but with a relatively good set of rights for resident workers as in the Turkey agreement. Third, the Euro-Med agreements with Maghreb states that grant no first entry rights but include an equal treatment guarantee with some implications for residence rights. Fourth, agreements with the rest of the world that are very limited in terms of rights for resident migrant workers;[7] because of their limited relevance, these agreements will not be discussed. Concerning the sectoral labour migration directives, I give an overview

---

[5] Article 63(3) and (4) EC afforded the EU competence to adopt measures in:

(a) conditions of entry and residence, and standards on procedures for the issue by Member States of long-term visas and residence permits, including those for the purpose of family reunion, and
(b) illegal immigration and illegal residence, including repatriation of illegal residents;

(4) measures defining the rights and conditions under which nationals of third countries who are legally resident in a Member State may reside in other Member States.

[6] Full references are provided for each source when they are discussed more fully later in this chapter.
[7] As Thym argues, since the CJEU has used the Turkish agreement to strengthen the position of Turkish workers, Member States have been particularly careful when drafting migration provisions in agreements with partner countries. As a result, subsequent agreements focus on controlling migration flows rather than providing rights for resident workers. See, D Thym, 'Constitutional Foundations of the Judgments on the EEC-Turkey Association Agreement' in D Thym and M Zoeteweij-Turhan M (eds) *Right of Third-Country Nationals under EU Association Agreements. Degrees of Free Movement and Citizenship* (Leiden/Boston: Brill, 2015).

of key provisions of the directives on highly skilled workers, seasonal workers, students and volunteers and the single permit. While the sectoral directives are not meant to apply to domestic workers, examining them comparatively sheds light on the fragmentation of the EU's labour migration regime. I then argue, in Section 3, that this highly fragmented regime resting on a hierarchy of statuses, which, in its turn, reflects a bias on the value of work. Section 4 discusses the legal sources on non-EU nationals' integration while Section 5 analyses EU legal provisions on illegally resident workers in light of their potential impact on domestic workers. Section 6 concludes by drawing broader conclusions on the role of EU migration law in shaping the migrant domestic workers' vulnerability to exploitation.

EU Sources on the Movement of EU and Non-EU Workers

Fully Mobile EU Citizens

When juxtaposed with Member States' national immigration regimes, the EU regime on the free movement of EU national workers is considerably liberal.[8] Article 45 TFEU,[9] Regulation 492/2011 on freedom of movement of workers within the Union as well as secondary law – the Citizens' Directive 2004/38/EC[10] – shapes a unique labour migration regime. Under EU law, EU citizens, regardless of their educational background, skills or salary level, enjoy certain 'core rights' when they cross national borders within the EU for the purpose of work.[11]

An EU domestic worker may enter the Member State of her choice to look for work without having to rely on intermediaries or sponsorship by an employer.[12]

---

[8] S Peers, 'Aliens, Workers, Citizens or Humans? Models for Community Immigration Law' in E Guild and C Harlow (eds), *Implementing Amsterdam Immigration and Asylum rights in EC Law* (Oxford: Hart Publishing, 2001) 291–308.

[9] TFEU, art 45 states: '1. Freedom of movement for workers shall be secured within the Union. 2. Such freedom of movement shall entail the abolition of any discrimination based on nationality between workers of the Member States as regards employment, remuneration and other conditions of work and employment. 3. It shall entail the rights, subject to limitations justified on grounds of public policy, public security or public health: (a) to accept offers of employment actually made; (b) to move freely within the territory of Member States for this purpose; (c) to stay in a Member State for the purpose of employment in accordance with the provisions governing the employment of nationals of that State laid down by law, regulation or administrative action; (d) to remain in the territory of a Member State after having been employed in that State, subject to conditions which shall be embodied in regulations to be drawn up by the Commission. 4. The provisions of this Article should not apply to employment in the public service.'

[10] Regulation (EU) No 492/2011 of the European Parliament and of the Council on freedom of movement for workers within the Union [2011] OJ L141/1.

[11] E Guild, 'The EU's Internal Market and the Fragmented Nature of EU Labour Migration' in Costello C and Freedland M (eds), *Migrants at Work: Immigration and Vulnerability in Labour Law* (Oxford: Oxford University Press, 2014) 98–121.

[12] The right to 'accept offers of employment actually made' under TFEU art 45 entails the right to enter a Member State and stay for up to three months for the purpose of looking for employment. See Case C-292/89 *Antonissen* [1991] ECR I-00745 and recital 9 of Directive 2004/38/EC.

In a state where domestic workers are in high demand, she can meet up with a few potential employers and negotiate the terms and conditions of work before deciding on an offer. Once on the job, she can freely change employers or sector – she will, in other words, be as legally mobile as any worker who is a citizen. In addition, she is entitled to equal treatment with national workers in relation to pay and other conditions of work.

EU migrant workers have EU law-derived rights for their family members, including those who are not EU citizens. When an EU domestic worker moves, she can therefore bring her family members, who, in their turn, will also have rights to residence and to work comparable to those of nationals and EU citizens. Beyond the human rights' dimension of the right to family reunion as guaranteeing the right to respect for private and family life, at a more practical level, the right is important for the creation of a supportive network the migrant worker can turn to when things go wrong.

An EU domestic worker will also have strong protection against removal, including access to justice mechanisms to challenge an expulsion decision.[13] While not entirely shielded from removal as full protection is reserved only for a state's own nationals, she will nonetheless enjoy a high level of protection especially when compared to that of non-EU workers. The circumstances under which an EU national can become irregular and deportable while working in another Member State are narrowly construed under EU law which guarantees EU workers a high level of residence stability.[14] Residence stability places EU migrant workers in a uniquely privileged position vis à vis most categories of non-EU workers whose right to reside is highly precarious. Bringing a complaint against one's employer is challenging for any worker, be it a national or migrant. For non-EU migrant workers, however, their precarious migration status adds another layer of vulnerability; when deportation is at stake, seeking to enforce rights at work becomes highly unlikely. The kind of residence stability EU law guarantees to EU migrant workers is therefore a key protection against vulnerability to exploitation. Finally, EU migrants have the right to intra-EU mobility which means that they can move freely between Member States for the purpose of employment or become circular migrants and move back and forth between their country of origin and place of work.[15]

Overall, an EU migrant domestic worker moves and takes up employment under a legal framework which has the potential to reduce the vulnerabilities typically associated with the migration experience. Fully mobile and protected, EU migrant domestic workers are not normally exposed to more vulnerabilities than

---

[13] Directive 2004/38, art 31.

[14] However, non-economically active EU citizens are at a higher risk of becoming illegal and removable. See BM Queiroz, *Illegally Staying in the EU. An Analysis of Illegality in EU Migration Law* (Oxford: Hart Publishing, 2018), especially ch 2.

[15] Marchetti's study on care givers in Italy shows that circularity is very much the preferred migration and employment pattern for Eastern European women in the sector. S Marchetti, 'Dreaming Circularity?: Eastern European Women and Job-sharing in Paid Home Care' (2013) 11(4) *Journal of Immigrant and Refugee Studies* 347–63.

national domestic workers; this partly explains why this category is not a major source of migrant domestic labour in the EU today. However, for many domestic workers who are fully mobile EU nationals, transitional citizenship was their first step towards full EU citizenship.

EU Migrant Workers and Transitional Citizenship: A8, EU2 and Croatian Nationals

Transitional arrangements are temporary restrictions of up to seven years on workers' free movement. In the context of EU enlargements, Member States have the discretion to temporarily derogate from EU free movement provisions and apply national immigration rules to workers from acceding countries. The enactment of transitional arrangements in the enlargements of 2004 and 2007 attracted attention because it was the first time that such large numbers of people from significantly lower-income countries had become EU nationals. Yet, transitional arrangements are not a novelty for the EU. The Treaty of Rome had postponed Member States' obligation to give full effect to the free movement of workers until 1968.[16] In subsequent enlargements, transitional arrangements were enacted every time existing Member States feared an influx of workers from poorer acceding Member States. In 1981 a seven-year period of transitional arrangements was implemented for Greek workers; the same as for Spanish and Portuguese workers in 1986. Conversely, no transitional arrangements were enacted in 1973 when the UK, Ireland and Denmark joined the Union, or in 1995 when the accession of Sweden, Finland and Austria took place.[17]

In the 2004 enlargement, when ten new states joined the EU,[18] Member States could enact a seven-year period of transitional arrangements for workers from the Central and Eastern European states (A8), while workers from Malta and Cyprus were immediately granted full mobility rights.[19] Most old EU-15 Member States enacted restrictions for A8 nationals except for the UK, Ireland and Sweden who

---

[16] E Guild, 'The EU's Internal Market and the Fragmented Nature of EU Labour Migration' in *Migrants at Work* (n 11) above, 98–121.
[17] Ibid.
[18] The Czech Republic, Slovakia, Hungary, Slovenia, Estonia, Poland, Lithuania, Latvia, Malta and Cyprus.
[19] The formula of the arrangements was the following: during the first two years of accession each Member State had to notify the Commission of its intention to apply transitional arrangements. After two years – in 2006 – Member States had to notify the Commission of their intention to continue applying arrangements for three more years; at this point, their decision had to be justified on the basis of a real threat of disturbance to their labour market. For the remaining two years any decision to continue applying mobility restrictions had to be based on well-founded indications that the free movement of workers would lead to serious disturbances in the labour market. Adinolfi notes that Member States' right to derogate from free movement provisions was exceptionally wide in the context of the 2004 enlargement as compared to the previous ones. See, A Adinolfi, 'Free Movement and Access to Work of Citizens of the New Member States: The Transitional Measures' (2005) 42 *Common Market Law Review* 469–98.

opened their labour markets immediately. This decision influenced the direction of migration flows; the UK – and to a lesser extent Ireland – who offered more opportunities for casual employment had a disproportionately high share of A8 nationals.[20]

Many of those migrants, especially women, found work in care services. As discussed in Chapter 1, some of the EU 15 Member States who applied transitional restrictions, exceptionally allowed access to A8 migrant workers provided they would work in care services for the elderly, channelling, in this way, transitional citizens in care and domestic work.

In 2007 Bulgaria and Romania joined the EU. This time enlargement coincided with the beginning of the economic downturn in Europe which might have influenced some Member States' decision to impose restrictions on Bulgarian and Romanian (EU2) workers. Yet not all Member States made use of the possibility to restrict the free movement of workers. Sweden and Cyprus, along with Finland and all A8 states except Hungary, fully opened their labour markets to Bulgarian and Romanian workers; the rest of the EU and the UK enacted restrictions.[21] As with the 2004 enlargement, Member States who enacted restrictions allowed Bulgarian and Romanian workers access for the purpose of working as carers.

The same formula of transitional arrangements applied in relation to Croatian workers in 2013. Member States made different use of the possibility to impose transitional arrangements on Croatian workers. Spain and Cyprus, as well as the majority of Member States, initially applied restrictions but lifted them in July 2015 after the first two years had elapsed. On the other hand, the UK, Austria and the Netherlands required Croatians to hold a work permit until the end of the transitional period in July 2020.

How does transitional citizenship shape a migrant domestic worker's vulnerability to exploitation? Transitional citizens are differently legally vulnerable from both fully mobile EU nationals and from non-EU nationals. Because transitional restrictions are only placed on the right to take up employment, a domestic worker with transitional citizenship status is still entitled to free movement; she can thus enter the Member State of her choice as self-employed or for up to three months as jobseeker. In this respect, she is less vulnerable from those non-EU nationals with no first entry rights under EU law. However, to stay beyond the initial three-month

---

[20] J Gordon, 'Free Movement and Equal Rights for Low Wage Workers? What the United States can Learn from the New EU Migration to Britain' (Fordham Law Legal Studies Research Paper, May 2011).

[21] Spain requested a job offer and employer's authorisation to grant a work permit. At the end of the first phase, in January 2009, Spain decided to fully open its labour market to EU2 nationals. However, in July 2011, Spanish authorities, following an emergency procedure, re-introduced the work permit system for Romanian workers only. The reintroduced restrictions were applicable only to new entrants seeking employment and did not affect the status of Romanian workers already residing and working in Spain. However, the hasty change of rules targeting the nationals of a single Member State, as well as the EU Commission's lax reaction, received negative criticism. For commentary, see E Guild and S Carrera, 'Labour Migration and Unemployment. What Can We Learn from EU Rules on the Free Movement of Workers?' (CEPS Paper in 'Liberty and Security in Europe' Series, February 2012).

period, she would need to obtain a work permit according to each state's national migration rules. As discussed in Chapter 1, national migration regimes governing domestic work in Europe vary significantly; the difficulty to obtain a permit and the restrictiveness of some regimes post-entry can push new entrants into informality, bogus self-employment or even illegality of stay.

In addition, transitional citizens' intra-EU mobility rights are compromised because to move to another Member State they must apply for a work permit according to that country's immigration rules; this is a significant difference between transitional and fully mobile EU citizens. Eventually though, transitional citizens become EU citizens with full mobility rights and protections under EU law. Conversely, for non-EU nationals the route to full legal inclusion is much more uncertain and highly dependent on Member States' discretion.

Domestic Workers under the Association and Cooperation Agreements with Third Countries

EFTA Workers

The EEA agreement signed between the EU, Iceland, Liechtenstein and Norway[22] creates a regime on workers' free movement akin to that of fully mobile EU citizens.[23] Similarly, the Free Movement of Persons Agreement between EU Member States and Switzerland[24] creates a set of coterminous rights: the right of first entry,[25] non-discrimination on the basis of nationality,[26] unrestricted access to the labour market including full occupational and geographical mobility,[27] equality of treatment in employment conditions,[28] residence rights,[29] as well as family reunification, including residence and labour market access rights for family members irrespective of their nationality.[30]

Given that domestic work is a generally low-paid occupation, migrants from high-income countries such as Switzerland and the rest of EFTA countries, do not normally work as domestic workers. They are nonetheless likely to move as au pairs; the agreements contain no specific provisions on au pairs, but do not exclude them either. Given their quasi-EU migrant status, EEA au pairs have more chances to experience genuine cultural exchange through the scheme than to find themselves working as low-cost substitute for domestic work. However, EFTA

---

[22] Agreement on the European Economic Area OJ No L1, 3 January 1994.
[23] Article 28 of the EEA agreement on the freedom of movement of workers replicates TFEU, art 45.
[24] Agreement between the European Community and its Member States, of the one part, and the Swiss Confederation, of the other, on the free movement of persons OJ No L11/6, 30 April 2002.
[25] Free Movement of Persons Agreement, art 3.
[26] Ibid, art 2.
[27] Ibid, art 7(b).
[28] Ibid, art 7(a).
[29] Ibid, arts 2, 4 and 7(c).
[30] Ibid, art 7(d) and (e).

states, being prosperous countries with ample work opportunities, are attractive destinations for EU nationals looking for work which can include domestic work. In addition, EFTA states' policies attract EU citizens in domestic work services. For example, Switzerland grants very limited access to non-EU/EFTA citizens to work as domestic workers which results in the need for care and other domestic work being largely met by EU citizens.[31] When an EU domestic worker migrates to one of the EFTA states for work, she does so under a regime that reduces many of the risks normally associated with migration.

Turkish Workers

Under the Ankara Agreement signed by Turkey and the EU in 1963 and complemented by the Association Council Decision 1/80, Turkish workers residing in an EU Member State enjoy a relatively privileged status under EU law. Contrary to EFTA workers, Turkish workers have no first entry rights under EU law but are admitted under the diverse migration regimes of Member States. However, once admitted for at least a year, the application of EU law is triggered which grants Turkish workers a set of rights for gradual access to the labour market. These include an entitlement to renew their work permit after the first year provided work is available, the right to change employer after three years and full access to any paid employment after four years.[32]

Even though the EU-Turkey agreement does not provide for family reunification rights, Turkish workers, as other non-EU nationals, can rely on the provisions of the Family Reunification Directive.[33] After three years of legal residence, the family members of a Turkish worker can take up any employment provided that the post has first been offered to EU nationals and access any paid employment without restrictions after five years.[34] Additionally, a standstill clause prohibits Member States from imposing any new restrictions on the labour market access of Turkish workers and their family members.[35]

A Turkish domestic worker who gains admission to the labour market of an EU Member State can gradually access a status that is comparable to that of EU nationals; the important differences being the lack of first-entry and intra-EU mobility rights.[36] EU law provisions on Turkish workers are therefore an important resource to challenge more restrictive national migration regimes on migrant domestic workers who are Turkish nationals. Even though there are no indications that significant numbers of Turkish nationals are employed as domestic workers in

---

[31] G Medici and A Blackett, 'Ratification as International Solidarity. Reflections on Switzerland and Decent Work for Domestic Work' (2015–2016) 31 *Connecticut Journal of International Law* 187–215.
[32] Decision 1/80, art 6(1).
[33] Directive 2003/86/EC on the right to family reunification [2003] OJ L251/12.
[34] Ibid, art 7.
[35] Ibid, art 13.
[36] They can access intra-EU mobility rights if they qualify for long-term residence status.

Maghreb Nationals

The EU has concluded the Euro-Mediterranean Agreements with Tunisia, Morocco and Algeria.[38] While none of these agreements grants first entry rights, once legally admitted into an EU Member State, labour migrants from the Maghreb derive some limited rights under EU law. The most important right is that to equal treatment with nationals in relation to working conditions, pay and social security; equal treatment covers temporary workers as well.[39] In *El Yassini*, the CJEU held that the equality clause in the Euro-Med agreements has direct effect which allows individuals to rely on it before the national courts.[40] However, the CJEU refused to grant Maghreb nationals an EU law status similar to that of Turkish resident workers. When asked in *El Yassini* whether certain provisions for Turkish workers could be applied by analogy to Maghreb nationals, the CJEU held that Decision 1/80 is qualitatively different because of the prospect of Turkey's accession to the EU and of the progressive realisation of the free movement of workers regime in the case of Turkish nationals.[41]

The Euro-Med agreements are, nonetheless, a relevant legal source for EU Member States where a considerable number of domestic workers are Maghreb nationals, such as Spain.

Non-EU Workers under Labour Migration Directives

The admission of migrant workers is traditionally a very sensitive issue for Member States. Attempts to harmonise the entry and stay conditions of labour migrants at the EU level are generally met with resistance. Member State reluctance to cede to the EU part of their sovereign power regarding the admission of labour migrants was manifested in 2001 when the European Commission

---

[37] See, for example, H Theobald, 'Care Workers with Migrant Backgrounds in Formal Care Services in Germany: A Multi-level Intersectional Analysis' (2017) 1(2) *International Journal of Care and Caring* 209–26.

[38] Euro-Med agreements with Tunisia [1998] OJ L97, Morocco [2000] OJ L70 and Algeria [2005] OJ L265. The Euro-Med agreements replaced earlier cooperation agreements signed between the EU, Tunisia, Morocco and Algeria in 1978.

[39] J Apap, *The Right of Immigrant Workers in the European Union. An Evaluation of the EU Public Policy Process and the Legal Status of Labour Immigrants from the Maghreb Countries in the New Receiving States* (Hague: Kluwer Law International, 2002).

[40] *El-Yassini v Secretary of State for Home Department* (Case C-416/96) EU:C:1999:107, para 32. See also the discussion in B Ryan, 'The European Union and Labour Migration: Regulating Admission or Treatment?' in A Baldaccini, E Guild and H Toner (eds), *Whose Freedom, Security and Justice? EU Immigration and Asylum Law and Policy* (Oxford/Portland: Hart, 2007), 512–13.

[41] *El Yassini*, paras 57 and 58.

proposed a single, horizontal directive to regulate conditions of entry and stay for all non-EU workers irrespective of skill.[42] Member States rejected the proposal and the Commission finally withdrew it in 2005.[43] The rejection was due to the very diverse labour migration regimes of Member States and the Commission's failure to convince of the added value of harmonisation at the EU level.[44]

Following the failure to attract support for the initial proposal, in 2005 the Commission adopted a policy plan on legal migration.[45] According to the 2005 policy plan, the comprehensive approach to labour immigration was to be abandoned in favour of a sectoral approach. The new sectoral approach entailed setting differentiated conditions and procedures for admission as well as rights for a few selected categories of economic migrants. The 2005 Plan proposed the adoption of four sectoral directives in the field of labour immigration, each targeting one of the following categories of migrant workers: highly skilled, seasonal workers, remunerated trainees and intra-corporate transferees. A framework directive for a single permit and residence rights for non-EU workers was also proposed.[46] The UK, Ireland and Denmark opted out of all migration directives and have thus always exclusively applied their national regimes on labour migration issues.

The stated aims of the EU labour migration regime are to attract highly skilled non-EU workers, able to benefit from the economic prosperity of the EU and to facilitate the admission of low-skilled workers for specific sectors with fluctuating needs.[47] Petra Herzfeld Olsson accurately notes that the approach in EU labour migration law has been to grant more favourable conditions and a robust set of rights to labour migrants in highly paid jobs and substandard conditions and fewer labour protections for those in low-paid sectors.[48] This approach has

---

[42] European Commission, Proposal for a Directive on the conditions of entry and residence of third-country nationals for the purpose of paid employment and self-employed economic activities, COM (2001)386 final, 11 November 2001.

[43] European Commission, Communication from the Commission to the Council and the European Parliament: Outcome of the Screening of Legislative Proposals Pending before the Legislator, COM (2005)462 final, 27 September 2009.

[44] See Ryan (n 40) above, 512–13.

[45] European Commission, Communication from the Commission: Policy Plan on Legal Migration, COM(2005) 669 final, 21 December 2005. The policy plan was adopted in the framework of the Hague Programme, a multi-annual agenda which set the Union's priorities in the field of freedom, security and justice. It was approved by the European Council in 2004 following the expiration of the Tampere Programme which lasted from 1999 to 2004. Council of the European Union, *The Hague Programme: strengthening freedom, security and justice in the European Union* (16054/04 JAI 559 of 13 December 2004).

[46] The choice of legislative tool, ie directives instead of regulations even though the adoption of the latter would have been legally possible, is telling of Member States' eagerness to maintain control over immigration issues and particularly over the admission of migrant workers from outside the EU. TFEU art 288 stipulates that: 'To exercise Union's competences, the institutions shall adopt regulations, directives, decisions, recommendations and opinions.'

[47] The Hague Programme in 2004 made the link between migration and economic prosperity when it highlighted that legal migration has an important role in advancing economic development.

[48] P Herzfeld Olsson, 'The Development of an EU Policy on Workers from Third Countries – Adding New Categories of Workers to the EU Labour Market with New Combinations of Rights' in S Evju (ed) *Regulating Transnational Labour in Europe: The Quandaries of Multilevel Governance* (Oslo: University of Oslo, 2014).

significant implications for domestic workers who are considered low skilled and are thus excluded from both the scope of directives targeting skill and from the directive on seasonal workers.

Highly Skilled Labour Migrants

The Blue Card Directive on the admission of highly skilled non-EU workers was adopted in 2009.[49] This introduces a new migrant status, that of blue card holder, a privileged status with an important set of rights and protections. It is available only to those TCNs with 'high professional qualifications'.[50] Several provisions of this directive have the potential to reduce migrant worker vulnerability. First, blue card holders, as long as they work in highly skilled sectors, have a progressive right to circulate freely on the labour market and the right to change employer.[51] Second, they enjoy some residence security if they become unemployed.[52] Third, the directive includes a clause on equal treatment with nationals in a wide range of fields, such as: wages, dismissals, health and safety, associational rights, education and vocational training, social security, access to goods and services as well as in relation to geographical mobility in the territory of the host Member State.[53] Fourth, they enjoy a facilitated access to long-term residence status and a privileged treatment in relation to their family reunification rights.[54] Finally, EU blue card holders and their family members enjoy intra-EU mobility rights.[55] The possibility to relocate to another state within the EU expands personal freedom as it allows

---

[49] Council Directive 2009/50/EC on the conditions of entry and residence of third-country nationals for the purposes of highly qualified employment [2009] OJ L155/17. Even though the Blue Card Directive concerns highly skilled migrants, a less controversial issue than low-skill migration, this instrument was adopted following a heated political debate. See SA Espinoza and C Moraes, 'The Law and Politics of Migration and Asylum: The Lisbon Treaty and the EU' in D Ashiagbor, N Countouris and I Lianos (eds), *The European Union after the Treaty of Lisbon* (Cambridge: Cambridge University Press 2012), 156–84.

[50] Attested by a higher education degree or relevant professional experience of at least five years, Blue Card Directive, art 2(g).

[51] Under Blue Card Directive, art 7(2), Member States grant blue card holders' residence and work permits for a period of between one and four years. Article 12(1) states that, during the first two years, the migrant is restricted to a specific sector; after this period, she may take up employment in any other highly skilled sector. Article 12(2) allows a change of employer, subject to Member State permission, only during the first two years.

[52] Blue Card Directive, art 13 stipulates that temporary unemployment of up to three months may not lead to loss of status; while seeking new employment, the blue card holder may legally reside in the host Member State.

[53] Ibid, art 14. Working time and paid leave are not expressly mentioned. However, the word 'including' indicates that the list of working conditions is open-ended, thus equality in working time and paid leave could be included as well.

[54] Ibid, art 16. Blue card holders can accumulate stays for the purpose of qualifying for long-term residence under Directive 2003/109/EC. Article 15 establishes a derogation from Directive 2003/86/EC on family reunification that exempts blue card holders from the requirement to have prospects of acquiring long-term residence to qualify for family reunification and sets a fast-track procedure to examine applications.

[55] Ibid, art 18. After 18 months of residence in a Member State, they may relocate with their family to another Member State for the purpose of highly skilled work.

the migrant worker to improve her conditions by looking for better opportunities elsewhere; it can therefore be a tool in reducing one's vulnerability to exploitation. Overall, the status of blue card holder may not be as robust as that of EU and quasi-EU nationals, but it certainly places highly skilled TCNs in a comparable position.

In 2014, the EU adopted a second directive dealing with non-EU highly skilled workers, Directive 2014/66/EU on intra-corporate transferees.[56] This sets conditions of entry and residence for managers, specialists and trainee employees for the purpose of temporary secondment in a Member State. It seeks to facilitate multinational corporations to temporarily assign highly skilled workers in their subsidiaries in other Member States, while also setting a common set of EU rights for transferees. Intra-corporate transferees receive a permit of at least one year which guarantees some residence stability to the migrant worker.[57] Like blue card holders, intra-corporate transferees have access to facilitated family reunification provisions and enjoy intra-EU mobility rights during their secondment.[58] The directive also stipulates intra-corporate transferees' right to equal treatment with the host states' nationals in a range of areas: terms and conditions of employment, freedom of association, branches of social security, access to goods and services.[59]

Low-Skilled Labour Migrants

The Seasonal Workers Directive is the first EU directive adopted to regulate migration for low-skilled work.[60] The directive's preamble cites addressing seasonal workers' vulnerability and risk of exploitation as a central aim.[61] The extent to which the directive's provisions are directed towards achieving this aim is, however, limited especially when juxtaposed to the EU law provisions applicable to highly skilled migrants.

To be sure, the directive introduces various provisions aimed at the protection of seasonal workers as workers. Article 20, a novelty for EU labour migration instruments, specifies standards in relation to seasonal workers' living conditions and obliges Member States to require proof that these standards are met throughout the whole duration of their stay. Article 23 stipulates seasonal workers' right to equal treatment as national workers in relation to wages, dismissals, working time,

---

[56] Directive 2014/66/EU of the European Parliament and of the Council on the conditions of entry and residence of third-country nationals in the framework of an intra-corporate transferee [2014] OJ L157/1.

[57] Under the Intra-corporate Transferees Directive, art 13(2), the permit can be extended for up to three years for managers and specialists and up to one year for trainees.

[58] Ibid, arts 19 and 20.

[59] Ibid, art 18.

[60] Directive 2014/36/EU of the European Parliament and of the Council on the conditions of entry and stay of third-country nationals for the purpose of employment as seasonal workers [2014] OJ L94/375. Under the Seasonal Workers Directive, art 2(2) seasonal work is work that is dependent on the passing of the seasons. While Member States can determine which sectors require seasonal workers, it is expected to be relevant mainly for agriculture and tourism. See recital 13 of the directive's preamble.

[61] Ibid, recital 43.

paid leave, health and safety, freedom of association, collective bargaining and the right to strike.[62] Crucially, seasonal workers are entitled to back payments.[63] To ensure effective enforcement, Article 25 requires Member States to set mechanisms where seasonal workers can lodge complaints directly or through representatives to ensure protection from victimisation and retaliation. Member States are also required to ensure the effective inspection of seasonal workers' workplaces either through national labour inspection authorities or worker's organisations.[64]

Yet, the potential of the directive's worker-protective provisions to reduce vulnerability to exploitation is significantly compromised by provisions that exercise migration control over seasonal workers. To begin with, a seasonal worker's permit is precarious and of short duration. Member States can determine the permit's maximum duration at anywhere between five and nine months in any 12-month period.[65] Seasonal workers can, however, lose their permit on several grounds.[66] Some depend entirely on the employer's conduct, such as employing illegally resident migrants, failing to pay social security contributions or not complying with labour legislation and contractual obligations.[67] Such provision is problematic not only because it undermines security of residence but also because it has a chilling effect on migrant workers filing a complaint against the employer. Secondly, seasonal workers, in contrast to highly skilled migrants, have no freedom to circulate on the labour market. Seasonal workers are restricted to work only in the sector specified on their permit and may not take up work in another seasonal sector.[68] Importantly, the directive stipulates no clear-cut right for seasonal workers to change employers; Member States *may*, but are not obliged to, allow them to change employers.[69] This is a significant drawback given the importance of the

---

[62] The rationale of equality of treatment is not only to guarantee seasonal workers' labour rights but also to protect national workers from social dumping practices. J Hunt, 'Making the CAP Fit: Responding to the Exploitation of Migrant Agricultural Workers in the EU' (2014) 30 *International Journal of Comparative Labour Law and Industrial Relations* 131–52. In general, the fair treatment of TCN workers is seen as a means of establishing a level playing field within the EU by reducing the unfair competition between the nationals of a member state and TCNs. This point was highlighted by the Commission in its 2005 Policy Plan on Legal Immigration and is reiterated in the Directive's recital 19. See also the joint statement by a number of civil society organisations, *Joint NGO statement, EU Seasonal Migrant Workers Directive: Full Respect of Equal Treatment Necessary*, (20 April 2011). Member States can, however, restrict seasonal workers' equal treatment in relation to unemployment and family benefits, to education and vocational training.

[63] Seasonal Workers Directive, art 23(c).

[64] Ibid, art 24.

[65] Ibid, art 14. The procedure for granting seasonal work permits is different for stays of up to 90 days and for stays beyond 90 days. See ibid, art 12. In any case the maximum period of stay is that stipulated in art 14.

[66] Ibid, art 9. This lists the reasons that can cause the withdrawal of the permit which include the falsification of documents and the violation of the permit's terms by the worker.

[67] Ibid, art 9(3).

[68] Ibid, art 22(c).

[69] Ibid, art 15. Judy Fudge and Petra Herzfeld Olsson trace the articulation of a discretionary instead of a mandatory provision on the right to change employers to a disagreement between the Council and the Parliament during pre-adoption negotiations. See, J Fudge and P Herzfeld Olsson, 'The EU Seasonal Workers Directive: When Immigration Controls Meet Labour Rights' (2014) 16 *European Journal of Migration and Law* 439–66.

right to change employers for migrant workers, especially those in low-skilled, low-paid jobs who are at a greater disadvantage vis à vis the employer than highly skilled workers. Yet, EU labour migration directives afford this protection only to blue card holders. Having no labour market mobility undermines the effectiveness of the directive's worker-protective provisions. Thirdly, seasonal workers have no long-term residence and no family reunification rights.[70] Given that the maximum duration of their permit is nine months, seasonal workers cannot rely on the Family Reunification Directive which requires a minimum of one-year continuous legal residence before the non-EU migrant can sponsor family members.

Single Permit Directive

In 2011, the EU adopted Directive 2011/98/EU on a single permit for TCN workers.[71] The directive does not create any first-entry rights for non-EU migrants nor does it harmonise the diverse national migration regimes of Member States on the admission of labour migrants.[72] The purpose is rather to simplify the procedural rules by creating a one-stop shop to process applications and to create a common set of rights for TCNs once admitted for work in the EU.[73] The directive's implementation shows that the instrument has been more effective in harmonising Member States' procedural rules rather than TCN workers substantive rights.[74]

In contrast to the sectoral directives applicable to specific categories of workers, the Single Permit Directive is meant to be a horizontal instrument applicable to all TCN workers. Despite the claim of horizontality, several categories of migrants are excluded from the directive's personal scope: family members of EU nationals, long-term residents, intra-corporate transferees, posted workers, seasonal workers and au pairs.[75] For some of these categories, such as family members of EU citizens or long-term residents, the exclusion is justified as the excluded migrants are covered by more favourable EU law provisions. For others, though, such as seasonal workers and au pairs, the exclusion does not seem justified and weakens the directive's claim of horizontality.

---

[70] Given the temporariness of their stay, seasonal workers are expressly excluded from accessing long-term residence status. See, Long-term Residence Directive, art 3.
[71] Directive 2011/98/EU of the European Parliament and of the Council on a single application procedure for a single permit for third-country nationals to reside and work in the territory of a Member State and on a common set of rights for third-country workers legally residing in a Member State [2011] OJ L343/1.
[72] Recital 6 and art 1(2) reiterates Member States' exclusive competence in regulating and determining the volumes of admission. Under art 8(3), national authorities may declare an application as inadmissible and reject it on this basis.
[73] Recital 19 states that the directive aims at 'developing further a coherent immigration policy and narrowing the rights gap between citizens of the Union and third-country nationals legally working in a Member State'.
[74] A Beduschi, '"An Empty Shell?" The Protection of Social Rights of TCN Workers in the EU after the Single Permit Directive' (2015) 17(2–3) *European Journal of Migration and Law* 210–38.
[75] Single Permit Directive, art 3.

Single-permit holders may reside and circulate freely within the territory of the granting Member State, carry out the specific employment activity indicated on their permit and receive information on their rights under the directive.[76] The directive includes an equal treatment clause in relation to, inter alia, pay, dismissal, health and safety and associational rights.[77] Contrary to the instruments on highly skilled workers, the Single Permit Directive confers no intra-EU mobility rights, no rights to change employer and sector and no provisions to ensure the migrant's residence stability during unemployment periods.

The Single Permit Directive, therefore, confers much more limited rights than the directives targeting explicitly highly skilled migrants which adds to the fragmentation of the EU regime on non-EU workers. Despite the introduction of the Single Permit Directive, Member States still retain significant powers to determine the rights of non-EU workers who do not belong to one of the categories with more expansive equal treatment rights under EU law, ie EU and quasi-EU citizens and their family members and highly skilled TCNs.

Fragmentation, Different Hierarchies and the Value of Work: Implications for Migrant Domestic Workers

The analysis of the different EU legal sources on the entry and the rights of migrant workers reveals a complex and fragmented regime. The fragmentation results in the construction of a hierarchy of migrant statuses in EU law with a differentiated set of rights attached to each status. The hierarchy of migration statuses in EU migration law is relevant for all migrant workers construed as low skilled; as such, it also has significant implications for migrant domestic workers.

Migrant workers who are EU nationals, when not subjected to transitional arrangements, are clearly first in the hierarchy of migration statuses under EU law. They enjoy the right to first independent entry, residence stability, full access to and mobility in the labour market,[78] equality of treatment with nationals in a range of fields, as well as family reunification rights. The same holds true for EEA and Swiss nationals. The various Association and Cooperation Agreements create differentiated statuses for non-EU workers based on their nationality. Hence, EEA and Swiss workers are the most favoured non-EU nationals as their status is comparable to that of EU citizens. In fact, EEA and Swiss workers are paradoxically even higher in the hierarchy than transitional EU citizens.

Turkish workers hold a relatively robust set of entitlements when compared to other categories of non-EU nationals. Admitted Turkish workers enjoy a special status and a comprehensive set of rights under EU primary law. Crucially though,

---

[76] Ibid, art 11.
[77] Ibid, art 12.
[78] The only narrow exception is a position which entails exercising public authority.

Turkish workers have no first-entry rights under EU law; they are admitted in the EU under the diverse national migration rules of Member States. Maghreb nationals under the Euro-Med Agreements are next; their only entitlement under the agreements is a right to equal treatment with nationals which has some, albeit limited, implications for residence rights. Apart from EEA, Swiss and Turkish citizens, non-EU workers from the rest of the world derive no rights from the Association and Cooperation Agreements and, therefore, come last in the hierarchy of migration statuses.

It has been argued that the fragmentation of non-EU nationals' rights reflects the state of external relations the EU maintains with the respective country; if the agreement is part of a long-term plan of association with the EU, Turkey for instance, then the set of rights granted to the nationals of that country tends to be comprehensive; however, when the aim is that of cooperation and enhancing trade relations, then the rights' aspect is much weaker.[79] However, the EEA and Swiss Agreements constitute exceptions. Despite the fact that there is no prospect of EU accession, the bundle of rights granted to EEA and Swiss workers is robust, extensive and as close as it can get to that of EU citizens. Such preferential treatment and status turn EEA and Swiss into quasi-EU nationals. From this follows that the discrepancies of the regimes under each agreement cannot be explained only by taking into account the prospect of accession. Geographical proximity to the EU and, most importantly, the economic prosperity of the partner country are decisive factors for the EU to grant labour migration rights to non-EU nationals.

The overview of the secondary labour migration legislation adopted on the new legal basis provided by the Treaty of Amsterdam shows that the EU has opened up piecemeal paths for the entry of different categories of non-EU workers. Despite these developments, the personal scope of the adopted legislation remains restricted and the status of non-EU nationals therein very much fragmented. A non-EU migrant seeking independent entry into an EU Member State to work as a domestic worker cannot rely on any of the EU labour migration directives because they cover either highly skilled or seasonal workers. To gain lawful admission, she will instead have to navigate the diverse and even more fragmented migration regimes of Member States. As a result, her admission conditions will not be scrutinised for compatibility with EU law.

Under the labour migration directives, the differentiation on the status and entitlements of non-EU workers takes place based on their perceived market value. The perceived market value of the migrant worker is tightly associated with skill; the more highly skilled, the more desirable and welcome the migrant worker is. However, the skill of the migrant worker is not always relevant for EU law. In the case of EU and quasi-EU citizens – Swiss and EFTA nationals – skill is irrelevant when it comes to admission for the purpose of employment. The same holds true for Turkish and Maghreb nationals; their skill level is again irrelevant for EU law.

---

[79] K Eisele, *The External Dimension of the EU's Migration Policy. Different Legal Positions of Third-Country Nationals in the EU: A Comparative Perspective* (Leiden: Brill Nijhoff, 2014).

While Member States may determine to what extent skill is relevant when deciding for what kind of jobs they grant first-entry rights, once entry is granted, EU law comes into play and may result in the disapplication of national regimes for migrant workers if they restrict their EU law rights.

For the rest of non-EU workers, skill is of utmost importance and determines the position and rights the migrant worker has under EU law. The EU labour migration regime favours highly skilled migrant workers by carving out exceptions to facilitate their admission, stay and rights in the EU. While seasonal workers are an exception, evidently, the set of rights they derive under EU law is much less comprehensive and leaves many dimensions of their vulnerability to exploitation unchallenged. As more options exist for the highly skilled, those classified as low skilled run the risk of becoming irregular due to fewer opportunities to access an independent and stable legal migration status. Paradoxically, labour migration directives afford fewer rights and protections to those most vulnerable to exploitation, ie, low-skilled migrants, than highly skilled workers who have more bargaining leverage vis à vis their employer. Additionally, the conditions of admission and stay of the low-skilled are regulated almost exclusively under national legal regimes.

When skill is relevant for EU migration law, it is narrowly construed as the possession of professional or higher education qualifications, associated with the ability to access highly paid jobs. Therefore, EU law grants a robust set of admission and stay rights to those non-EU nationals with qualifications that secure employment in highly paid sectors, while the entry of lower-skilled workers, such as domestic workers, takes place through the, often restrictive, Member State migration regimes. As Elspeth Guild argues, the EU labour migration regime, which prioritises highly skilled workers, falls short of serving the diverse labour market realities and needs of the different Member States.[80] Additionally, the regime's fragmentation fails to guarantee a fair treatment to those non-EU workers whose work is actually required in many EU states.

The example of Cyprus illustrates this claim. As a matter of EU law compliance, Cyprus amended its immigration legislation and incorporated word-for-word the provisions of the EU Blue Card Directive. However, a separate Parliamentary decision set the volume of admissions at zero.[81] Even though zero admissions in essence mean that Cyprus grants no permits for highly skilled migrants, the Commission has not challenged this practice which clearly contravenes the effectiveness of the Blue Card Directive. At the same time, the majority of non-EU workers enter and work in Cyprus as domestic workers in private households under a highly restrictive national regime. By not regulating the area of migrant domestic workers' admission, the EU fails to provide harmonised and fair conditions of

---

[80] E Guild, 'Equivocal Claims? Ambivalent Controls? Labour Migration Regimes in the European Union' (Nijmegen Migration Law Working Paper Series 2010/05, 2010).

[81] TFEU, art 79(5) gives Member States the discretion to decide how many TCNs to admit under EU labour migration directives.

entry, stay and work for a large group of workers that is very much needed in many Member States.

Domestic Workers under EU Law Sources on the Integration of Non-EU Migrants

With the newly acquired legislative competences in the field of immigration under the Treaty of Amsterdam, the EU adopted two instruments concerning the integration of non-EU migrants legally residing in a Member State: Directive 2003/109/EC on long-term residence and Directive 2003/86/EC on family reunification.

Directive on Long-Term Residents

The Long-Term Residence Directive was adopted in 2003 following a long period of negotiations.[82] The directive has two central aims: to integrate non-EU nationals who have been lawfully residing in the EU on a long-term basis and to approximate their status and rights to those of EU nationals.[83] It seeks to meet these aims by establishing a new status for non-EU nationals, that of long-term resident, which should be acquired through harmonised rules and procedures across the Member States.[84] The status of long-term resident is an innovative legal source for the integration of non-nationals; it creates a path to legal inclusion and allows non-EU nationals to become part of the European polity.[85]

Once granted, the status is meant to be permanent;[86] Member States can exceptionally withdraw the status under narrow circumstances.[87] Additionally, long-term residents have enhanced protection against expulsion in comparison to other TCNs,[88] which creates residence security akin to that of EU nationals. The directive's equality clause entitles long-term residents to equality of treatment with nationals in accessing employment, self-employment, wages, dismissal, associational rights and a range of other fields.[89] Crucially, long-term residents have

---

[82] The Long-term Residence Directive was the first instrument the Commission proposed in the area of immigration. See, European Commission, Proposal for a Council Directive concerning the status of third-country nationals who are long-term residents (COM (2001)127 final, 13 March 2001.
[83] Long-term Residence Directive, recitals (4) and (12).
[84] Council of the European Union Directive 2003/109/EC concerning the status of third-country nationals who are long-term residents [2004] OJ L16/44.
[85] T Kostakopoulou, 'Invisible Citizens? Long-term Resident Third-country Nationals in the EU and their Struggle for Recognition' in R Bellamy and A Warleigh (eds) *Citizenship and Governance in the European Union* (London/New York: Continuum, 2001).
[86] Long-term Residence Directive, art 8(1).
[87] If the status was acquired fraudulently, if an expulsion order is adopted, or in case of absence from the territory of the EU for 12 consecutive months. Ibid, art 9.
[88] Ibid, art 12, which stipulates that expulsion may take place only if the TCN poses an actual and serious threat to public policy or public security.
[89] Ibid, art 11(1) and subject to the derogations in art 11, paras 2, 3 and 4.

full intra-EU mobility rights; they may enter another Member State as jobseekers, reside there for work purposes and be joined by family members while enjoying equality of treatment with national workers. Overall, the rights of long-term residents are robust and turn the holders into quasi-EU citizens.

What, then, are the conditions for accessing this protective status and to what extent can domestic workers meet those conditions? The first condition is length of stay; applicants must complete five years of legal and continuous residence in an EU Member State.[90] Apart from the residence requirements, applicants must also prove a level of income that is sufficient to sustain themselves and their dependants without having to resort to social assistance in the Member State where they reside.[91] The income requirement is the first significant hurdle for migrant domestic workers and other migrants in low-paid jobs. Another obstacle for domestic workers is Article 3, which introduces several exemptions from the directive's personal scope. The most relevant to domestic workers is the exemption under Article 3, paragraph 2(e) which reads:

> the Directive does not apply to TCNs who reside solely on temporary grounds such as au pair or seasonal worker, or as workers posted by a service provider for the purposes of cross-border provision of services, or as cross-border providers of services or in cases where their residence permit has been formally limited.

It follows clearly from the provision's wording that au pairs are excluded. What is less clear, however, is the meaning of the phrase 'where their permit has been formally limited' and its implications for migrant domestic workers. As discussed in Chapter 1, the migration regimes of European states do not grant unlimited residence permits to domestic workers. On the contrary, their permits are formally limited in many respects: length of stay, sector of employment and often employer. Despite such formal limitations, domestic workers still renew their permits and may, in practice, end up residing in the same Member State on a long-term basis – even longer than the five years the directive requires. Does the 'formally limited' exemption mean that Member States can deny long-term residence status to a non-EU domestic worker who was admitted on a limited permit but who has, nonetheless, effectively resided lawfully in that Member State for five years or more? If the answer is yes, then what is the point of having a five-year qualifying period if this can be circumvented by granting limited residence permits?[92] In its first implementation report, the Commission also stated that interpreting the exemption too broadly so as to exclude those who have resided lawfully for five years or more would be against the directive's effectiveness.[93]

---

[90] Ibid, art 4(1).
[91] Ibid, art 5, para 1(a).
[92] E Guild, *The Legal Elements of European Identity: EU Citizenship and Migration Law* (Hague: Kluwer International, 2014), 224.
[93] European Commission, Report from the Commission to the European Parliament and the Council on the application of Directive 2003/109/EC concerning the status of third-country nationals who are long-term residents, COM(2011)585 final, 28 September 2011.

In *Singh*, the CJEU was called to clarify the meaning of the 'formally limited' exemption. *Singh* concerned a a non-EU resident who had been residing in the Netherlands for about six years on a fixed-term residence permit which was restricted to the exercise of activities as a spiritual leader.[94] Dutch authorities had renewed Mr Singh's residence permit twice. When he applied for long-term residence status, they rejected his application on the basis that the permit, being fixed term, fell under the 'formally limited' requirements of the Long-Term Residence Directive.

When deciding on the correct interpretation of the exemption, the CJEU first noted that, as there is no reference to national law, the phrase 'formally limited' is an autonomous EU law concept; as such, it must be interpreted at the EU level and applied uniformly across the Member States. The Court then differentiated between, on the one hand, residence 'solely on temporary grounds' such in the case of au pairs or seasonal workers and, on the other hand, permits with a 'formal restriction'.[95] In the first case, the Court held, that the temporary nature of those permits prevents the non-EU migrant from settling. In the second case, however, the permit's formal limitation is not an indication of whether the non-EU national can settle. The Court concluded that if the 'formal limitation *does not prevent* the long-term residence', then the TCN falls under the directive's personal scope.[96] Thus the test established in *Singh* is whether the formal limitation prevents long-term residence.[97]

Singh is largely a positive development but does not fully clarify the matter. The judgment is a message that the 'formally limited' exemption does not give Member States *carte blanche*. Member States may not circumvent their obligations under the directive simply by labelling certain permits as limited when they can be, and in practice are, renewed or extended.[98] However – and this is the judgment's limitation – the Court did not hold that all TCNs whose permits are renewed beyond the five-year period will automatically fulfil the residence requirement and qualify for long-term residence. For the Court, renewal is only a 'strong indication' that the limitation in question does not preclude the TCN's long-term residence.[99] The Court finally stated that assessing whether an exclusion is legal – by applying the test established in *Singh* – is a matter for national courts.

After *Singh* doubt remains about what kind of permits can be considered 'formally limited'. Importantly, challenging the way national migration regimes construe and apply the exemption requires litigation in front of national courts or the intervention of the European Commission. In his Opinion, Advocate General Bot proposed a much clearer stance than that finally adopted by the Court.

---

[94] *Staatssecretaris van Justitie v Mangat Singh* (Singh) (Case C-502/10) EU:C:2012:636, paras 42–43.
[95] *Singh*, para 50.
[96] Ibid, para 51.
[97] National courts are to apply this test on a case-by-case basis. See, *Singh*, ibid, para 52.
[98] See also, S Peers, 'The Court of Justice Lays the Foundation for the Long-term Residents Directive: Kambaraj, Commission v. Netherlands, Mangat Singh' (2013) 50 *Common Market Law Review* 529–52.
[99] *Singh*, para 52.

He argued that a 'formally limited' permit is just another type of temporary permit; to the extent that it is renewed beyond the five years, it follows that the TCN has fulfilled the duration of residence requirement to be eligible for long-term residence status.

Even though the law after *Singh* is not entirely clear, the judgment still challenges the implementation of the Long-term Residence Directive in some Member States. For instance, in Cyprus, following the Supreme Court case in *Motilla*[100] – a case decided before *Singh*[101] – non-EU migrants legally residing in the country on successive fixed-term permits do not qualify for long-term residence status. In 2011, the Commission criticised the broad interpretation of the exemption in Cyprus and in a number of other Member States but took no measures as the judgment in *Singh* was pending at the time.[102] In its latest implementation report, the Commission considers that Member States no longer interpret the 'formally limited' exemption too broadly which indicates that there is no appetite to pressure them any further on this issue.[103]

Overall, the Long-term Residence Directive introduces important citizenship-like provisions for TCNs who are long-term residents: security of residence, full equality with nationals and intra-EU mobility.[104] Carrera and Wiesbrock have argued that this is an 'indication of the loss of discretionary power by the nation-state as well as a signal that a new European citizenship of TCNs is already in the making'.[105] It is true that, once granted, long-term residence status, approximates considerably the position of TCNs to that of EU citizens and, consequently, to that of nationals.[106] Crucially, however, the conditions of first entry are not set at EU but at Member State level; permits are also renewed on the basis of national provisions. It is therefore national immigration law which determines whether a TCN will be able to reach the five years of legal and continuous residence threshold, meet the income requirements and qualify for the status. For example, personal scope

---

[100] *Cresencia Cabotaje Motilla v The Republic of Cyprus*, (2008) 3 Supreme Court Judgment 29. The case concerned a migrant domestic worker who had resided in the country for more than nine years. See ch 1.

[101] This shows that, when deciding *Motilla*, the Supreme Court overlooked the CJEU's exclusive competence in interpreting EU law and, instead of sending a reference for a preliminary ruling, proceeded with a wrongful interpretation of the Long-term Residence Directive.

[102] COM(2011) 585 final, at p 2.

[103] European Commission, Report from the Commission to the European Parliament and the Council on the implementation of Directive 2003/109/EC concerning the status of third-country nationals who are long-term residents COM(2019) 161 final (Brussels, 29.03.2019).

[104] In this respect, Acosta Arcarazo has characterised long-term resident status as a form of subsidiary EU citizenship. D Acosta Arcarazo, *The Long-Term Residence Status as a Subsidiary Form of EU Citizenship* (Martinus Nijhoff Publishers 2011).

[105] S Carrera and A Wiesbrock (2010) 'Whose European Citizenship in the Stockholm Programme? The Enactment of Citizenship by Third-Country Nationals in the EU' 12 *European Journal of Migration and Law* 337–59 at 358.

[106] Groenedjik identifies three narrow aspects where the treatment of long-term residents can still diverge from that of EU nationals: political participation in local elections, access to jobs in public service and equal treatment in relation to social assistance. See K Groenendijk, 'Citizens and Third Country Nationals: Differential Treatment or Discrimination?' in JY Carlier and E Guild (eds), *The Future of Free Movement of Persons in the EU* (Brussels: Bruylant, 2006).

exemptions aside, it is practically impossible for a migrant domestic worker under the Cypriot regime, which stipulates salaries way below comparable minimum wages in other occupations, to meet the directive's minimum income requirements. In addition, the fact that EU labour migration directives set differentiated paths to long-term residence is another indication that the status is not inclusive but selective, favouring those whose market value is considered to be higher.

Directive on Family Reunification

Directive 2003/86/EC (the Family Unification Directive) provides for common rules on the right of legally resident non-EU nationals to be joined by their family members in the Member State where they reside.[107] It establishes the conditions under which Member States are to grant family reunification[108] and sets the rights family members should enjoy.[109] To qualify as sponsor, the migrant must hold a residence permit valid for a year or more and have 'reasonable prospects of obtaining the right to permanent residence'.[110] The way Member States implement the residence requirement varies significantly. In Sweden, sponsors must be permanently resident to be eligible – a higher threshold than the directive. As noted in Chapter 1, TCN domestic workers in Cyprus are granted non-renewable four-year permits and are denied long-term residence; it thus follows that they are excluded from the scope of family reunification as well. In Spain, TCNs on temporary permits can act as sponsors as long as they have secured renewal of their permit for at least another year.[111] In addition, Member States may – but are not obliged to – require that sponsors provide proof of suitable accommodation as well as stable and regular resources to support themselves and their family members without recourse to public funds. Again, Member States made different use of these possibilities. Sweden, for instance, introduces no accommodation and income requirements, while Spain and Cyprus do but without specifying either accommodation standards or income levels.[112]

For migrant domestic workers, the obstacles in qualifying as sponsors for the purpose of family reunification under the directive are many. The requirements to have reasonable prospects of long-term residence or even permanent residence, adequate financial means and suitable accommodation are incompatible not only with their admission and stay conditions – as discussed in Chapter 1 – but often with their working and living conditions as well. The conditions to qualify

---

[107] Council Directive 2003/86/EC on the right to family reunification [2003] OJ L251/12.
[108] Ibid, art 1.
[109] Ibid, arts 13, 14 and 15.
[110] Ibid, art 3.
[111] European Commission, Report from the Commission to the European Parliament and the Council on the application of Directive 2003/86/EC on the right to family reunification, COM(2008)610 final, 8 October 2008.
[112] Ibid.

for family reunification under EU law seem to have been drafted with the highly skilled, well-paid migrant worker in mind.

EU Migration Law Norms on Illegally Resident Domestic Workers

Prior to the adoption of the Treaty of Amsterdam, the EU lacked competence to legislate in the area of irregular immigration. Instead, the Member States' Home Affairs Ministers adopted soft law measures in the framework of intergovernmental cooperation. On a discourse level these soft law measures pursued a twofold aim: to prevent irregular immigration and to guarantee the rights of irregular migrants. In practice though, the measures favoured a security-based approach to immigration matters over one that would ensure migrants' protection.[113] The security-based approach, which tends to conflate security, criminality and migration, persists in the post-Amsterdam era.[114]

Currently, the EU's competence to legislate on illegal immigration is based on TFEU, Article 79(2)(c).[115] The Returns and Employers Sanctions Directives are the two instruments that form part of the EU's legal framework for fighting illegal immigration.[116] Directive 2008/115/EC on common standards and procedures for returning illegally resident TCNs[117] requires Member States to issue a return decision against irregularly staying TCNs, remove them and, under certain circumstances, imposing an entry ban on removed TCNs.[118] Directive 2009/52/EC on sanctions against employers[119] aims to curb the flow of irregular migrant workers into the EU by addressing what is perceived as the 'pull factor' of illegal migration, that is, the prospects of finding employment despite the lack of authorisation.[120] The directive, therefore, requires Member States to prohibit the

---

[113] R Cholewinski, 'The EU *Acquis* on Irregular Migration Ten Years On: Still Reinforcing Security at the Expense of Rights?' in E Guild and P Minderhoud (eds), *The First Decade of EU Migration and Asylum Law* (Leiden: Nijhoff Publishers 2012).

[114] H Askola, (2010) '"Illegal Migrants", Gender and Vulnerability: The Case of the EU's Returns Directive' 18(2) *Feminist Legal Studies* 159–78.

[115] It reads: 'The European Parliament and the Council acting in accordance with the ordinary legislative procedure, shall adopt measures in the following areas: ... c) illegal immigration and unauthorised residence, including removal and repatriation of persons residing without legal authorisation;'

[116] The fight against illegal immigration is one central aims of the EU's common immigration policy decided with the Tampere Conclusions in 1999.

[117] Directive 2008/115/EC of the European Parliament and the Council on common standards and procedures in Member States for returning illegally staying third-country nationals [2008] OJ L348/98.

[118] See Returns Directive, arts 6(1), 8(1) and 11.

[119] Directive 2009/52/EC of the European Parliament and of the Council providing for minimum standards on sanctions and measures against employers of illegally staying third-country nationals [2009] OJ L168/24.

[120] European Commission, Commission Staff Working Document, Accompanying document to the Proposal for a Directive providing for sanctions against employers of illegally staying third-country nationals, Impact Assessment, SEC(2007)603, 16 May 2007.

employment of illegally resident non-EU nationals and impose 'effective, proportionate and dissuasive sanctions' against employers violating the prohibition.[121]

In addition, the directive requires Member States to impose several obligations on employers when hiring non-EU nationals, such as conducting pre-employment checks, keeping records on the migrant's permit to facilitate inspections and notifying national authorities when hiring a TCN.[122] In essence, these administrative burdens transfer part of a state's immigration control onto the employer. Such administrative burdens can have a discriminatory effect on employers' recruiting practices as they may become reluctant to consider non-EU applicants. Discrimination can also have spill-over effects on legally resident TCNs and other ethnic minority communities as employers who are not familiar with immigration rules and procedures may be reluctant to employ them altogether.[123] Regrettably, the Commission's report on the implementation of the Employers Sanctions Directive does not examine whether implementation has had any negative impacts on the labour market experience and prospects of non-EU nationals.[124] However, civil society organisations, with first-hand knowledge of the situation on the ground, report that the introduction of employers' sanctions has largely worsened the situation of irregular migrant workers.[125]

Interestingly, the directive establishes more lenient rules and obligations for the employers of domestic workers. For example, Member States enjoy the discretion to 'provide for reduced financial sanctions where the employer is a natural person who employs an illegally staying third-country national for his or her private purposes and where no particularly exploitative working conditions are involved'.[126] Member States can also simplify employers' obligations to notify national authorities when they employ a migrant domestic worker.[127] While such provisions may make it easier for domestic workers to find work, they mirror gendered ideas around household work being construed outside of the labour market.

---

[121] The Employers Sanctions Directive, arts 3(1) and 5. This requires the imposition of sanctions against private employers, legal persons (art 8) and subcontractors (art 11). The sanctions are primarily financial; Article 5 stipulates fines proportional to the number of illegally resident TCNs employed and the payment of costs incurring from the TCN's return. There are also provisions concerning the imposition of criminal and administrative sanctions. Article 9 requires Member States to establish criminal offences in the following cases: (a) the employment of the irregular TCN is continuous or persistent, (b) the infringement involves the employment of a significant number of irregular TCNs, (c) the employer is knowingly employing a TCN who is a victim of human trafficking and (d) the irregular TCN is a minor. On administrative sanctions, see art 7.

[122] Employers Sanctions Directive, art 3(1).

[123] M Bell, *Anti-Discrimination Law and the European Union* (Oxford: Oxford University Press, 2002).

[124] European Commission, Communication from the Commission to the European Parliament on the Application of Directive 2009/52/EC, COM (2014)286 final, 25 May 2014.

[125] Platform for International Cooperation on Undocumented Migrants (PICUM), *Employers' Sanctions: Impacts on Undocumented Migrant Workers' Rights in Four EU Member States* (Brussels, April 2015).

[126] Employers Sanctions Directive, art 5(3).

[127] Ibid, art 4(2).

In its proposal for the adoption of the Employer Sanctions Directive, the Commission acknowledged the vulnerability of illegally resident migrant workers stemming from the risk to be deported.[128] While the adopted text does not explicitly engage with TCNs' vulnerability, the directive introduces three provisions with a worker-protection focus. First, the directive requires Member States to ensure that illegally resident migrant workers can recover any outstanding wages.[129] To facilitate access to the right to back payments, Member States must create mechanisms where illegally employed TCNs can file unpaid wage claims and enforce judgments against their employers.[130] But apart from the right to receive back payments, the directive does not guarantee any other substantive labour rights for illegally resident migrant workers. Second, the directive requires Member States to have effective mechanisms in place for illegally employed migrant workers to file complaints against employers either directly or through a representative, such as trade unions.[131] Finally, the directive contemplates the possibility for Member States to grant short-term residence permits to irregular migrants who initiate legal proceedings against employers.[132]

The Commission's implementation report draws attention to the fact that the directive's worker-protective measures lack robust implementation in the Member States.[133] Crucially, the potential of the rights to recover unpaid wages and to file complaints to reduce vulnerability to exploitation is seriously undermined because of irregular migrant's deportability. Without residence security, it is highly unlikely that illegally resident migrants will make use of these provisions to challenge their exploitation. Fear of deportation makes them reluctant to seek legal protection or engage with authorities in any way. Without a 'firewall' – to use Joseph Carens' famous term – between immigration law enforcement and access to legal protection, including labour rights enforcement, migrants employed in breach of immigration rules have almost no prospects of accessing complaint mechanisms.

Granting residence permits to those illegally resident migrant workers who initiate proceedings against the employers is not an adequate firewall between immigration and rights' enforcement. First of all, granting a permit depends entirely on national discretion; there is no obligation under the directive. Secondly, the possibility to access a temporary residence permit is limited to situations where the employer has committed a criminal offence under the directive, namely

---

[128] Commission of the European Communities, *Proposal for a Directive of the European Parliament and of the Council providing for sanctions against employers of illegally staying third-country nationals*, COM 2007(249) final, 16.05.2007, p 2.

[129] Employers Sanctions Directive, art 6(1).

[130] Ibid, art 6(2). Migrants should be able to enforce judgments against the employer even if they have been returned to the country of origin.

[131] Ibid, art 13.

[132] Ibid, art 13(4).

[133] European Commission, Communication from the Commission to the European Parliament and the Council, on the application of Directive 2009/52/EC of 18 June 2009 providing for minimum standards on sanctions and measures against employers of illegally staying third country nationals, COM(2014)286, 22 May 2014.

employing an irregular TCN under 'particularly exploitative working conditions' or employing a minor.[134] 'Particularly exploitative conditions' are defined as 'working conditions, including those resulting from gender-based or other discrimination, where there is a *striking* disproportion compared with the terms of employment of legally employed workers which, for example, affects workers' health and safety, and which offends against human dignity'[135] (emphasis added). The provision's wording implies that a certain level of discriminatory treatment at work between illegally and legally employed workers would be allowed as long as it is not strikingly disproportionate. What kind of treatment would amount to 'particularly exploitative conditions' is unclear. Clearly, an illegally resident domestic worker who files a complaint against her employer must meet a very high threshold before she can have residence security during proceedings. It seems that a short-term residence permit is contemplated only for those irregular migrants found working in slavery-like conditions.

Overall, the Employers Sanctions Directive concerns, first and foremost, immigration law enforcement and does not establish a comprehensive set of rights and protections for migrant workers. The application of the directive's limited worker-protective provisions is triggered only after the TCN has been detected and faces deportation. It thus follows that illegal domestic workers have very limited protection under EU migration law; it is the norms of national illegality regimes, discussed in Chapter 2, that are most relevant in regulating their status and determining their access to labour rights. In the case of the UK, national norms on migrant workers' illegality have always applied exclusively because of the UK's opt-out from the Employers Sanctions Directive. It is telling that one of the main reasons that motivated the UK's opt-out was precisely the directive's worker-protective norms. As the then UK Home Affairs Minister framed the government's position at the parliamentary debate concerning the opt-out:

> The directive also guaranteed additional rights to illegally staying employees, including provision of back payments where an employee has earned less than the minimum national wage, which would be difficult to administer and would send the wrong message by rewarding breaches of immigration legislation.[136]

Conclusion

This chapter set out to examine the contribution of EU migration law sources in shaping migrant domestic workers' vulnerability to exploitation. The map of migrant statuses under the different EU migration law sources reveals a highly fragmented picture. I have argued that the fragmentation and different migrant

---

[134] Employers Sanctions Directive, art 9(1)(c) and (e).
[135] Ibid, art 2(i).
[136] Damian Green, HC Deb, 24 May 2011, c50WS.

status hierarchies created by EU migration law reflect a bias on the value of work which is conflated with the capacity to earn a high wage. As opposed to the regime on the free movement of domestic workers who are EU nationals that is comprehensive and protective, most categories of non-EU national domestic workers, and even transitional EU citizens, must navigate a much more complex and fragmented legal landscape when seeking independent admission and stay as workers in the EU. The fragmentation of the regime does not just aim to leave migrants with fewer economic means outside the EU, but also to ensure that when EU Member States decide to admit labour migrants from poorer countries, they are subject to as few EU law constraints as possible.

Additionally, juxtaposing the EU labour migration directives on highly skilled and low-skilled migrant workers shows that the tension between migration control and worker-protective provisions is much more pronounced in the low-skilled instruments than those regulating highly skilled migrants. The most protective EU migration law norms, norms that could challenge migrant vulnerability, such as the right to change employers or fast-track access to permanent residence and intra-EU mobility, are largely inaccessible to those migrant workers who are considered low skilled.

4

Using EU Labour Law Sources to Challenge Domestic Workers' Vulnerability

Introduction

Despite growing scholarly and policy interest in improving migrant domestic workers' conditions, there has been little discussion concerning the potential of EU labour law sources in challenging the ways national regimes structure their vulnerability to exploitation. Yet, EU labour law sources contain important rights and protections against many problems at work such as long and unregulated working hours, constant availability to the employer, pregnancy and maternity discrimination, harassment and lack of information concerning terms and conditions of work. Many of the rights and protections EU labour law offers are of importance to domestic workers, including those who are migrants. Additionally, the supremacy of EU law over national law means that whenever there is a mismatch, EU law prevails over national law; this makes EU law sources particularly promising tools for challenging vulnerability structured in national law and practice.

Why is it, then, that there has been little academic discussion of EU labour law sources' utility and no advocacy strategies invoking compliance with EU law as a tool to pursue change at the domestic level? There are, I believe, two main reasons that have led scholars and activists alike to largely ignore the potential of EU labour law in the fight against domestic workers' vulnerability. The first is the misplaced scholarly debate concerning the inclusion of domestic workers in the personal scope of EU labour law sources. The second is the tendency to associate migrant domestic workers with non-EU citizens and, at times, even with illegally resident migrants. The assumption that migrant domestic workers are mostly non-EU citizens without the right to work and reside in the EU and thus excluded from EU law protection has led legal scholars to overlook EU labour law sources in the fight against vulnerability to exploitation.

However, migrant domestic workers are often EU migrants exercising their free movement rights and are therefore fully entitled to the protections of EU labour law. Most importantly, as I show in this chapter, EU labour law sources, with the exception of EU free movement rights, apply fully to non-EU nationals, including those who lack legal status in migration law terms.

In an article published in 2016 in the *European Law Review* (the 2016 article), I challenged the view that EU labour law sources do not apply to domestic workers.[1] By providing a more nuanced account on the place of domestic work under EU labour law sources, I wished to show when these sources apply to paid work in the private household and to outline the rights and protections domestic workers can derive.

In this chapter, I take the argument a step further and show how specific EU labour law sources can be used to challenge national provisions and practices that make domestic workers vulnerable to exploitation. With a focus on the UK, Cyprus, Sweden and Spain, I discuss specific areas of national labour law regimes which fall short of EU law requirements. My analysis shows that such provisions or practices should be challenged on the basis of incompatibility with EU law and, consequently, reformed. I also highlight areas where, while national regimes do not exclude domestic workers, more work needs to be done to make EU law-derived rights effective for those working in private households.

One might ask, what is the value of discussing the compatibility of UK law with EU law as the country has now left the EU? As the discussion in this chapter shows, several UK labour law provisions relevant to domestic workers are incompatible with EU law. Post-Brexit, relying on EU labour law as a strategy to reform national law and boost rights at work will no longer be possible in the UK. However, while the UK was a member of the EU, there was ample scope to challenge and eventually disapply national law provisions contrary to EU law. Unfortunately, the strategy of invoking compliance with EU law to challenge domestic workers' exclusion from important rights and protections at work was never pursued in the UK, which represents a missed opportunity.

The discussion is structured as follows. Section 2 provides a summary and updates my discussion in the 2016 article on domestic workers' inclusion into the personal scope of EU labour law sources. The focus is on primary and secondary sources conferring rights and protections to individual workers. Hence, I do not examine EU collective labour law sources because of their limited relevance for domestic workers. I also examine the inclusion of illegally resident domestic workers in the personal scope of EU labour law following the Court of Justice of the European Union (CJEU) judgment in *Tümer*.[2] Section 3 outlines the substantive rights and protections domestic workers could derive under selected areas of EU law: pregnancy and maternity rights, working time and the right to receive information on terms and conditions of employment. This is by no means an exhaustive account of all the areas of EU labour law that are relevant to domestic workers, but a discussion of sources with the potential to address key vectors of vulnerability.

---

[1] V Pavlou, 'Domestic Work in EU Law: The Relevance of EU Employment Law in Challenging Domestic Workers' Vulnerability' (2016) 41(3) *European Law Review* 379–98.

[2] *Tümer v Raad van bestuur van het Uitvoeringsinstituut werknemersverzekeringen* (Tümer) (Case C-311/13) EU:C:2014:2337.

Section 4 discusses the regulation of domestic work in the UK, Cyprus, Sweden and Spain to identify any mismatches with EU law requirements in the selected areas. Section 5 concludes.

Domestic Work and the Personal Scope of EU Labour Law Sources

When it comes to the inclusion of domestic workers in the personal scope of EU labour law, in the 2016 article I identified three types of inclusion. First, *straightforward inclusion* as in the areas of free movement of workers and gender equality law which have broad and autonomous personal scopes. Secondly, *non-straightforward inclusion* as in the Framework Health and Safety Directive[3] and its individual directives. In this context, I revisited a debate on the relationship between the personal scopes of the framework and individual directives and argued that both the Pregnant Workers[4] and the Working Time Directives[5] apply fully to domestic workers. Thirdly, *inclusion linked to national law* as in the case of directives delegating the definition of 'worker' to national law. The third cluster includes the directives on employer's insolvency,[6] atypical work[7] and the two recently adopted directives on transparent and predictable working conditions[8] and on work/life balance.[9]

Straightforward Inclusion: Free Movement of Workers and Gender Equality

The areas of free movement of workers and gender equality law have broad personal scopes which are defined in EU law and therefore apply autonomously

---

[3] Directive 89/391 on the introduction of measures to encourage improvements in the safety and health of workers at work (Health and Safety Directive) [1989] OJ L183/1.
[4] Directive 92/85 on the introduction of measures to encourage improvements in the safety and health at work of pregnant workers and workers who have recently given birth or are breastfeeding (Pregnant Workers Directive) [1992] OJ L348/1.
[5] Directive 2003/88 concerning certain aspects of the organisation of working time (Working Time Directive) [2003] OJ L299/9.
[6] Directive 2008/94 on the protection of employees in the event of insolvency of their employer (Insolvency Directive) [2008] OJ L283/36.
[7] Directive 97/81 concerning the framework agreement on part-time work concluded by UNICE, CEEP and ETUC (Part-time Work Directive) [1997] OJ L14; Directive 1999/70 concerning the framework agreement on fixed-term work concluded by ETUC, UNICE and CEEP (Fixed-term Work Directive) [1999] OJ L175/43; Directive 2008/104 on temporary agency work [2008] OJ L327/9.
[8] Directive (EU) 2019/1152 of the European Parliament and of the Council of 20 June 2019 on transparent and predictable working conditions in the European Union [2019] OJ L186/105.
[9] Directive (EU) 2019/1158 of the European Parliament and of the Council of 20 June 2019 on work/life balance for parents and carers and repealing Council Directive 2010/18/EU [2019] OJ L188.

of Member States' national definitions. These sources allow for no exemptions entrenched in national law; thus national rules with more restricted personal scopes contravene EU law and must be disapplied.

Article 45(1) TFEU lays down the free movement of workers, one of the EU's four fundamental freedoms. The CJEU has had a pivotal role in developing the notion of 'worker' who is to enjoy free movement rights. In the 1980s, in the case of *Lawrie-Blum* the Court set out the three essential criteria for an individual to be considered a worker for the purpose of free movement law: (1) to be under the direction or supervision of another; (2) to provide services for a certain period of time; and (3) to receive some remuneration for these services.[10] Over the years, the Court has consistently applied the broad notion of worker set in *Lawrie-Blum* to strike down narrower national definitions and to provide protection to individuals seeking to exercise their free movement rights regardless of the type of work they do or the level of remuneration they receive for their work.[11] There is, therefore, nothing to suggest that a domestic worker would not be entitled to all the rights and protections EU workers enjoy when exercising their free movement rights under Article 45 TFEU and associated secondary legislation.[12] Even when working on a casual basis or for a very low salary, an EU migrant working as a domestic worker undoubtedly falls within the personal scope of free movement of workers' law.

In the area of gender equality law, the CJEU, drawing on its free movement of workers' jurisprudence, defines an equally broad and inclusive personal scope. For example, in *Allonby*, the Court held that the concept of 'worker' under Article157(1) TFEU on equal pay between men and women has an autonomous EU law meaning which corresponds to that set out in *Lawrie-Blum*.[13] Gender equality is a fundamental principle of EU law and, as such, calls for a broad and inclusive personal scope which cannot but include domestic workers as well. It thus follows that secondary EU legislation which constitute specific expressions of the gender equality principle apply to anyone who provides work under the direction of another in exchange of remuneration.[14]

The view that domestic workers are not entitled to the rights and protections EU law provides in areas such as equal pay, protection against harassment at work, is clearly untenable.

---

[10] *Lawrie-Blum v Land Baden-Württemberg* (Case C-66/85) EU:C:1986:284, paras 16–18.
[11] *Athanasios Vatsouras (C-22/08) and Josif Koupatantze (C-23/08) v Arbeitsgemeinschaft (ARGE) Nürnberg 900 (Vatsouras)* (Case C-22/08) EU:C:2009:34, paras 26–30.
[12] See discussion in ch 3.
[13] *Allonby v Accrington & Rossendale College, Education Lecturing Services, trading as Protocol Professional and Secretary of State for Education and Employment* (Case C-256/01) EU:C:2004:18, paras 66–67.
[14] Such as Directive 2006/54/EC of 5 July 2006 on the implementation of the principle of equal opportunities and equal treatment of men and women in matters of employment and occupation (recast).

Non-Straightforward Inclusion: Reconsidering the Framework Health and Safety Directive and its Individual Directives

Even though the Health and Safety Directive defines its personal scope broadly to cover all workers, including trainees and apprentices, in both public and private sectors,[15] it explicitly excludes domestic workers in private households.[16] Interestingly, in its draft proposal on the directive, the European Commission did not intend to exclude any category; the concept of 'worker' was defined as 'any person who performs work in some form, including students undergoing training and apprentices'.[17] It was Member States who inserted the domestic worker exemption into the directive's personal scope during the legislative process. In the late 1980s when the directive was adopted, there was little challenge to the idea that health and safety standards were unsuitable for private households. Additionally, the prevailing assumption that paid domestic work was in decline in Europe might have led those drafting the directive to believe that the exclusion would not affect a significant number of workers.

Many years have passed since the entry into force of the Health and Safety Directive. It is now clear that paid domestic work, far from declining, is a growing sector in Europe and plays a key role in the sustainability of our families, communities and economies. Our understanding of health and safety issues has also shifted, not least because of relevant developments in EU law. In its jurisprudence in this area, the CJEU endorses what Anne Davies calls, a 'dignitarian understanding of health and safety'.[18] What is meant by this is an understanding of health and safety issues as being intrinsically linked to workers' dignity and general wellbeing, as opposed to a narrow view limited to the prevention of occupational risk.[19] Because of the link with workers' dignity, it is necessary to design health and safety standards that can be adapted and applied in all workplaces, including private households when they become workplaces, by employing a domestic worker.[20]

---

[15] See Health and Safety Directive, art 2.

[16] Article 3 states: 'For the purposes of this Directive the following terms shall have the following meanings: (a) worker: any person employed by an employer, including trainees and apprentices but excluding domestic servants.'

[17] European Commission, Proposal for a Council Directive on the introduction of measures to encourage improvements in the safety and health of workers at the workplace, COM (88)73 final.

[18] A Davies, *EU Labour Law* (Cheltenham: Edward Elgar Publishing, 2012) 201.

[19] In *UK v Council*, the CJEU famously said that health and safety should be understood 'as a state of complete physical, mental and social-wellbeing that does not consist only in the absence of illness or infirmity'. See, *United Kingdom of Great Britain and Northern Ireland v Council of the European Union. Council Directive 93/104/EC Concerning Certain Aspects of the Organization of Working Time – Action for annulment* (*UK v Council*) (Case C-84/94) EU:C:1996:431, para 15.

[20] As I discuss in ch 2, Spanish health and safety law includes a provision stipulating the introduction of adapted health and safety measures for private households employing a domestic worker.

Throughout the years, European Parliament resolutions have highlighted the need to apply the health and safety directive to a range of sectors at risk, including domestic work.[21] At the same time, the development of ILO standards on domestic work – especially Convention 198 on decent work for domestic workers and Recommendation 201 – reinforce states' obligation to redesign health and safety laws so that they deliver effective protection to those working in and for private households.[22]

There could be no better example than the COVID-19 pandemic to illustrate the importance of having suitable health and safety measures in all workplaces. It is no exaggeration to say that domestic workers across the world have been on the front line of the global health crisis, providing essential care for children, the elderly and other people in need. With schools closed, imposed lockdowns and people teleworking for extended periods in most European countries, there has been an increased need for home-based childcare and other types of care and domestic work. As domestic workers have no possibility to telework, those who continue to work during the pandemic do so while exposing themselves and their families to health risks. A survey on the impact of COVID-19 on platform-mediated work, for instance, reports cases of domestic workers who have had to turn up to work with their children.[23] The nature of their work, especially when it involves care, requires being in close proximity with individuals often considered at risk of contracting the virus. Because of the exclusion of domestic work from health and safety legislation in most countries, there has been lack of guidance by governments on the kind of measures employers and service providers should take to ensure adequate health and safety at work for domestic workers. Having to work without personal protective equipment and other health and safety measures exposes both domestic workers and communities to risk.[24]

It is clear that the blanket exclusion of domestic workers from the EU Health and Safety Directive and, consequently, from national legislations implementing the directive, is no longer defensible and must be reconsidered.[25] The EU should

---

[21] European Parliament, Resolution of 15 January 2008 on the Community strategy 2007–2012 on health and safety at work, point 42; European Parliament, Resolution of 28 April 2016 on women domestic workers and carers in the EU.

[22] See ILO C.189, art 13(1) on domestic workers which stipulates that: 'Every domestic worker has the right to a safe and healthy working environment. Each Member shall take, in accordance with national laws, regulations and practice, effective measures with due regard for the specific characteristics of domestic work to ensure the occupational safety and health of domestic workers.'

[23] Fairwork 'The Gig Economy and Covid-19: Fairwork Report on Platform Policies' (Oxford, United Kingdom, 2020).

[24] Developing guidelines specific to working in a private household and providing personal protective equipment to domestic workers are two of the claims put forward by a number of European social partners – trade unions and employers' associations. See, EFFAT, EFFE, EFSI, UNI-Europa, Joint statement on the COVID-19 pandemic in Personal and Household Services (Brussels, 1 April 2020).

[25] For recent successful litigation on behalf of workers in the so-called 'gig economy' in challenging their exclusion from UK legislation implementing EU health and safety provisions, See *IWUGB v SSWP and Others* [2020] EWHC 3050(Admin). The case was brought by the Independent Workers Union of Great Britain, representing mainly precarious migrant workers in transportation, such as taxi drivers, chauffeurs and van drivers, whose health and safety risks have been exacerbated in the context of the

take urgent action to remove the exclusion and provide guidance to Member States on how to effectively protect the health and safety of domestic workers.

Directive 89/391 stipulates the adoption of individual directives to address specific health and safety issues.[26] Two are most relevant to domestic workers: the Pregnant Workers' Directive and the Working Time Directive.[27] Now, a separate issue concerns the relationship between the personal scope of the Health and Safety Directive and that of its individual directives. Since the Health and Safety Directive excludes domestic workers, does that mean that they are also excluded under the individual directives?

Various doctrinal analyses consider the personal scope of the Health and Safety Directive as being directly applicable to the directives on working time and pregnant workers.[28] These analyses, however, do not discuss the implications of this finding for domestic workers. However, the critiques of Deirdre McCann and Catherine Barnard, that did look into this issue, concluded that domestic workers are excluded from the personal scope of the working time and pregnant workers directives because of their exclusion in the Health and Safety Directive.[29]

In the 2016 article, I challenged McCann's and Barnard's findings and provided several arguments as to why both individual directives should be considered fully applicable to domestic workers. My critique drew on the directives' structure, the status of certain labour rights as fundamental rights in EU law and the practice of the EU Commission which, as early as the late 1990s, had challenged Member States' exclusion of domestic workers from national measures implementing the Pregnant Workers' Directive.[30] More recently, the EU Commission challenged the exclusion of domestic workers from several Member States' national measures implementing the Working Time Directive, confirming, therefore, the view that the Commission considers both directives fully applicable to domestic workers.[31]

COVID-19 pandemic. The UK High Court held that the UK, by excluding categories of workers such as those represented by the claimant from the implementation of the EU framework health and safety directive and the directive on personal protective equipment, failed to meet its obligations under EU law.

[26] Framework Health and Safety Directive, art 16.

[27] Directive 92/85/EEC on the introduction of measures to encourage improvements in the safety and health at work of pregnant workers and workers who have recently given birth or are breastfeeding (Pregnant Workers Directive) [1992] OJ L348/1; Directive 2003/88/EC concerning certain aspects of the organisation of working time (Working Time Directive) [2003] OJ L299.

[28] See, for example, G Ricci, 'Tutela della salute e orario di lavoro' in S Sciarra (ed), *Manuale di Diritto Sociale Europeo* (Torino: G Giappichelli Editore, 2010) 51–87; K Riesenhuber, *European Employment Law. A Systematic Exposition* (Cambridge: Intersentia, 2012); B Valdés de la Vega, 'Occupational Health and Safety: An EU Law Perspective' in E Ales (ed) *Health and Safety at Work. European and Comparative Perspective* (Alphen aan den Rijn: Kluwer Law International, 2012) 1–27.

[29] D McCann 'New Frontiers of Regulation: Domestic Work, Working Conditions and the Holistic Assessment of Nonstandard Work Norms' (2012) 34 *Comparative Labor Law & Policy Journal* 167–84; C Barnard, *EU Employment Law*, 4th edn (Oxford: Oxford University Press, 2012). Mantouvalou made the same argument but only in relation to the Working Time Directive. See, V Mantouvalou, 'Human Rights for Precarious Workers: The Legislative Precariousness of Domestic Labour' (2012) 34 *Comparative Labor Law & Policy Journal* 133–65.

[30] Report of the Commission on the implementation of Council Directive 92/85, COM(1999) 100 final.

[31] See, European Commission (2017) Report on the implementation by Member States of Directive 2003/88/EC concerning certain aspects of the organisation of working time, COM(2017) 254 final.

Additionally, CJEU jurisprudence has repeatedly held that the Health and Safety Directive does not determine the personal scope of the Working Time Directive. Building on its earlier case law on working time, the Court confirmed in *Matzak* that the term 'worker' for the purpose of the working time directive has an autonomous EU law meaning which prevails over more restrictive national definitions.[32] The Court went on to hold that Mr Matzak, a volunteer firefighter in Belgium, met the criteria to be legally characterised a worker under EU law and was therefore entitled to the directive's rights and protections, most importantly, including limits to on-call hours. How is it that a volunteer firefighter is covered by EU working time legislation, but a domestic worker is not?

Inclusion Linked to National Law

A third cluster of EU labour law directives has no autonomous personal scope. Their scope of application is tied to national definitions of the notions of 'employee' or 'worker'. In other words, to be entitled to the directive's rights and protections, an individual would have to fall within the national definition. What does the technique of linking application to national definitions imply for domestic workers? Can Member States use their discretion to define who is an employee or worker to exclude domestic workers from national measures implementing the directives without autonomous personal scope? To answer this question, I examine the construction of personal scope of directives included in the third cluster: employer's insolvency, atypical work, work/life balance and transparent and predictable working conditions.

The Employer's Insolvency Directive provides some rights and protections for employees, most importantly in relation to unpaid wage claims, when their employer becomes insolvent.[33] This directive is not the first legal source that comes to mind when one thinks of domestic workers' labour rights. Understandably so, because those who employ domestic workers are natural persons who do not normally have the legal capacity to be declared insolvent. There can be, however, situations where the directive's application would be triggered – think, for instance, of an employer with commercial activities who becomes insolvent and also happens to employ a domestic worker.

Interestingly, and despite its potentially limited importance, the Employer's Insolvency Directive includes a standstill provision in relation to domestic workers. While it applies to 'employees' as defined under national law,[34] a Member State may only exclude domestic workers if the exclusion already existed in its national

---

[32] *Ville de Nivelles v Rudy Matzak (Matzak)*, (Case C-518/15) EU:C:2018:82. See also, *Union Syndicale Solidaires Isère v Premier Ministre and others (Isère)* (Case C-428/09) EU:C:2010:612; *Gérard Fenoll v Centre d'aide par le travail "La Jouvene" and Association de parents et d'amis de personnes handicapées mentales (APEI) d'Avignon (Fenoll)* (Case C-316/13) EU:C:2015:200.

[33] Directive 2008/94, recital 3.

[34] Ibid, arts 1(1) and 2(2).

legislation before the directive was adopted.[35] This was the case only for a limited number of Member States, namely France, the Netherlands, Poland, Malta and Spain; it thus follows that all other Member States should include domestic workers in their national measures implementing the Employer's Insolvency Directive.

The construction of personal scope under the Employer's Insolvency Directive adds nuance to the debate concerning the scope of application of EU labour law in general and of domestic workers' place in particular. The directive's standstill provision in relation to domestic workers is an example of how sometimes we can find sources of legal protection in unlikely, overlooked places.

The three so-called atypical work directives use the same technique to define their personal scope of application. They apply to either part-time,[36] fixed-term,[37] or temporary agency workers,[38] which are notions defined in the directives, while the definition of the term 'worker' is essentially a matter for national law. It thus follows that atypical work directives would apply to a domestic worker as long as they are legally characterised as a worker under national law. Given the trend of convergence on the legal notion of 'worker' across European jurisdictions,[39] this will often be the case. Tying the directives' scope of application to national definitions does not, in any case, provide Member Stares with carte blanche to exclude categories of workers. As the CJEU ruled in *O'Brien* when construing the term 'worker' for the purpose of implementing EU legislation – in this case the Part-Time Work Directive – Member States must have due regard to the objectives of the legislation and respect its effectiveness.[40] In *Ruhrlandklinik*, the CJEU held that while Member States have the discretion to define the term 'worker' under their national law, the EU legislator retains the right to define the notion for the purpose of EU law – in this case the Temporary Agency Work Directive. The Court went on to hold that, for the purposes of the directive, a worker is

> any person who carries out work, that is to say, who, for a certain period of time, performs services for and under the direction of another person, in return for which he receives remuneration, and who is protected on that basis in the Member State concerned [...][41]

In other words, national discretion does not extend to excluding from the directive's protection contractual relationships that do not substantially differ from those that national law considers to be employment/work relationships.

---

[35] Ibid, art 1(3).
[36] Part-Time Work Directive, cl 3.
[37] Ibid, cl 3(1).
[38] Temporary Agency Work Directive, arts 1(1) and 3(1)(c).
[39] G Davidov, N Freedland and N Kountouris, 'The Subjects of Labor Law: "Employees" and Other Workers' in M Finkin and G Mundlak (eds), *Research Handbook in Comparative Labor Law* (Cheltenham, Northampton, MA: Edward Elgar Publishing, 2015), 115–31.
[40] *Dermod Patrick O'Brien v Ministry of Justice, formerly Department for Constitutional Affairs* (*O'Brien*) (Case C-393/10) EU:C:2012:110.
[41] *Betriebsrat der Ruhrlandklinik gGmbH v Ruhrlandklinik gGmbH* (*Ruhrlandklinik*) (Case C-216/15) EU:C:2016:883, para 43.

In June 2019 the EU adopted two directives giving content to some of the principles and rights contained in European Pillar of Social Rights: the Transparent and Predictable Working Conditions Directive and the Work/life Balance Directive.[42] The Transparent and Predictable Working Conditions Directive replaces earlier legislation in the area of employers' obligation to inform workers of terms and conditions of work – the Written Statement Directive.[43] Recital (8) of the new directive's preamble notes the developments in the CJEU's jurisprudence on the notion of 'worker' and affirms that domestic workers, as long as they fulfil the criteria under EU law, fall within its scope; the directive intends to exclude only the genuinely self-employed. Article 1(2) of the directive's main body sets a broad personal scope:

> The directive applies to every worker in the Union who has an employment contract or employment relationship as defined by the law, collective agreements or practice in force in each Member State with consideration to the case-law of the Court of Justice.

The reference to the case law of the Court is a new addition to the technique of tying the scope of application to national definitions. While, as we saw, directives with no autonomous personal scope still place restrictions on Member State discretion, the explicit reference to the Court's case law reflects the drafters' aim to make the directive as inclusive as possible. This nod to the EU definition of 'worker' is a strong indication that the CJEU will interpret the directive's personal scope broadly to include all those who, for a certain period of time, provide services under the direction or supervision of another in exchange for remuneration. After all, this directive was adopted with the rights of atypical, often on-demand, workers in mind. Closing the protective gap for those susceptible to misclassification is one of its stated aims, a task which requires extra scrutiny of national definitions.[44]

When compared to its predecessor, the new Transparent and Predictable Working Conditions Directive is an improvement in terms of personal scope. Under the, now repealed, Written Statement Directive, Member States could exclude those with employment contracts or relationships of a casual or specific nature provided the exemption was justified on 'objective considerations'.[45] Several Member States had used this possibility to exclude domestic workers from the right to receive information on terms and conditions of employment: Austria, the Netherlands, Sweden and Spain before reforming its specific legislation on domestic work.

Member States might, of course, still enact exclusions when implementing the new directive. The broader personal scope with its reference to the Court's jurisprudence, however, now provides a tool to effectively challenge such exclusions. Domestic workers, to the extent that they provide services under the direction

---

[42] The Transparent and Predictable Working Conditions Directive is based on Principle 5 on secure and adaptable employment and Principle 7 on information about employment conditions and protection in dismissals.

[43] Directive 91/533 on an employer's obligation to inform employees of the conditions applicable to the contract or employment relationship [1991] OJ L 288/32.

[44] See, for example, recitals (5) and (12) in the Preamble.

[45] Article 1(2)(b), Written Statement Directive.

of another in exchange for remuneration should be considered as workers and should, therefore, fall within the directive's scope of application.

The new Work/Life Balance Directive replaces the previous directive on parental leave and creates several individual rights to different types of leave from work: paternity, parental, carer's leave and time off work on *force majeure* grounds as well as the right to request flexible working arrangements. All these entitlements aim to support workers in combining paid work with unpaid caring responsibilities.

This directive's personal scope is almost identical to that on transparent and predictable working conditions:

> This Directive applies to all workers, men and women, who have an employment contract or employment relationship as defined by the law, collective agreements or practice in force in each Member State, taking into account the case-law of the Court of Justice.[46]

There are, therefore, equally strong indications that the personal scope of the Work/Life Balance Directive will also be interpreted broadly. Nothing in the directive suggests that domestic workers could be excluded from its different substantive provisions. Besides, as an instrument promoting equality between men and women,[47] its personal scope should be understood as broad and inclusive. One, of course, cannot but notice that the directive on work/life balance – unlike the directive on transparent and predictable working conditions – makes no explicit reference to domestic workers. This is surprising given the important difficulties domestic workers face in meeting the needs of their own family members while working to take care of others. An explicit reference would have pre-empted domestic workers' exclusion from national implementing measures. As the various Member States prepare to implement the directive, it is important that unions and other stakeholders advocate for domestic workers' inclusion in national measures.

Illegally Resident Migrant Workers and the Personal Scope of EU Labour Law

Thus far, I have examined the inclusion of domestic workers in the personal scope of EU labour law. What happens with those migrant workers who lack legal residence under immigration law? Can Member States exclude them from rights and protections derived from EU labour law? At the outset, it should be noted that no EU labour law directive explicitly excludes illegally resident migrant workers from its scope of application.[48] An issue that arises, especially in the third cluster

---

[46] Directive on Transparent and Predictable Working Conditions, art 2.
[47] Work/Life Balance Directive, see recitals (2), (6) and (10) of the Preamble.
[48] S Peers 'Legislative Update: EC Immigration and Asylum Law Attracting and Deterring Labour Migration: The Blue Card and Employer Sanctions Directive' (2009) 11 *European Journal of Migration and Law* 387–426.

directives with no autonomous personal scope, is whether Member States can use their discretion to exclude illegally resident migrant workers. The CJEU's answer in *Tümer* is no.

Tümer concerned a non-EU migrant living and working in the Netherlands on a series of fixed-term residence permits. When the renewal of his latest permit was refused, he became illegally resident but continued working. When his employer was declared insolvent, Tümer applied for an insolvency benefit under the Dutch Unemployment Law, the national instrument implementing the Insolvency Directive. His application was rejected on the basis that the Dutch Unemployment Law did not consider illegally resident migrants to be 'employees' and thus exempted them from the insolvency benefit.

When examining the compatibility of Mr Tümer's exclusion with EU law, the Court first noted that the EU's competence to legislate in the area of working conditions, ie under Article 151 TFEU, is not limited to EU nationals but also covers the working conditions of non-EU nationals. While Member States may enjoy discretion to determine the terms 'employee' or 'worker', when the application of EU law is triggered, such discretion must be exercised in ways that uphold the social objectives of the EU legislation in question.[49] In the case of the Insolvency Directive, the social objective of guaranteeing a minimum of EU law protection when the employer becomes insolvent does not allow the exemption of individuals who would normally, ie under labour law terms, be considered employees.

In his Opinion, Advocate General Bot usefully divided EU law provisions into three categories: provisions applying specifically to non-EU nationals – such as directives on immigration – provisions applying exclusively to EU nationals – such as free movement of workers – and provisions applying irrespective of nationality – such as labour law directives. The personal scope of the third type of provisions, he notes, is determined in light of their pursued objectives. EU labour law directives cover individuals regardless of nationality because their objectives do not justify the exemption of non-EU nationals.[50] If Member States were allowed to make the right to receive insolvency benefits conditional upon legal residence, the objectives and effectiveness of the directive would be undermined, while the exclusion of illegally migrant workers would be against the general EU law principle of non-discrimination.[51]

The implications of the judgment and of AG Bot's analysis clearly extend beyond the insolvency directive. The judgment upholds the autonomy of labour law against immigration law interference and makes clear that Member States may not exclude illegally resident workers from the application of EU labour law. Of course, this finding applies to domestic workers as well. The effect of *Tümer* is that migrant workers, irrespective of status under migration law, are entitled

---

[49] *Tümer v Raad van bestuur van het Uitvoeringsinstituut werknemersverzekeringen (Tümer)* (Case C-311/13) EU:C:2014:2337, para 42.
[50] Opinion of AG Bot in *Tümer* (C-311/13) EU:C:2014:1997.
[51] Ibid, paras 69 and 70.

to all claims deriving from EU labour law. The judgment therefore challenges national illegality regimes to the extent that they bar access to EU law rights such as working time limits, maternity protection or the right to receive information on working time.

To sum up this section, domestic workers should be able to rely on the full range of EU individual labour law sources with two exceptions: the framework Health and Safety Directive because it contains a textual exclusion and the Employer's Insolvency Directive because the exclusion applies only in a limited number of Member States. Free movement law applies to migrant domestic workers who are EU nationals. Equality law should be considered to apply to all domestic workers without exception. For example, a migrant domestic worker, regardless of their migration status, is covered by equal pay and other equality provisions such as protection against workplace harassment. Similarly, the Pregnant Workers and Working Time Directives apply fully to domestic workers. In relation to the third cluster directives with personal scope tied to national definitions, Member States are restricted by EU law in enacting blanket exclusions. Domestic workers should, in principle, be able to rely on directives on part-time, fixed-term and temporary agency work, as well as the directives on transparent and predictable working conditions and work/life balance. Any exclusions structured in national provisions should be scrutinised with due regard to each directive's purpose and effectiveness.

Substantive Rights in Selected Areas

Having clarified the inclusion of domestic workers in the personal scope of EU labour law sources, I now review the substance of protections and entitlements domestic workers can derive from EU law sources in the areas of information on terms and conditions of work, pregnancy and maternity rights and working time. I focus the analysis on these areas because of their importance in addressing some of the most common vulnerabilities migrant domestic workers face.

Information on Terms and Conditions of Work

The new directive on transparent and predictable working conditions obliges employers to provide workers with written information on essential aspects of the employment relationship.[52] Employers should provide information on a range of aspects indicated in Article 4, such as, the identities of the parties, their usual place of work, specification or description of the work, notice periods and procedures to terminate the relationship, paid leave, remuneration, the normal length of

---

[52] Directive on Transparent and Predictable Working Conditions, arts 3 and 4.

working day or week and arrangement for overtime and its remuneration.[53] As the wording of the provision suggests – 'the information […] shall include *at least* the following' – the list is open-ended; therefore other aspects not mentioned might also be considered essential and create an obligation for the employer to provide information.[54]

Lack of information is a major vector of vulnerability to exploitation for domestic workers, especially migrants with additional linguistic and cultural barriers, when navigating complex legal systems to make sense of their rights and obligations. Their having no accurate information on important aspects of their employment relationship can lead to lax enforcement of protective legislation and exploitation. For instance, temporary migrants are often restricted by the terms of their permit to work for a named employer. A clear statement on who the employer and workplace are can help protect against abusive practices such as requiring migrant domestic workers to work for additional employers.

Having access to information on terms and conditions at work does not, of course, lead to straightforward enforcement of any rights. However, written, timely and accurate information on rights and obligations at work is the first and necessary step towards better enforcement. Additionally, the directive carries a symbolic value which should not be underestimated. A binding obligation on employers to provide their workers written information helps formalise a relationship often not regarded as a proper employment relationship by the very parties participating in it. Those who employ domestic workers tend not to view themselves as 'real' employers and domestic workers are often unaware of the full range of rights available to them.[55] By framing the relationship in labour law terms, with rights and obligations, the directive is a step towards shifting perspectives around paid household work.

Pregnancy and Maternity Rights

The Pregnant Workers Directive introduces several rights and protections for women who are pregnant or have recently given birth. These include the right to refuse night work,[56] entitlements to a period of maternity leave[57] and to paid time-off to attend ante-natal appointments.[58] Importantly, the directive requires Member States to prohibit the dismissal of a worker who is pregnant or has

---

[53] The explicit inclusion of overtime and its remuneration as an essential aspect is a new addition which consolidates CJEU case law. See, Judgment of 8 February 2001, *Lange*, C-350/99, EU:C:2001:84.

[54] See, in this respect, case law on the now-repealed Written Statement Directive, *Wolfgang Lange v Georg Schünemann GmbH (Lange)* (Case C-350/99) EU:C:2001:84, paras 21 and 25.

[55] See generally, A Triandafyllidou and S Marchetti, *Employers, Agencies and Immigration: Paying for Care* (Abingdon: Routledge, 2015).

[56] Pregnant Workers Directive, art 7.

[57] Ibid, art 8.

[58] Ibid, art 9.

recently given birth except in 'exceptional cases' not connected with the worker's pregnancy; this provision has generated rich case law.[59]

According to the Court's established case law, the prohibition of dismissal under the Pregnant Workers Directive has direct effect; claimants can therefore invoke the protection in national courts even if the national implementing measure excludes them.[60] While formally based on health and safety provisions, the directive has an undeniable equality dimension;[61] the CJEU has reiterated the directive's sex equality objectives in several judgments concerning especially protection against dismissal.

The directive diverges from the classical anti-discrimination model found in other areas of equality legislation such as equal pay. Dismissing, for instance, a pregnant worker is a form of direct discrimination which admits no justification. Crucially, there is no requirement for a comparator to substantiate a claim. Finding a suitable comparator as a requirement to access protection against workplace discrimination is a real barrier for domestic workers because their employers are usually natural persons who do not normally employ anyone else.[62] This departure from the comparator approach, therefore, makes it possible for domestic workers to bring claims of pregnancy and maternity discrimination against their employers.[63]

The protection against dismissal under Article 10 of the directive has generated a rich body of CJEU case law which has potential to address many domestic workers' vulnerabilities, including those structured in migration law, such as temporary permits, the employer's excessive power to dismiss or the exclusion of illegally resident workers from labour law protection. According to the Court's established case law, the protection against dismissal can be subject to no exceptions or derogations.[64] It can therefore be used to challenge the pregnancy-related dismissal of an illegally resident migrant domestic worker. The protection also extends to fixed-term workers.[65] Thus, dismissing a worker who was hired on a six-month fixed-term contract and notified her employer of her pregnancy one

---

[59] Ibid, art 10.

[60] *Maria Luisa Jiménez Melgar v Ayuntamiento de Los Barrios (Melgar)* (Case C-438/99) EU:C:2001:509.

[61] The need to establish an explicit link between the directive and the principle of equality is also reflected in efforts, albeit unsuccessful, to improve maternity protection. In its 2008 proposal for the amendment of Directive 92/85, the Commission argued that the legal basis can no longer be only health and safety; its equality dimension requires that it is also expressly based on TFEU, art 157.

[62] This is a common difficulty even for other workers in small establishments. See the discussion in E Albin, 'From "domestic servant" to "domestic worker"' in J Fudge, S McCrystal and K Sankaran (eds), *Challenging the Legal Boundaries of Work Regulation* (Oxford: Hart Oñati International Series in Law and Society, 2012) 231–51.

[63] For instance, Spanish tribunals and courts have issued several judgments on pregnancy dismissal cases brought by domestic workers. See *STS 591/2020*, ES:TS:2020:591; *STSJ EXT 581/2019*, ES:TSJEXT:2019:581.

[64] *George Lawrence Webb v Lawrence Desmond Webb (Webb)* (Case C-294/92) EU:C:1994:193.

[65] *Tele Danmark A/S v Handels- og Kontorfunktionærernes Forbund i Danmark (HK) (Tele Danmark)* (Case C-109/00) EU:C:2001:513.

month after recruitment was contrary to the directive despite the fact that the pregnancy prevented the worker from performing her tasks during a substantial part of the contract's duration.[66] Non-EU national domestic workers on temporary residence and work permits fall under the definition of fixed-term worker. The fact that they cannot be dismissed in the event of pregnancy is crucial, not least because their residence permit often depends on continuous employment. Therefore, the directive's dismissal protection can be used to protect temporary, non-EU, migrant domestic workers from losing their employment and becoming irregular because of their pregnancy. However, the non-renewal of a pregnant worker's fixed-term contract will not necessarily be considered unlawful under the directive. According to the judgment in *Melgar*, the non-renewal of a fixed-term contract can exceptionally constitute sex discrimination only if it was motivated by the worker's pregnancy.[67] While the directive prohibits the pregnancy-related dismissal of a temporary migrant domestic worker, it cannot be relied upon to extend a temporary permit.

In 2018, the Court's judgment in *Porras Guisado* attracted negative attention for the controversial finding that a collective redundancy is an 'exceptional case' that can justify the dismissal of a pregnant worker.[68] Yet the relevance of this ruling extends well beyond the area of collective redundancies. In *Porras Guisado*, the CJEU held that the prohibition of pregnancy-related dismissal under the directive should be implemented in a way that is not only reparative, ie providing remedies to dismissed workers, but also preventive. This is what the Court refers to as the 'double protection' the Pregnant Workers' Directive requires.[69] In a particularly incisive point of analysis, the CJEU acknowledges the:

> harmful effects which the risk of dismissal may have on the physical and mental state of workers who are pregnant, have recently given birth or are breastfeeding, including the particularly serious risk that pregnant women may be prompted voluntarily to terminate their pregnancy.[70]

What does it mean to have preventive protection against pregnancy-related dismissals? According to the Court, the very 'taking of a decision to dismiss' is against the protective aims of Article 10.[71] From this follows that even handing a dismissal notice to a pregnant worker can have the kind of serious detrimental effects the Pregnant Workers' Directive seeks to prevent. Reparation in the form

---

[66] Ibid.
[67] *Melgar*, para 47.
[68] *Jessica Porras Guisado v Bankia SA and Others (Porras Guisado)* (Case C-103/16) EU:C:2018:99. According to Directive 92/85, art 10(1), Member States shall take the necessary measures to prohibit the dismissal of pregnant workers during the period from the beginning of their pregnancy to the end of their maternity leave, 'save in exceptional cases not connected with their condition which are permitted under national legislation and/or practice and, where applicable, provided that the competent authority has given its consent'.
[69] Ibid, *Porras Guisado*, para 59.
[70] Ibid, para 62.
[71] Ibid, para 63.

of compensation for unfair dismissal or even re-admission to work cannot undo the harm and psychological pressure a pregnant worker experiences on receiving a dismissal notice: for a migrant domestic worker there is even more at stake. It is not difficult to imagine how devastating the threat of dismissal is for a migrant woman with a low-paid job who nevertheless depends on that job not only for subsistence, but also for lawful residence and even a roof. Having in place measures to prevent – instead of only remedying – the dismissal of a pregnant worker is crucial. I return to this point in section 4 below.

Working Time

The Working Time Directive introduces minimum standards for normal hours of work, weekly and daily rest periods, paid annual leave and guarantees for night work.[72] While not explicitly regulated in the directive, the issue of on-call hours has generated important case law which is relevant to domestic workers.

Under the directive, the maximum weekly hours of work, including any overtime, are 48.[73] The 48-hour weekly limit is subject to a derogation clause whereby Member States can exempt specific categories of workers whose working time is considered 'unmeasured'.[74] Novitz and Syrpis note that the UK has used this derogation clause to exclude domestic workers from important protections under the national implementing measure, the 1998 Working Time Regulations.[75] But does the directive permit Member States to enact a blanket exclusion of domestic workers as the UK did? What type of workers should be considered to have 'unmeasured' working time and should domestic workers be considered to fall within this category?

In recent CJEU jurisprudence, the right of every worker to a limitation of her maximum working hours as well as rights to daily and weekly rest periods are characterised as fundamental social rights.[76] According to the Court, the provisions on working time limits implement Article 31 of the EU Charter of Fundamental Rights (EUCFR) which guarantees to every worker 'the right to working conditions which respect his or her health, safety and dignity'.[77] Working time limits are therefore tightly linked to workers' dignity. Because workers are in a relationship of subordination and in an unequal bargaining position against the employer, working time

---

[72] Directive 2003/88 concerning certain aspects of the organisation of working time (Working Time Directive) [2003] OJ L299/9.
[73] Ibid, art 6.
[74] Ibid, art 17.
[75] T Novitz and P Syrpis, 'The Place of Domestic Work in Europe: An Analysis of Current Policy in the Light of the Council Decision Authorising Member States to Ratify ILO Convention No 189' (2015) 6(2) *European Labour Law Journal* 104–27.
[76] *Federación de Servicios de Comisiones Obreras (CCOO) v Deutsche Bank SAE* (Case C-55/18) EU:C:2019:402.
[77] See the Opinion of Advocate General Pitruzzella delivered on 31 January 2019, *Federación de Servicios de Comisiones Obreras*, EU:C:2019:87, para 12.

limits have an important function in safeguarding their dignity against managerial authority. Such function suggests that any exemptions must be construed narrowly so as to not frustrate the directive's protective purpose. It must therefore be understood that Member States may only exempt types of workers with complete control and autonomy over the organisation of their working time. This reading is further supported by the three examples of workers in an unmeasured work situation the provision provides: 'managing executives', 'family workers' and 'religious workers'.[78] These are examples of workers with a high degree of independence, who typically organise their hours autonomously. As they are not prima facie subjected to managerial authority to the same extent as other workers, Member States may exclude them from provisions limiting working time. This is clearly not the case for domestic workers, who have hardly any control over their working hours and its organisation.

Domestic workers cannot be exempted based on the 'family worker' derogation either as they do not fall under the definition of family worker. According to ILO definitions, a family worker 'holds a self-employment job in a market-oriented establishment operated by a *related* person living in the same household'.[79] Therefore, the 48-hour week must be considered the absolute maximum for domestic workers.

In relation to different types of rest periods the directive sets that, as a minimum, all workers are entitled to 11 consecutive hours of daily rest[80] as well as 35 hours of uninterrupted rest every week.[81] For those working at least six hours every day, the directive provisions a daily break, the specificities of which should be laid down in legislation or collective agreements.[82] Additionally, all workers are entitled to a minimum of four weeks of paid annual leave.[83] In CJEU's jurisprudence, the right to paid annual leave has long been considered a fundamental social right.[84] Finally, the directive sets limits and rights in relation to night work; night work should not exceed eight hours every 24 hours,[85] while those working regularly at night are entitled to free health assessments.[86]

While the directive does not regulate on-call hours, there is important CJEU jurisprudence in this area which clarifies the difference between working time and rest time.[87] According to this jurisprudence, on-call hours fall within the notion of

---

[78] Working Time Directive, art 17.
[79] See, ILO, International Classification by Status in Employment 1993.
[80] Working Time Directive, art 3.
[81] Ibid, art 5.
[82] Ibid, art 4.
[83] Ibid, art 7.
[84] The CJEU legally characterised the right to paid annual leave as a fundamental social right for the first time in *BECTU* C-173/99. Paid annual leave as a principle of EU law was reiterated and consolidated in the Court's jurisprudence in various subsequent judgments, such as *María Paz Merino Gómez v Continental Industrias del Caucho SA (Gomez)* (Case C-342/01) EU:C:2004:160; *Stringer and Others v Her Majesty's Revenue and Customs (Stringer)* (Case C-350/06) EU:2009:18.
[85] Working Time Directive, art 8.
[86] Ibid, art 9.
[87] Under the directive, working time is defined as 'any period during which the worker is working, at the employer's disposal and carrying out his activity or duties' and rest period is any time which is not working time. See ibid, arts 1(1) and (2).

working time which, therefore, means that they count towards working time limits and must be remunerated.

In *SIMAP*, the CJEU held that the hours the employer requires the worker to be physically present at the workplace count as working hours even if the worker is not actually performing any tasks.[88] In *Jaeger*, the criterion to be physically present was further refined. In this case, the CJEU held that the hours during which the worker is required to be physically present at a place specified by the employer count as working time even if there is a possibility to rest.[89] In other words, the critical issue when distinguishing between active and inactive time – working time and rest time – is the worker's autonomy to dispose of her time freely without being expected to attend to any requests from the employer.

More recently, in *Matzak*, the CJEU further reinforced the understanding that workers' autonomy and their right to disconnect from work must be at the heart of regulating on-call time.[90] The Court held that even though the worker was not required to be at a place specified by the employer, the requirement to reach the workplace in a short period of time – eight minutes in Mr Matzak's case – was so restrictive of the worker's autonomy and of any opportunities to engage in other activities that was incompatible with the notion of free time.

The Court's jurisprudence on on-call time is highly significant for domestic workers, especially those in live-in employment, as the issue is particularly complex and contentious. In domestic work, the very notions of working time and rest, workplace and private space merge to an extent that is unknown in any other type of work. Sharing the same living space with their employer often means that domestic workers are constantly available to respond to calls for work, without an effective right to disconnect and, crucially, without remuneration for their availability.[91]

The judgments in *SIMAP*, *Jaeger* and *Matzak* provide a useful framework to challenge domestic workers' constant and taken-for-granted availability. Following *SIMAP*, the time the employer requires the domestic worker to be physically present at the workplace counts as active working time even if she is not carrying out any tasks. According to *Jaeger*, even if the worker can rest, as long as she has to be present at a place determined by the employer, a place which could be the normal workplace or somewhere else accompanying, for instance, the employer during holidays or other activities, she is working. In line with *Matzak*, even the time a worker spends away from the workplace and in a place of her own choice but while expected to quickly respond to calls for work counts as working time. Rest time is, therefore, only the time during which the worker enjoys autonomy and can dispose of her time freely without having to worry that she might be called to work in any minute – having, in other words, a real possibility to disconnect.[92]

---

[88] *SIMAP v Conselleria de Sanidad y Consumo de la Generalidad Valenciana* (Case C-303/98) EU:C:2000:528.

[89] *Landeshauptstadt Kiel v Norbert Jaeger (Jaeger)* (Case C-151/02) EU:C:2003:437.

[90] *Ville de Nivelles v Rudy Matzak (Matzak)*, (Case C-518/15) EU:C:2018:82.

[91] See also ch 2.

[92] Similarly, ILO C.189 art 10(3) states that: 'periods during which domestic workers are not free to dispose of their time as they please and remain at the disposal of the household in order to respond to possible calls shall be regarded as hours of work'.

Having working time limits stipulated in legislation or collective agreements is only the first step towards enjoying these entitlements in practice. Effective enforcement can be particularly difficult especially in non-unionised workplaces and those with limited labour inspections. In 2019 the CJEU handed down a judgment concerning employers' obligations to monitor compliance with the directive's provisions. In *Federación de Servicios de Comisiones Obreras*, the CJEU held that the Working Time Directive obliges employers to measure and keep records of their workers' actual hours worked on a daily and weekly basis.[93] While there is no such express provision in the directive, the duty to keep records on working time is inferred from the dignitarian purposes of working time limits as provisions implementing Article 31 of the EU Charter of Fundamental Rights.[94] The duty to keep working time records extends fully to domestic workers' employers.

How Does National Law Fare?

After having outlined the different substantive rights domestic workers derive from EU law in the areas of information on terms and conditions of employment, pregnancy and maternity protection and working time, I now turn to discuss the regulation of these issues in the labour law regimes of the UK, Cyprus, Sweden and Spain with the aim of identifying any mismatches with EU law.

Information on Terms and Conditions of Work

During the last few years, there have been advances in national laws in relation to domestic workers' right to receive information on their terms and conditions of work.

In preparation for the ratification of ILO C.189, in 2018 *Sweden* amended its special law on household employment, the Domestic Work Act 1970, to include provisions on employers' obligations to provide a written statement within one month of employment.[95] Under the newly inserted provisions, the employer must provide information in relation to, at least, the parties' identity, specify tasks, state the contract's duration if fixed-term, any probation period, information on salary and any benefits, normal weekly and monthly hours, paid holidays and notice periods for termination.[96] Employers who do not comply with these obligations

---

[93] *Federación de Servicios de Comisiones Obreras (CCOO) v Deutsche Bank SAE* (Case C-55/18) EU:C:2019:402.

[94] See the Opinion of Advocate General Pitruzzella delivered on 31 January 2019, *Federación de Servicios de Comisiones Obreras*, C-55/18, EU:C:2019:87, para 12.

[95] Act 2018:179 amending Act 1970:943 on working hours etc in domestic work [SFS 2018:1719 *Lag om ändring i lagen (1970:943) om arbetstid m.m. i husligt arbete*].

[96] Act 1970:943 on working hours etc in domestic work, s 11(a) and (b).

may be liable to pay compensation.⁹⁷ Importantly, for contracts entered into before the amendments' entry into force –1 March 2019 – the employer is still obliged to provide information upon the employee's request.⁹⁸

Similarly, when *Spain* reformed its special law on domestic work in 2011, the new provisions mean that the employer is now obliged to provide a written statement to any domestic worker hired for more than four weeks. The written statement should contain all the information to which workers falling within the personal scope of generally applicable legislation are entitled. In addition, in line with Spain's sectoral approach, domestic workers should receive information in relation to payments in kind if any, any agreed on-call hours and their remuneration, as well as any arrangements in relation to living in the employer's household.⁹⁹

In *Cyprus*, the new contract of employment immigration authorities have distributed since May 2019 explicitly refers to the employer's obligation to provide the employee with a written statement under the provisions of generally applicable legislation. The reference is to the national legislation implementing the Written Statement Directive and is therefore an acknowledgment that this legislation applies to domestic workers.

In 2019, the *UK* widened the personal scope of its provisions on employers' obligation to provide a written statement on terms and conditions of employment. While prior to the amendment, only those legally characterised as employees were entitled to a written statement, the provision now applies to the wider category of workers.¹⁰⁰ The amendment creates more possibilities for domestic workers – whose contracts might not always meet the high threshold required to be legally characterised as employees under UK law – to benefit from the right to receive information on essential aspects of their work relationship.

Pregnancy and Maternity

In the area of pregnancy and maternity, Member States have overall transposed the different EU law requirements in their national legal regimes.¹⁰¹ On paper, all Member States prohibit the dismissal of pregnant workers, one of the most important protections the Pregnant Workers' Directive stipulates. Nothing in the national law of Member States suggests that domestic workers are exempt from this protection.

---

⁹⁷ Ibid, s 24.
⁹⁸ Act 2018:179 amending Act 1970:943 on working hours etc in domestic work [SFS 2018:1719 *Lag om ändring i lagen (1970:943) om arbetstid m.m. i husligt arbete*].
⁹⁹ Royal Decree 1620/2011, art 5(4).
¹⁰⁰ Employment Rights Act 1996, section 1(1) as amended by the Employment Rights (Miscellaneous Amendments) Regulations 2019 (SI 2019/734).
¹⁰¹ European Network of Legal Experts in Gender Equality and Non-Discrimination, 'A comparative analysis of gender equality law in Europe 2019' (Luxembourg: Publications Office of the EU, 2020).

At the same time, it is no secret that, despite the prohibition, the dismissal of pregnant workers continues to be a pressing issue. The phenomenon is only exacerbated in times of economic turmoil.[102] Survey studies on the impact of COVID-19 on pregnant workers show that low-paid workers are more at risk of discrimination, including termination of their contracts.[103] Migrant domestic workers are certainly not the only group who suffer from the gap between the 'law in the books' and the 'law in action', but they are traditionally vulnerable to losing their job if they become pregnant.[104] For example, in Cyprus, the Ombudsman has expressed concern over the not-so-uncommon practice of dismissing non-EU migrant domestic workers despite the prohibition.[105]

Of course, any dismissed pregnant worker, including a domestic worker, can challenge her dismissal as unlawful sex discrimination by bringing proceedings against her employer. Leaving the practical challenges of such an endeavour aside, the mere prohibition of dismissal does not meet the protection's preventive dimension the CJEU set in *Porras Guisado*. Employers can still proceed with dismissal relying on the fact that many, especially the most vulnerable workers, will be deterred from challenging such a decision and initiating litigation. And, of course, there are all the urgent practical issues a migrant domestic worker must solve if she suddenly finds herself without work while pregnant.

Clearly, more needs to be done for dismissal protection to be preventive and deliver what Article 10 of the Pregnant Workers' Directive promises. The starting point must be placing restrictions on employer's managerial prerogative to dismiss a worker who falls under the personal scope of the directive. Governments could, for example put in place a system whereby employers must obtain prior authorisation from a labour authority or equivalent body which verifies whether reasons unrelated to the worker's pregnancy justify dismissal.[106] At the same time, however, we would need broader supportive mechanisms for affected workers to enforce their rights, such as free and simplified extra-judicial procedures to deal with complaints, coupled with administrative fines for unscrupulous employers. More effectively, Member States could introduce a system of precautionary penalties that employers would need to pay before dismissing a pregnant worker; if the dismissal is deemed fair, employers can recover any sums paid.[107]

---

[102] N Busby and G James, 'Regulating Work/care Relationships in a Time of Austerity: A Legal Perspective' in S Lewis, D Anderson, C Lyonette, N Payne and S Wood (eds) *Work-Life Balance in Times of Recession, Austerity and Beyond* (Abingdon: Routledge, 2016) 78–92.

[103] Trades Union Congress, 'Report on Pregnant and Precarious: New and Expectant Mums' Experiences of Work during Covid-19' (11 June 2020).

[104] J Andall (2000) *Gender, Migration and Domestic Service: The Politics of Black Women in Italy* (Farnham: Ashgate); L Addati and LT Cheong '"Meeting the Needs of My Family Too": Maternity Protection and Work-family Measures for Domestic Workers' (Geneva: ILO, 2013).

[105] Office of the Ombudsman, 'Report against Social Welfare Services in relation to the handling of public fund claims by pregnant migrant women' (Nicosia: 29 December 2009).

[106] Directive 92/85, art 10(1) foresees the consent of a competent authority, but only as an option for Member States.

[107] I first presented these two proposals in V Pavlou, 'Whose Equality? Paid Domestic Work and EU Gender Equality Law' (2020) 20(1) *European Equality Law Review* 36–46.

Preventive measures are important for all working women. For women in precarious and non-unionised jobs, such as domestic workers, for those subject to immigration rules, for those who lack a supportive network, preventive measures are the only way to ensure that protection against pregnancy-related dismissal is not just an illusory promise.

Working Time

In the area of working time regulation, we can find several provisions excluding domestic workers in all four states that we focus on.

In the *UK*, domestic workers are explicitly excluded from important working time rights and protections.[108] First, they are excluded from the 48-hour weekly limit including overtime to which other workers are entitled. Normally, employers have an obligation to ensure that the weekly limit is complied with, to monitor, in other words, the actual hours worked by their employees.[109] Domestic workers' employers are, however, exempt from this obligation which means that domestic workers can legally be expected to work very long hours without any monitoring. Second, in relation to night work, domestic workers are excluded from the eight-hour limit applicable to other workers and limits designed for work that involves physical or mental strain,[110] eg think of the caretaker of an elderly person who works long night shifts. Third, domestic workers are also not entitled to a health assessment before taking up night work, nor can they be transferred to day work if they suffer from health issues.[111] Finally, domestic workers are excluded from protective measures – rest breaks – for those with monotonous patterns of work.[112] These exclusions, while clearly falling short of the minimum protections and entitlements in the Working Time Directive, have not been challenged for their incompatibility with EU law.

In *Cyprus*, the Working Time Directive has been transposed almost verbatim without any textual exclusion of domestic workers from the implementing legislation.[113] However, as Chapter 2 of this book showed, the state has created a regime that applies exclusively to non-EU domestic workers. The main source of this regime – the contract of employment that immigration authorities prepare and disseminate to migrant domestic workers and their employers – is an atypical source of employment regulation. It was prepared by immigration authorities, ie the state, to regulate a private law relationship, without any input from the parties in that relationship, while at the same time lowering the level of protection stipulated in generally applicable legislation. While the legal validity of this instrument

---

[108] All these exclusions are pursuant to UK Working Time Regulations 1998, reg 19.
[109] Ibid, regs 4(1) and (2).
[110] Ibid, reg 6(1), (2) and (7).
[111] Ibid, regs 7(1) and (6).
[112] Ibid, reg 8.
[113] Law on the organisation of working time 2002 (63(I)/2002).

is certainly dubious, there is no doubt that the state intends it to be binding, especially for the migrant worker who risks being deported if she does not respect its terms. As the contract makes no reference to the legislation as a supplementing source, it is clear that the state wants the parties to see the contract as the exclusive source regulating their relationship. Therefore, when assessing whether Cyprus meets its EU law obligations in the area of working time, one cannot just look at the law implementing the directive; one must look at the contract's provisions.

The contract states that:

> The Employee shall work for 6 days per week for 7 hours per day, either during the day or night as may be required by the Employer from time to time.[114]

While 42 hours per week is, in principle, within the directive's limit, the contract does not specify whether overtime and on-call hours count towards it. Given that the contract applies to non-EU migrants holding a domestic worker visa who are generally expected to live in the employer's household, these omissions are crucial. Live-in domestic work is well-known for the difficulties of establishing limits between work and free time. Constant availability is commonly expected of live-in domestic workers and a regulatory instrument that makes no effort to acknowledge and limit the phenomenon is perpetuating its normalisation. EU working time law requires that no worker works for more than 48 hours per week, including overtime and on-call hours and the Cypriot regime for migrant domestic workers must be amended to encompass, at the very least, that minimum standard.

Additionally, the contract makes no provision for daily rest breaks, nor is the issue regulated in any other instrument such as a collective agreement. Work performed during the night is essentially considered the same as daytime work without any of the guarantees EU working time law stipulates in relation to night work. Migrant domestic workers in Cyprus, therefore, have no right to limit their night work and no entitlement to health assessment.[115]

In *Sweden*, the special instrument regulating work within the private household stipulates a weekly limit of 40 hours; this is in line with the Working Time Directive.[116] However, if the domestic workers' tasks involve care, this weekly limit can be extended by 12 hours, that is 52 in total, to meet employer's needs; this exceeds the directive's limit. In addition to normal hours of work, domestic workers can be asked to work overtime for up to 48 hours over a reference period of four weeks and maximum limit of 300 hours during a calendar year.[117] Worryingly, domestic workers can be asked to work unlimited overtime if special and unforeseen circumstances so require; workers are expected to comply with such a request unless they have a 'valid obstacle'.[118]

---

[114] Contract of Employment for Domestic Workers, Section 2.1 A (Cyprus Ministry of Interior).

[115] The only reference the contract makes to health assessment is in the context of border control, whereby, upon arrival and before employment starts, employers bear the cost of medical examination to verify that the migrant worker is free of contagious diseases. See, Contract of Employment for Domestic Workers, Section 1.C (c) (Cyprus Ministry of Interior).

[116] Domestic Work Act (1970:943), s 2.

[117] Ibid, s 3.

[118] Ibid, ss 4 and 5.

Such provisions, regardless of how often they are actually triggered, are deeply problematic. They frame the domestic worker–employer relationship as exceptional and place on the worker obligations of care that are more akin to those of family members – an obligation to offer unlimited support to the employer in times of crisis. Apart from being deeply problematic, the Swedish provisions on domestic workers' overtime are also incompatible with EU working time law. To comply with the directive, overtime cannot exceed eight hours per week – or 32 per month – for all domestic workers irrespective of the tasks they perform.

In *Spain*, the special legislation on domestic work establishes a weekly maximum of 40 hours of work. This limit is, however, without prejudice to any extra hours the parties may agree for on-call work – referred to as 'presence time' – this is, in other words, time during which the domestic worker is available to the employer without carrying out any tasks.[119] This is problematic in terms of EU law compliance as, according to CJEU jurisprudence, the directive's 48-hour limit per week includes on-call hours. On the contrary, Spanish legislation creates the possibility for employers and domestic workers to agree up to 20 hours of on-call per week in a reference period of one month; this would far exceed the directive's limit on weekly hours. It seems that the Spanish legislator considers, contrary to CJEU's case law, that on-call hours do not count towards the maximum weekly time. To comply with the directive, the Spanish provision on on-call work for domestic workers should therefore be modified to specify that the parties can only agree up to eight extra hours for on-call on top of the regular 40-hour week.

In relation to daily rest, Spanish legislation establishes a minimum of 12 consecutive hours which is slightly more generous than the 11 hours stipulated in the directive.[120] However, there is a flexibility clause for live-in domestic workers whose daily rest can be reduced to 10 hours while the remaining two hours can be distributed over the course of four weeks. Spanish labour law scholars are critical of this as it reflects a tendency to prioritise employer interests over those of the worker.[121] To that critique it should be added that the flexibility clause is incompatible with the Working Time Directive. The EU considers that a minimum of 11 hours of daily rest is necessary to protect every worker's health and wellbeing. The fact that daily rest is not one of the provisions subject to reference periods under Article 16 demonstrates the importance of safeguarding the right to daily rest against employer needs or demands for flexibility.

Is this too much ado about nothing?. Will live-in domestic workers' lives change if they get, on paper that is, one extra hour of daily rest? My point is not about the value of one extra hour of daily rest but rather about the importance of insisting on the application of worker-protective laws for domestic workers, including those whose work is interwoven with the most intimate aspects of private life.

---

[119] Royal Decree 1620/2011, art 9(1).
[120] Ibid, art 9(4).
[121] J Gandía López and D Giménez Toscani, *El nuevo régimen laboral y de seguridad social de los trabajadores al servicio del hogar familiar* (Albacete: Bomarzo, 2012).

If we are to use the law to challenge the unjust law of the private household, as Adelle Blackett describes it,[122] we must start from the mundane and insist that live in domestic workers are treated equally. For there is nothing that can justify the instances of lower protection for the working time of domestic workers apart from the gendered construction of women's work within the private household as being inherently boundaryless. EU working time law, without explicitly intending to do so, gives us the tools to challenge and transform this construction.

Conclusion

In this chapter, I have argued that EU labour law sources are a useful but largely underutilised resource to challenge domestic workers' vulnerability structured in national laws and practices. By providing a nuanced account of the personal scope of different EU labour law sources and the place of domestic workers therein, I sought to show how these sources can open paths for transformative legal change for domestic workers, including migrants.

It is important to acknowledge, though, that EU law does not provide the full range of labour rights it does not regulate all issues that are important vectors of vulnerability for domestic workers. EU law sources cannot be used to challenge, for instance, domestic workers' disadvantage in the area of dismissals – with the exception of discriminatory dismissals within the meaning of EU law. Low pay or deductions from wages are other important aspects of working life that, for the time being, are not regulated under EU law.[123] The protection EU law provides is therefore limited in certain areas.

Notwithstanding any limitations, domestic workers can, however, derive rights and protections from EU law in important areas. I have shown here how domestic workers can rely, for example, on EU working time law to challenge their exclusion from key protections in national labour law, such as limits to on-call hours.

---

[122] A Blackett, *Everyday Transgressions. Domestic Workers' Transnational Challenge to International Labor Law* (Cornell University Press, 2019). On Blackett's notion of the unjust law of the private household, see the introduction.

[123] Note, however, that in late 2020 the European Commission published a proposal for an EU directive in the area of adequate minimum wages which, if finally adopted, may have implications for domestic workers' wages. European Commission, Proposal for a Directive of the European Parliament and the of the Council on adequate minimum wages in the European Union (Brussels: 28.10.2020) COM (2020) 682 final.

5
Challenging Vulnerability

Introduction

Having examined the role of different legal regimes in structuring and sustaining migrant domestic workers' vulnerability to exploitation, as well as the potential of EU labour law sources in challenging aspects of this vulnerability, in this chapter, I turn to comparatively examine national processes of reform and avenues for change. Using the examples of Sweden, Spain, Cyprus and the UK, I discuss the role and strategies of different actors in representing the interests of migrant domestic workers and in advocating for legal and policy changes to improve their rights. In Sweden, a controversial tax reform, implemented since 2008, has had the effect of changing the institutional setting of domestic work from direct recruitment by a private household to working via a private company. The change of institutional setting has, in its turn, created opportunities for trade unions to overcome some of the difficulties often associated with the collective organisation and representation of migrant domestic workers. In Spain, established trade unions took advantage of political momentum in 2011 and, in collaboration with domestic workers' associations, lobbied for and achieved a significant reform of the social security and labour law regimes applicable to domestic work. On the other hand, the very restrictive legal and institutional contexts in Cyprus and the UK have either hindered dynamic processes of change altogether or have forced actors advocating for domestic workers right to focus their efforts on fighting migration law fights at the expense of developing strategies that centre on labour issues.

By comparatively discussing the four case studies, this chapter informs the debate on whether changing the institutional setting of domestic work can contribute to reducing migrant domestic workers' vulnerability to exploitation.[1] The discussion in this chapter also provides insights on the role of different actors involved in challenging vulnerability and, by doing so, it informs the debate on whether change is more likely if pursued via a trade union or other civil society organisation. By presenting different actors' use of framing devices in challenging migrant domestic workers' vulnerability, the discussion here informs the debate on the role of ILO C.189 beyond ratification, as a mobilisation and law reform tool.

---

[1] FX Devetter and S Rousseau, 'The Impact of Industrialisation on Paid Domestic Work: The Case of France' (2009) 15(3) *European Journal of Industrial Relations* 297–316.

The chapter is organised as follows. In section 2, after discussing the obstacles facing migrant domestic workers in their collective organisation, I briefly present the debate on whether they can best pursue their interests in a trade union or other civil society organisation. Section 3 presents the case studies of Sweden, Spain, Cyprus and the UK. I am interested in how the legal and institutional framework of each national case shape debates on domestic workers' vulnerability and impact on different actors' roles and framing devices. Section 4 concludes by drawing broader lessons on mobilising the law to challenge vulnerability.

Organising Migrant Domestic Workers

Collective organisation is one of the main ways through which workers seek to improve their working conditions and enforce their rights; it is therefore key in challenging their vulnerability to exploitation. For domestic workers, especially migrants, organising collectively is, however, a particularly challenging endeavour. Migrant domestic workers are confronted with the barriers normally affecting temporary migrant and other non-standard workers, as well as with additional barriers specific to working within a private household.

There is a large body of scholarship discussing common difficulties to collectively organise and represent 'non-standard' workers, including migrants.[2] The notion of a non-standard, or atypical, worker is frequently used in juxtaposition to the category of standard or typical worker. Generally speaking, a standard worker is someone with a legal status entitling him or her to the full range of employment rights, who is directly hired by an employer and works full-time under an open-ended contract. In contrast, a non-standard worker might be legally excluded from all or certain rights and protections at work, works part-time under temporary contracts and may be hired via an agency. Migrant domestic workers often share characteristics of non-standard work, such as working on a fixed-term contract or via an agency. Certain working arrangements can also cast doubts on their employment status. When a domestic worker works for one employer, it is difficult to argue that there is no employment relationship because the employer normally exercises a high degree of control. If, however, she works for several employers – think of a live-out cleaner or carer – there is a higher risk of being legally characterised as self-employed and thus falling outside the scope of labour rights and protections, including the right to be represented by a trade union. Non-standard workers face barriers that are both legal and practical in nature. The legal characterisation of the relationship as one of employment is often a prerequisite of accessing collective labour rights.

---

[2] See, for example, R Gumbrell-McCormick, 'European Trade Unions and "Atypical" Workers' (2011) 42(3) *Industrial Relations Journal* 293–310; L Vosko, 'Tenuously Unionised: Temporary Migrant

Practical barriers stem from non-standard workers' limited income and time to invest in trade union activities, as well as the fear that these might jeopardise current and future employment opportunities.[3]

Migrant workers, especially those from outside the EU, face additional barriers to collectively organise and have their interests represented through a trade union. The temporariness of their stay and the associated deportability risk can dissuade migrant workers from joining a trade union and engaging in workplace activities. Additionally, ethnic and linguistic diversity can make building solidarity on the basis of worker identity more difficult, as migrants might feel more affinity to members of their own ethnic group rather than their colleagues. For established trade unions, organising migrants and other non-standard workers requires significant effort and resources, as well as overcoming conflicts of interests – both real and perceived – with the representation of standard and national workers. Traditionally, established trade unions have therefore been reluctant or even unable to organise and represent migrant and other non-standard workers.

In addition to the barriers relevant to non-standard and migrant workers, working in and for a private household brings more challenges. The very framing of domestic work as a 'labour of love', as work that women are expected to perform out of duty and without pay, distorts its employment character and can further act as a barrier for the creation of worker consciousness which is necessary for collective organisation. Domestic workers often work in isolation, without contact with colleagues and dispersed in different households; this makes contact with a trade union difficult.

Due to all these barriers, migrant domestic workers have often been assumed to be 'unorganisable', a group for whom 'collective mobilisation appears highly unlikely'.[4] However, there have been several successful stories of domestic workers' collective organisation and mobilisation. Historical and contemporary studies demonstrate that the barriers to domestic workers' trade union organisations have made them engage in alternative forms of organising that are not union-based, such as community associations, often based on ethnicity or nationality.[5]

Guy Mundlak and Hila Shamir usefully distinguish between three types of organisations that collectively organise migrant domestic workers: trade unions,

---

Workers and the Limits of Formal Mechanisms Designed to Promote Collective Bargaining in British Columbia' (2014) 43(4) *Industrial Law Journal* 451–84.

[3] ACL Davies, 'Half a Person' A Legal Perspective on Organising and Representing Non-standard Workers, in A Bogg A and T Novitz, *Voices at Work* (Oxford: Oxford University Press, 2014) 122–37.

[4] Z Jiang and M Korczynski (2016) 'When the 'Unorganizable' Organize: The Collective Mobilization of Migrant Domestic Workers in London' 69(3) *Human Relations* 813–38.

[5] E Boris and P Nadasen, 'Domestic Workers Organize!' (2008) 11 *The Journal of Labor and Society* 413–37; see Jiang and Korczynski (n 4) above; B Anderson, 'Mobilising Migrants, Making Citizens: Migrant Domestic Workers as Political Agents (2010) 33(1) *Ethnic and Racial Studies* 60–74; S Ally, 'Caring about Care Workers: Organizing in the Female Shadow of Globalization' (2005) 38(1–2) *Labour, Capital and Society* 184–207.

workers' rights centres and community-based associations.[6] Trade unions perform a number of functions which include representing their members' interests collectively and individually, collectively bargaining on terms and conditions of work, but also providing political representation through their engagement in developing and implementing governmental policies.[7] Workers' rights centres and community-based associations are civil society organisations which, while not membership-based, provide a range of different services for individual migrant workers, such as language classes, legal advice and practical support. Workers' rights centres are normally led by nationals and, in addition to service-provision, they also lobby and mobilise for wider law and policy changes in support of migrants' rights. Community-based associations, on the other hand, are normally run by migrants themselves and bring workers together based on religious or national affiliations; their role is to offer a space for socialisation and networking, as well as broader social support to migrant communities. As Mundlak and Shamir argue, for migrant workers, organising in a trade union has unique added value compared to having their interests represented by other types of civil society organisations. Only trade unions can give migrant workers a political voice, the possibility, in other words, of representation in political affairs and decisions. This possibility is crucial because, as they note, migrant workers, as non-citizens, are normally barred from participating in the polity of the host state and of expressing their voice in political debates and decision-making processes that concern them.[8]

However, Virginia Mantouvalou and Einat Albin defend participation in civil society organisations as an equally valuable form of active industrial citizenship and argue that it can well be the preferred option for a marginalised group such as domestic workers.[9] In their comparative study on efforts to collectively organise migrant domestic workers in Israel and the UK, Mantouvalou and Albin find that, for migrant domestic workers, especially those who lack a legal migration status, non-governmental organisations (NGOs) are easier to approach and engage with than trade unions.[10] They conclude their analysis by affirming that:

> [...] active participation in society and the workplace can take different forms for different workers and that it is not only trade unions that foster industrial citizenship: NGOs and other civil society organizations also play a very significant role in active participation on an equal basis.

---

[6] G Mundlak and H Shamir, 'Organising Migrant Care Workers in Israel: Industrial Citizenship and the Trade Union Option' (2014) 153(1) *International Labour Review* 93–116.
[7] KD Ewing, 'The Function of Trade Unions' (2005) 34(1) *Industrial Law Journal* 1–22.
[8] See Mundlak and Shamir (n 6) above.
[9] V Mantouvalou and E Albin, 'Active Industrial Citizenship of Domestic Workers: Lessons Learned from Unionising Attempts in Israel and the United Kingdom' (2016) 17(1) *Theoretical Inquiries in Law* 321.
[10] Ibid.

In a similar vein, labour sociologists Joyce Jiang and Marek Korczynski argued that community-based associations offer valuable 'communities of coping' for marginalised migrant workers.[11] Communities of coping are informal groups and networks that bring people together and allow them to share the burdens of their day-to-day life and work.[12] As such, communities of coping offer a forum for micro-mobilisation for marginalised workers. In their study of the self-help group for domestic workers in London, Justice for Domestic Workers (J4D), Jiang and Marek note that participation was important for developing both individual and collective agency.[13] Participating in group meetings and activities boosted participants' self-confidence which then allowed them to better negotiate their working conditions on an individual basis. On a collective level, participation in J4D contributed to migrant domestic workers' development of labour consciousness.[14] Joining a supportive community-based group can therefore be beneficial for individual migrant workers while, at the same time, fostering a very much needed sense of solidarity and collectivism. Yet, as Jiang and Korczynski admit: 'communities of coping may be crucial, but they may not be enough for a nascent collectivism to develop into a resistive solidarity'.[15]

I do not contest the view that participation in civil society organisations, especially those that are community based, can be an empowering and transformative experience for marginalised individuals. The case studies I discuss in this chapter, however, provide evidence that trade union engagement in challenging domestic workers' vulnerability is essential in achieving substantial and sustainable change.

Processes of Reform and Avenues to Challenge Domestic Workers' Vulnerability

Sweden: Shifting the Institutional Setting of Domestic Work through Policy Change

In Sweden, the change of institutional setting has had the effect of reducing some of domestic workers' vulnerabilities structured in the labour law regime.[16] Improving domestic workers' labour rights was not the result of any overarching policy and legislative reform with that aim in mind, but rather the side effect of a controversial tax deduction implemented in 2007. In 2007, the centre-right government of the

---

[11] See Jiang and Korczynski (n 4) above.
[12] M Korczynski, 'Communities of Coping: Collective Emotional Labour in Service Work' (2003) 10(1) *Organisation* 55–79.
[13] Jiang and Korczynski (n 4) above.
[14] Ibid.
[15] Ibid.
[16] See discussion of the labour law regime in ch 2.

136 *Challenging Vulnerability*

time introduced a tax deduction of 50% on the labour costs for a range of household and personal services – such as cleaning, babysitting, household maintenance and personal care – when these are purchased by a private individual or household. The scheme's acronym in Swedish, RUT, tellingly stands for cleaning, maintenance and laundry.[17] RUT – for which the proposal dates back to the 1990s – was very much debated in Sweden for more than a decade before its final adoption.

For its proponents, the tax deduction was a well-suited measure to serve a number of policy aims.[18] First, one of RUT's stated aims was that of tackling tax evasion by reducing undeclared work. Even in Sweden, the personal and domestic services sector is notorious for its informality.[19] Hiring a cleaner, a babysitter or a gardener for a few hours a week and paying them cash-in-hand without relevant tax and social security contributions is not uncommon. To claim the RUT tax deduction, however, an individual or household must purchase these services through a registered company which therefore reduces the incentive for cash-in-hand payments. Second, proponents framed the scheme as a measure to tackle unemployment by creating new and formal jobs in personal and household services. Not only could those who were already working informally now access formal jobs with declared income, but the tax deduction would additionally create more demand for these services and therefore more employment opportunities. Because jobs in personal and household services are generally considered low-skilled, creating more jobs in this sector was presented as a tool for labour-market integration for people who lack formal qualifications. Third, as the deduction promotes contracting the services through a company instead of directly from the worker, RUT could function as a tool to professionalise household and personal services and therefore improve their quality. Finally, and more controversially, the RUT was framed as a gender equality measure. By creating incentives to outsource unpaid domestic work, the tax deduction, proponents argued, would not only allow working women to dedicate more time to their work and career, but it would also support dual-wage households in achieving a better work/life balance.

The RUT's introduction in 2007, combined with the 2008 liberalisation of national labour immigration rules[20] and the 2004 enlargement of the EU, were

---

[17] *Rrengöring, Underhåll och Tvätt*.

[18] There is a large body of scholarship discussing the different arguments surrounding the debate on the RUT's introduction and implementation. See, for example, K Carlsson, 'Public Care Work in Private Contexts. A Historical Perspective on the Swedish Welfare State' in L Widding Isaksen (ed), *Global Care Work Gender and Migration in Nordic Societies* (Lund: Nordic Academic Press, 2010) 195–216; E Platzer, 'Care Work and Migration Politics in Sweden' in Widding Isaksen, ibid, 159–72; E Kvist and E Peterson, 'What Has Gender Equality Got to Do with It? An Analysis of Policy Debates Surrounding Domestic Services in the Welfare States of Spain and Sweden' (2010) 18(3) *Nordic Journal of Feminist and Gender Research* 185–203; L Lane and B Jordansson, 'How Gender Equal is Sweden? An Analysis of the Shift in Focus under Neoliberalism' (2020) 50(1) *Social Change* 28–43.

[19] Interviews with Kommunal officers, 20 September 2013, Stockholm.

[20] See discussion in ch 1.

catalysts for the expansion of private domestic services in Sweden. Private companies, both small and large, offering a range of personal care and domestic services proliferated. Newly arrived migrants from diverse countries of origin and migration statuses started working in these companies under a variety of contractual arrangements. As my trade union informants confirmed, for many migrant workers, especially women, working as a cleaner or care assistant through a private company is often their first job in Sweden and the only type of work available to them.[21] The rapid expansion of the private domestic services sector and the diversification of its workforce further diminished trade unions' ability to oversee the enforcement of labour standards in a sector where enforcement is anyway notoriously difficult.

Critics – who include academics, trade unions and political parties on the left – have argued that, far from promoting equality, the RUT actually contributed to deepening societal inequalities based on class, gender and citizenship status. Several feminist scholars have emphasised that subsidising the marketisation of care through the RUT does nothing but undermine the very foundations of the Swedish welfare state: its egalitarian and social democratic traditions.[22] The state's gradual withdrawal from the public provision of care has created distributive conflicts, which initiatives such as the RUT normalise and further exacerbate. At the heart of these distributive conflicts is the issue of who can afford to buy domestic services, even at a tax-subsidised rate, and who must make a living working in these services. For its critics, the tax deduction has mainly benefitted households with medium to high incomes – the majority of whom also happen to be ethnic Swedes – while those destined to work in domestic services are predominantly migrant, working class women.[23]

Most migrant and working-class women who take up employment in domestic services do so out of a lack of better alternatives. The RUT, by indirectly expanding the sector of domestic services, has indeed created employment opportunities for otherwise marginalised individuals. Yet, the working conditions in this relatively new sector are often precarious. In their evaluation of the RUT 13 years after its introduction, scholars Lane and Jordansson, report that the scheme's implementation 'produced of a growing workforce of part-time and casual contract labour at the bottom of the employment pool'.[24] All of my trade union informants also confirm the many challenges facing those in domestic services: bogus self-employment, casual contracts, involuntary part-time work, higher risks of discrimination including harassment by service recipients, unpaid wages, unfair dismissals, victimisation if they seek to enforce their rights, as well as increased health and

---

[21] Interviews with Kommunal officers, 6 September 2018, Stockholm.
[22] See, for example, A Gavanas (2012) 'Migrant Domestic Workers, Social Network Strategies And Informal Markets for Domestic Services in Sweden' Women's Studies International Forum; N Morel, 'The Political Economy of Domestic Work in France and Sweden in a European Perspective' (LIEPP Working Paper, 2012); see Lane and Jordansson, (n 18) above.
[23] Lane and Jordansson (n 18) above.
[24] Ibid at 28–43, 37.

safety risks.²⁵ This is not surprising. The RUT's focus was, after all, on creating jobs; the quality of these jobs was not considered nor was there any discussion on how to improve the working conditions in domestic services.²⁶

From a workers' rights perspective, the RUT did achieve domestic workers' inclusion in the personal scope of generally applicable labour law and brought them closer to the Swedish model of industrial relations. As households have an incentive to purchase domestic services via a registered company instead of directly from the worker, a domestic worker is now more likely to be employed by a company instead of directly by a private individual. When employed by a company, domestic workers no longer fall within the personal scope of the 1970 Domestic Work Act but are entitled to the same rights and protections available to other workers under generally applicable labour law. Essentially, the company becomes the employer and directs and pays the domestic worker for the services she provides, while the private individual becomes the client or service recipient.

The change of institutional setting has also facilitated trade union efforts to unionise domestic workers. Kommunal, the largest trade union in Sweden and which organises service workers, can now access domestic workers more easily than in direct recruitment. The rapid expansion of the domestic services sector in recent years and the prevalence of migrant workers has made it more challenging for Swedish unions to oversee the enforcement of labour standards in these new and diverse workplaces. Kommunal, however, is trying to mitigate the adverse effects of these changes. Traditionally, trade unions in Sweden seek to maintain good relationships with large employers which they use as contact points to approach and recruit new members; evidently, this is easier when the employer is a company rather than a private individual.²⁷

Yet, in addition to their standard practices, Kommunal has been developing new strategies to reach out to migrant domestic workers, inform them about their rights and obtain information from them about the conditions in their workplaces. Since domestic workers often work isolated in private households, Kommunal is being proactive in its efforts to reach out to them. Their strategies include extensive use of social media networks as contact points where domestic workers can post work-related questions and concerns and get advice directly from a union member. Occasionally, they organise informal social events for domestic workers. For example, Kommunal organised an evening out to the theatre to watch a play on the life of a cleaner; the union rented the theatre for one night, invited domestic workers and then organised a discussion where participants shared experiences about their work. Kommunal also prepares multilingual information material on labour legislation and practice and the union's role, which they disseminate regularly in the areas where migrant communities live

---

²⁵ Interview with Kommunal officers, 6 September 2018, Stockholm.
²⁶ C Calleman, 'Domestic Services in a "Land of Equality": The Case of Sweden' (2011) *Canadian Journal of Women and the Law* 121–39.
²⁷ Interviews with Kommunal officers, 20 September 2013, Stockholm.

or socialise. It also organises monthly workshops targeting both employers and workers. Kommunal representatives report that their efforts have been fruitful and their membership numbers are increasing significantly every year. For example, in 2009 Kommunal had fewer than 1,000 members in the cleaning sector; by 2018, it had almost 5,000 members.[28]

Sweden ratified ILO C.189 in 2019. Even though Swedish trade unions had the issue of ratification on their agendas since 2011 when the instrument was adopted, the general understanding has been that C.189 brings little added value to domestic workers in Sweden. The trade union representatives I interviewed in 2013 and 2018 thought that the pressing issues for the cleaning and care assistance sectors was to grow their membership and extend the coverage of collective agreements. Ratification was seen as an important goal, but not for the direct implications it would have for the domestic legal order. Rather, the value of ratification was seen as 'setting a good example' for other countries.[29]

Spain: Reforming Labour Legislation on Domestic Work

In late 2011, rather unexpectedly and just before the country had a general election, the Spanish government introduced new progressive labour legislation on domestic work. Royal Decree 1620/2011 entered into force in November 2011 and marked a significant improvement in the labour law rights and protections available to those working in private households.[30] The opportunity to improve domestic workers' treatment under labour law emerged in the process of reforming the national social security system earlier in the same year. By 2011, Spain was already in a deep economic crisis; unemployment was on the rise and social security was losing affiliations at an accelerated pace. The socialist government of the time, under Zapatero's leadership, was seeking ways to increase employment rates and social security affiliations. Paid domestic work in Spain had been increasing since the late 1990s; it was generally well known that a large share of domestic workers were working informally, ie with cash-in-hand payments, so they were not making any social security contributions.[31] The government therefore saw an opportunity to create formal employment in the domestic work sector by facilitating the inclusion of domestic workers into the social security system.[32]

---

[28] Ibid.
[29] Interviews with Kommunal officers, 20 September 2013, Stockholm; Interview with Kommunal officers, 6 September 2018, Stockholm. See also the press communication LO, the Swedish confederation of trade unions representing service workers, issued shortly after Sweden ratified C.189: Available at: www.lo.se/english/news/swedish_riksdag_adopts_ilo_convention_189_a_triumph_of_dedicated_progressive_efforts (6 April 2021).
[30] See discussion of the content of this legislation in ch 2.
[31] Z Ibañez and M León, 'Resisting Crisis at What Cost? Migrant Care Workers in Private Households' in B Anderson and I Shutes (eds) *Care and Migrant Labour: Theory, Policy and Politics* (Palgrave, 2014).
[32] Interview with officers of the trade union UGT (Madrid, 29 January 2014).

At the time, Spain had a special social security regime for domestic workers dating from the late 1960s. As this special social security regime was created before the domestic work relationship was included in the personal scope of labour legislation, it provided a significantly lower level of social security protection compared to that of other workers.[33]

Reforming social and labour legislation on domestic work was formally on the political agenda of the socialist party, PSOE, since coming into power 2004.[34] Improving domestic workers' legal rights and protections was framed as a necessary step towards greater gender equality given that those who work in paid domestic work are mostly women. Moving the project forward, however, required the initiative of certain individuals in key positions in the government of the time, such as the Secretary of Employment, who seized the opportunity and started working in close cooperation with the two most representative trade unions, *Unión General de Trabajadores* (UGT) and *Comisiones Obreras* (CC.OO). The result of these concerted efforts was new social security legislation for domestic work which entered into force in August 2011.[35] The new legislation integrated the special regime for domestic workers into the general social security regime, albeit under a separate system which maintained some specificities for this group of workers.

The integration of domestic workers into the general social security regime was an important reform which granted domestic workers all protections and benefits available to other workers with the exception of unemployment benefits. Traditionally, the exclusion of domestic workers from unemployment benefits has been justified on the special characteristics of domestic work that make labour inspection challenging and supposedly increase the risk of fraudulent affiliations. While this argument could be made for the majority of workers in small establishments, it has only been invoked to exclude domestic workers. Spanish labour law scholars argue that it is more plausible to consider that the motives behind domestic workers' exclusion are financial, to avoid, in other words, a burden on the state from having to pay unemployment benefits to a large workforce.[36] Accessing unemployment benefits is one of the key claims put forward by trade unions and domestic workers' associations in Spain.

As the project of improving domestic workers' social security rights was progressing, UGT started negotiating with the government for a parallel reform of the labour law regime. Due to its traditionally close ties with the Socialist Party, UGT was well-placed to negotiate directly with the government. With

---

[33] See, J López and D GandíaToscani Giménez, *El nuevo régimen laboral y de seguridad social de los trabajadores al servicio del hogar familiar* (Albacete: Editorial Bomarzo, 2012).

[34] M León, 'A Real Job? Regulating Household Work: The Case of Spain' (2013) 20(2) *European Journal of Women's Studies* 170–88.

[35] Law 27/2011, of 1 August, on the update, adequacy and modernization of the social security system.

[36] E Desdentado Daroca, Las reformas de la regulación del trabajo doméstico por cuenta ajena en España (2016) 7(1) *Revista de Investigaciones Feministas* 129–48.

significantly improved social protection, domestic workers' rights and protections under a regime created almost three decades earlier[37] seemed outdated and inadequate.[38] The adoption of ILO Convention 189 earlier in the summer of the same year created further impetus for the reforms at the national level.[39] The fact that the ILO initiated standard setting in the largely neglected area of domestic workers' rights legitimised the national reform project. UGT therefore convinced the government of the need to update the legislation regulating domestic workers' working conditions.

Initially, the other large trade union, CC.OO, was not completely in tune with UGT's approach. CC.OO was in favour of a different arrangement to improve working conditions for domestic workers. CC.OO advocated that the institutional setting for domestic work should move away from direct recruitment by private households and be re-organised by incentivising employment through agencies, companies or cooperatives. In CC.OO's view, moving away from direct recruitment, would not only improve legal rights, but it would also create more favourable conditions for domestic workers' collective organisation.[40] UGT, however, has been traditionally against restricting direct recruitment by private employers in any way. Officially, UGT is not favour of incentivising agency work which it sees as problematic for the regularisation of migrants as self-employed workers.[41] The divergent views of the two trade unions on the institutional setting of domestic work could well indicate a power struggle between them because, if domestic work is reorganised through private agencies or cooperatives, CC.OO which traditionally organises service sector workers, would have more control over the newly-formed collective of workers.

Despite the disagreement between the two trade unions, the labour law reform was important not only for the outcome it produced – an improved labour law regime – but also because the process of reform offered a key opportunity for domestic workers' mobilisation. In Spain, apart from trade unions, there are a number of associations advocating for domestic workers' rights. Some of these are run by migrant domestic workers themselves, while others are civil society organisations with broader agendas that include domestic workers' issues in their sphere of work. The majority of these associations function as workers' rights centres, providing legal advice and practical support to domestic workers as well as engaging in mobilisation and lobbying for wider changes in the sector. The 2011 law reform process created a crucial opportunity for domestic workers' associations to actively participate in the debate by articulating concrete proposals on the draft legislation.[42]

---

[37] Royal Decree 1424/1985.
[38] Interview with UGT officers (Madrid, 29 January 2014).
[39] See León (n 34) above, 170–88; Desdentado Daroca (n 36) above.
[40] Interview with CC.OO officers (Madrid, 5 February 2014).
[41] Interview with UGT officers (Madrid, 29 January 2014).
[42] A number of organisations across Spain formed the National Platform of Domestic Workers' Associations which provided detailed comments on the proposal for the new labour legislation Aportaciones de la plataforma estatal de asociaciones de trabajadoras de hogar al borrador de proyecto de Real Decreto por el que se regula la relación laboral de carácter especial de servicio del hogar familiar (21 July 2011).

Importantly, equipped with newly gained visibility, domestic workers' associations in Spain have, for over a decade now, sustained an active public debate concerning their rights at work, as evidenced by numerous mobilisations and protests they have organised over the years.[43] Trade unions and domestic workers' associations have repeatedly mobilised demanding that different Spanish governments ratify C.189. For domestic workers' associations especially, ratification is seen as a way to endorse and consolidate their rights at the national level.[44]

The official registration of the first trade union for domestic and care workers in early 2021 further illustrates the dynamism that exists in the area of domestic workers' rights in Spain.[45] While the union is open to migrant domestic workers and advocates changes to migration law, its key claims centre on labour issues such as the ratification of ILO C.189, the full integration of domestic work in the general social security regime and the application of health and safety legislation.

Cyprus: Constrained by Migration Status

In Cyprus, there have been no dynamic processes of legislative or policy change to improve domestic workers' rights; the migration and labour regimes that govern their conditions of entry, stay and work have remained almost completely unchanged since their adoption in the early 1990s. Even though the majority of non-EU migrants in Cyprus work as domestic workers, public debate about their conditions of life and work is exceptional and is limited to moments of crisis. By moments of crisis, I refer to specific incidents of extreme abuse that are widely reported in the local media. One such moment of crisis took place in the spring of 2019, when it was revealed that a local man had brutally murdered five migrant women and two of their children. Following public outrage denouncing systemic failures in the way migrant women are treated in Cyprus, the right-wing government in power hastily changed some provisions in the model contracts of employment for migrant domestic workers.[46]

Limiting the debate in such moments of crisis, however, often means that extreme abuse predominates any discussion. While it is true that the legal and institutional context in Cyprus makes migrant domestic workers vulnerable to extreme forms of abuse and exploitation, focusing the anyway limited public discussion on these issues does not allow for a more comprehensive consideration of their problems at work and of the kind of reforms needed to address vulnerability to day-to-day exploitation. As I discuss in this section, in Cyprus, the lack of

---

[43] See, for example, 'Empleadas del hogar se concentran en Madrid para visibilizar la precariedad del sector y exigir sus derechos laborales' (*El Diario*, 31 March 2019); 'Las empleadas del hogar se organizan a nivel nacional para reclamar sus derechos' (*Público*, 28 February 2019); 'Las empleadas del hogar se movilizan para exigir más derechos laborales' (*El País*, 27 June 2018).

[44] Interview with SEDOAC representatives, 22 March 2014, Madrid.

[45] The name of the union is SINTRAHOCU which stands for Sindicatio de Trabajadoras del Hogar y los Cuidados (domestic and care workers' union).

[46] See ch 2.

collective organisation in trade unions and associations focusing on labour rights hinders migrant domestic workers' development of a collective voice that would allow their participation and representation in debates on their conditions of life and work.

The social location and social context of migrant domestic labour in Cyprus severely restrict their chances of collectively organising and mobilising as workers. Social scientists use the notion of social location to denote the combination of characteristics such as gender, race, social class, citizenship, and migration law status. Social context, on the other hand, is the specific context where social interactions take place, such as the type of work or industry and geography. For feminist social scientist Leah Vosko, considering both social location and social context highlights the broader social processes that shape certain types of precarious labour.[47] In Cyprus, domestic workers are women migrants, much poorer than the local population, who work on temporary visas that tie them to their employers and legally restrict their chances of working in a different type of job. They work isolated in private households – mostly in cities but sometimes in remote and sparsely populated rural areas – under poor working conditions, without collective representation or at least a collective voice. The interaction of all these factors locates migrant domestic workers at the lowest segments of the Cypriot labour market and society more broadly. Most importantly, the interaction of these factors makes it very difficult for migrant domestic workers to resist and mitigate their vulnerability to exploitation.[48]

The state shapes and reinforces this positioning in numerous ways. The structural dependence on the employer, the risk of deportation emphasised repeatedly in the regulatory regimes that govern their stay and work in the country, complaints procedures that are replete with bias favouring the employer have all contributed to erecting both real and perceived barriers to collective organisation.[49] An illustrative example of the role of the state is the clause restricting the right to freedom of association, which migration authorities included in the model contract of employment for non-EU domestic workers.[50] This was clearly unlawful being contrary to a freedom enshrined in the national constitution as well as in international and European human rights instruments. Yet, it remained in place for several decades and had obvious chilling effects, preventing migrant domestic workers from attempting to organise as a collective and challenge the vectors of their vulnerability. While this problematic clause was

---

[47] L Vosko, *Precarious Employment: Understanding Labor Market Insecurity* (McGill-Queen's University Press, 2006). See also, J Fudge, 'The Precarious Migrant Status and Precarious Employment: The Paradox of International Rights for Migrant Workers' (2012) 34(1) *Comparative Labor Law and Policy Journal*, 95–132.

[48] I do not mean that migrant domestic workers are powerless or that no acts of individual resistance take place. I would like to highlight the many practical and legal barriers in developing and sustaining collective action with the potential to transform vulnerability.

[49] For a detailed discussion of these issues, see ch 2.

[50] Ibid.

removed in 2019, its legacy remains, not least because state authorities took no steps to rectify in practice – as opposed to just formally – the long-term effects of restricting freedom of association.

In addition to the constraints shaped and sustained by the state, even the actors normally engaged in defending workers' interests, ie trade unions, have been absent from any attempts to improve migrant domestic workers' rights. Local trade unions have traditionally been reluctant to organise and support migrant workers in general.[51] In relation to migrant domestic workers, reluctance turns into indifference towards an overwhelmingly female collective who are located in the most atypical of workplaces, the private household. Organising domestic workers would have required trade unions to devise innovative and proactive strategies to approach them. Yet, the practical difficulties are not the only reason for trade unions' indifference. The artificially low salaries the state stipulates makes employing a migrant domestic worker affordable for a large share of the local population. Many employers are often workers themselves who rely on the affordability of migrant domestic labour to meet their care needs and facilitate their own access to paid work. Thus, for local trade unions, making claims on behalf migrant domestic workers would seemingly create a conflict of interest between representing national workers – who are also employers – and domestic workers. It is telling that trade unions in Cyprus have not even used the adoption of ILO C.189 as an opportunity to place the issue of domestic workers on their agenda.

As a result, migrant domestic workers in Cyprus have only been able to form and participate in nationality-based associations.[52] Nationality-based associations provide a supportive network for migrants and their communities and occasionally organise public events of solidarity. Participation in these associations can, of course, be a source of empowerment for individual domestic workers who gain moral support and even a better understanding of their labour rights. A recent survey study conducted in collaboration with the Office of the Ombudsman showed that those migrant domestic workers who have contacts with a community-based association are more likely to have a better understanding of their legal rights.[53] However, migrant associations have no leverage in public and political debates, even those that directly concern migrant domestic workers. The following example is illustrative. In 2013 the Ministerial Committee, which sets rules on the employment of migrant workers, reduced migrant domestic workers' minimum wage by 5% and eliminated their entitlement to an annual raise.[54]

---

[51] N Trimikliniotis, 'Racism and New Migration to Cyprus: The Racialisation of Migrant Workers' in F Anthias and G Lazarides (eds) *Into the Margins: Exclusion and Migration in Southern Europe* (Aldershot: Ashgate, 1999); PICUM, 'Migrants and the right to equal treatment in Cyprus' (Workshop Report, 2013).

[52] The most notable associations in terms of size are those of Filipino nationals, such as the group Obreras Empowered. See N Hadjigeorgiou, Commissioner for the Administration and the Protection of Human Rights, 'Report on the Status of Foreign Domestic Workers in Cyprus' (Nicosia, 18 December 2020). Filipinos have traditionally been one of the largest groups of domestic workers in Cyprus.

[53] See Hadjigeorgiou, ibid.

[54] Ministerial Committee on the Employment of TCNs in Cyprus (Nicosia, 11 June 2013).

In 2014, following an amendment of social security legislation, domestic workers' net minimum wage was further reduced. Overall, from 2012 to 2014 migrant domestic workers' monthly net salary was reduced from €326 to €309. Even though the reductions were framed as an inevitable response to the global 2008 financial crisis that reduced households' purchasing capacities, migrant domestic workers' state-mandated salaries have been stagnant for over a decade now, despite the prevalent discourse being that the country has now overcome the 2008 crisis. No migrant domestic workers' association was in a position to publicly challenge the reduction of their already extremely low wages. Similarly, there were no signs of any consultation with domestic workers' associations when the government decided to amend their contract of employment in 2019. This demonstrates their lack of representation even when the most important decisions about them are being made.

A number of non-governmental organisations (NGOs) with a human rights and equality agenda gather data, publish reports and organise events with the purpose of stirring a debate on the situation of migrant domestic workers in Cyprus. As these organisations depend on external funding that they receive on a project basis, the specific angle of their projects is, understandably, shaped by their funders' agenda. A number of NGO projects on migrant domestic workers have therefore focused on forms of extreme abuse, such as trafficking.[55] Beyond documenting abuse and formulating law and policy reform recommendations – which are ignored by state authorities with decision-making powers – local NGOs have not been able to develop more dynamic interventions aimed at transforming domestic workers' labour conditions.

An institution that has generally been receptive to migrant domestic workers' claims is the Ombudsman. The Ombudsman's competences include the examination of individual complaints against public authorities and the preparation of *ex officio* reports on human rights issues. In the area of non-discrimination at work, the Ombudsman can examine complaints against both public and private employers. Over the years, the Ombudsman has issued a number of reports on migrant domestic workers' conditions of life and work in Cyprus.[56]

---

[55] For example, in 2014, the Embassy of the USA in Cyprus (Bi-communal programme) funded a study titled 'Mapping out the Situation of Labour Trafficking in Cyprus' which was conducted by two local NGOs: Equality, Support, Antiracism and the Turkish Cypriot Human Rights Foundation. Between 2013 and 2015, the European Commission (Prevention of and Fight against Crime Programme) funded a multi-country study titled 'Combatting Trafficking in Women for Labour Exploitation in Domestic Work'. The report on Cyprus was prepared by a local NGO, the Mediterranean Institute of Gender Studies.

[56] 'Report of the Ombudsman as National Independent Human Rights Authority as regards the Status of Domestic Workers in Cyprus' (Nicosia, 2 July 2013); 'Report of the Ombudsman as Equality Body in relation to a Complaint on Restrictions of the Freedom of Association of Migrant Domestic Workers, Complaint No 2/2005' (Nicosia, 2005); ' Report on the Procedure of Labour Dispute Settlement between Migrant Workers and their Employers' (Nicosia, 12 March 2010); 'Report of the Ombudsman as National Independent Human Rights Authority in relation to the Arrest and Deportation of a Domestic Worker due to Health Conditions, Complaint No 1649/2012' (Nicosia, 7 January 2014); 'Report of the Ombudsman as Equality in Relation to the Protection of the Wages of Domestic Workers Employed by Recipients of Public Allowance, Complaint No 951/2013' (Nicosia, 31 July 2014).

While some reports were issued following individual complaints filed by domestic workers and local NGOs, other reports were prepared on the Ombudsman's initiative to identify problematic aspects of the legal and policy framework on migrant domestic labour in the country. In the process of preparing its reports, the Ombudsman has the competence to request that relevant public authorities collaborate and provide information. This process has been very important in terms of revealing state failures towards migrant domestic workers and in allowing the Ombudsman to make specific recommendations for legislative and policy reforms explicitly directed at the state.

Even though the Ombudsman lacks expertise on labour issues, its broad mandate to protect human rights and to combat discrimination in several areas, including work, means that the institution is potentially well placed to achieve transformative change for a vulnerable group who are experiencing structural barriers in accessing justice and enforcing their rights at work. How effective have the Ombudsman's interventions been? Not very if one considers that state authorities blatantly disregard its adverse findings and do not act upon its recommendations. There have been, for instance, no corrective responses to the Ombudsman's calls to end wage discrimination against migrant domestic workers.[57] In 2014 the Ombudsman urged immigration authorities to develop specific guidelines to handle situations where migrants are diagnosed with a contagious disease instead of deporting them without any consideration for their humanity. At the time of writing (2021) such guidelines are yet to be adopted. Similarly, even though the Ombudsman had asked state authorities to remove the clause prohibiting any engagement in political activities from migrant domestic workers' model employment contracts in 2005, it took 14 years for this to actually happen and for reasons unrelated to the institution's intervention. Against this background, inevitably one wonders how many reports documenting the same institutional failures will be produced before we can expect some form of change. If anything, the Ombudsman's engagement with the issue of migrant domestic workers over the years illustrates the institution's inability to instigate transformative change in this area.

UK: Efforts to Organise in a Restrictive Legal Context

Similar to the situation in Cyprus, the very restrictive institutional and legal framework governing migrant domestic labour in the UK highly restricts their chances of collectively organising to challenge the vectors of their vulnerability. Non-EU domestic workers have always been in a vulnerable position. To lawfully enter the UK, they traditionally depended on a pre-existing work relationship with a named employer. Once in the country, they worked as live-in domestic workers for long and largely unregulated hours and were paid very low wages. Surely, the features of

---

[57] Office of the Ombudsman, 'Report of the Ombudsman as National Independent Human Rights Authority as regards the status of domestic workers in Cyprus' (Nicosia: 2 July 2013).

their work – the structural dependence on one employer, long working days and isolation in a private household – are not conducive to workers' collective organisation. Despite these restrictions, migrant domestic workers' efforts to organise and resist vulnerability collectively have a long history in the UK.[58]

Following the changes of their visa conditions in 2012, however, migrant domestic workers face even more barriers to collective organisation. For almost a decade now, they have only been allowed to enter the UK on very short-term and non-renewable visas that do not allow them to change employers. The impact of this enlarged dependence on the employer and the temporariness of their stay not only exacerbates the risk of being deported, but also to make collective organisation highly unlikely. What are the chances that an overworked migrant domestic worker, who often knows no one else in the UK other than her employer and whose lawful stay is limited to six months, will be willing or even able to join a trade union? Probably close to none. Therefore, while migrant domestic workers are technically allowed to collectively organise as workers, in reality, when the legal and institutional framework is so restrictive, their prospects of doing so are very limited.

Importantly, the 2012 visa changes have not only increased the practical barriers to collective organisation but they have also shaped the direction of the debate on migrant domestic labour in the UK. As the visa conditions have so dramatically increased vulnerability to exploitation, civil society organisations advocating for migrant domestic workers' rights have had to direct their scarce resources to lobbying and mobilising to restore the previous visa regime that granted a more stable migration status and the right to change employers. Since the new visa conditions came into force, the use of the so-called 'fight against modern slavery' slogan became very prominent in the UK debate on migrant domestic workers' rights. In a context where anti-immigration sentiments and discourses are dominant – as vividly reflected in the debates surrounding Brexit – depicting migrant domestic workers as modern slaves and invoking anti-slavery arguments are often the only plausible avenues to gain sympathy and convince people of the need to have legal protections in place. As a result, during the last decade or so, mobilisation for migrant domestic workers' rights in the UK has centered on migration status issues as drivers of extreme abuse at the expense of more transformative framings and claims that centre on labour rights. The double criminalisation introduced by the 2016 Immigration Act, ie criminalising not just employing someone without legal migration status but also taking up work against immigration rules, has strengthened the focus on immigration issues.[59]

---

[58] For an overview of past efforts see Mantouvalou and Albin (n 9) above, 321–50; B Anderson, 'Different Roots in Common Ground: Transnationalism and Migrant Domestic Workers in London' (2001) 27(4) *Journal of Ethnic and Migration Studies* 673–83.

[59] See, for example, a policy report prepared on behalf of a community association for domestic workers, the Voice of Domestic Workers, Z Jiang, 'A Special Vulnerability: Migrant Domestic Workers Enslaved by the Non-renewable Six-month Overseas Domestic Worker Visa in the UK' (London, 2019). See, also, a range of campaigns developed by the charity organisation Kalayaan on domestic workers' rights. Available at: www.kalayaan.org.uk/news/campaigns/ (13 April 2021).

When it comes to the actors involved in the fight against vulnerability to exploitation at work, it should first be noted that established trade unions have largely been absent from efforts to collectively organise migrant domestic workers. The organisations involved in the collective representation of migrant domestic workers in the UK are primarily workers' rights centres and community-based associations. There are a number of UK associations that are led by migrant domestic workers. The most well-known is Kalayaan, a London-based charity which was established in 1987 to support migrant domestic workers lobbying for legal migration status.[60] Today, Kalayaan offers a range of services to migrant domestic workers: legal advice, training and practical support, as well as opportunities to meet and socialise. Kalayaan is best described as a workers' rights centre, rather than a community organisation, because it provides support to domestic workers regardless of their national or other affiliations and, more importantly, because it is active in lobbying for broader law and policy changes. Other similar organisations include Justice for Domestic Workers (J4DW), a self-help group for domestic workers established in 2009 which was affiliated for some time to the hotel and restaurant branch of the trade union Unite and Kalayaan.[61] Ratification of the ILO Convention 189 was a key claim put forward by domestic workers' groups in the UK, especially the first years following its adoption. However, as the UK was one of the only eight ILO Member States to vote against the Convention's adoption in 2011, ratification has always been unlikely. As a result, domestic workers' organisations have now focused most of their efforts on restoring the previous visa regime by invoking anti-slavery arguments.

Conclusion

What broader lessons can we draw from these four case studies about different avenues to challenge migrant domestic workers' vulnerability to exploitation? Examining Sweden, Spain, Cyprus and the UK through a comparative lens yields interesting insights on at least three interconnected issues: the potential impact of changing the institutional setting of domestic work, the role of different actors in advocating for domestic workers' rights and the likelihood of ILO C.189 to be transformative.

In relation to the change of institutional setting, the Swedish case demonstrates that there can be improvements to domestic workers' rights and protections when they are employed by a company instead of directly by an individual employer. Where there are special regimes applicable exclusively to domestic workers whose employer is a natural person – as the 1970 Domestic Work Act in Sweden – these

---

[60] See Anderson (n 5) above.
[61] Jiang and Korczynski (n 4) above.

will give way to generally applicable legislation. When special regimes on domestic work provide substandard rights and protections – such as in Sweden, Cyprus and the UK –[62] shifting the institutional setting to promote the industrialisation of domestic work will therefore result in improvements to the substance of rights and protections. Of course, that is only on paper. The problem of how to then effectively exercise and enforce them, while somewhat lessened in a regulatory setting where the employer is not a natural person, is still existent and pressing when the provision of domestic work is mediated through a third party. However, I believe that it is precisely in the area of enforcement where changing institutional setting carries the most transformative potential. As the case of Sweden shows, changing the institutional setting opens up vital space for trade unions to organise and represent domestic workers' interests collectively, including through the conclusion of collective agreements. Trade unions play – or should play – a crucial role in strengthening workers' rights and protections and ensuring their effective enforcement. For this potential to be realised, however, trade unions must be willing to adapt their strategies to a workforce that is heterogeneous and atypical when compared to their traditional members.

I do not mean to paint a rosy picture of industrialisation as the cure for all evils, nor am I denying the many problems that privatising domestic work entails. The regulatory context and starting point in each national context are crucial. In Sweden, the growth of private companies providing domestic and care services signals a drifting away from a welfare system committed to the provision of high quality and publicly funded care services on the principle of equality. Against this background, the implementation of the RUT was rightly seen and criticised as a retreat of the welfare state which is driving the racialisation of care services and the deterioration of working conditions. However, in national contexts where there are already large numbers of domestic workers with highly individualised, status-like relationships with a single employer, initiatives encouraging a shift to employment by a third party can help challenge domestic workers' vulnerability to exploitation. Incentivising employment by a third party does not have to be in a way that undermines workers' rights by making their conditions of work more precarious.

While there can be a range of actors involved in representing migrant domestic workers' interests, by comparing the four case studies, we can draw broader lessons on their potential to effectively challenge vulnerability to exploitation. In Sweden, it is clear that the main actors involved are trade unions. Their strategies against vulnerability at the workplace are focused on unionising migrant domestic workers and concluding collective agreements to enforce their rights. In doing so, Kommunal acknowledges migrant domestic workers' unique obstacles to unionise and devises innovative strategies to approach workers that depart from the strategies they would typically use for an ethnically homogeneous workforce with

---

[62] See ch 2.

standard working arrangements. While trade unions do voice their critique of migration rules, their focus is clearly centred on a labour law paradigm. In Spain, established trade unions have not placed that much focus on collective organisation and representation of domestic workers. Nonetheless, they took advantage of a favourable political momentum and, using their contacts with the party in power at the time, lobbied for and achieved legislative change. While not giving a direct voice to domestic workers, trade unions collaborated with associations led by domestic workers, including migrants, and incorporated their claims in the proposal for reform. The role of other civil society associations, while important, is supplementary to the role played by trade unions.

Conversely, in Cyprus and the UK the lack of meaningful trade union engagement with the issue of migrant domestic labour has left restrictive legal and institutional frameworks largely unchallenged. In both countries different community associations and other NGOs have tried to fill in the gap in the representation of domestic workers' interests. While these organisations can play an important role in terms of providing a range of services and a safe space, they lack the political leverage needed to achieve transformative and sustainable change. In their efforts to gain public support for migrant domestic workers in restrictive migration landscapes, NGOs understandably turn to 'modern' slavery and trafficking as framing devices. However, these framings are unable to provide holistic responses to vulnerability because they centre on migrant domestic workers as migrants instead of as workers.

ILO C.189 on decent work for domestic workers offers a normative language to challenge restrictive national regimes. Local actors advocating for domestic workers' rights can use the Convention as a framing device and the claim of ratification as an opportunity to place domestic work on the political agenda. While the potential is there, the case studies discussed here show that, with the exception of Spain, C.189 has had little impact on national debates, while local actors have made limited use of its provisions. In Spain, despite the lack of ratification, local actors have drawn inspiration on C.189 to shape their proposal for legislative reform. As the concern with domestic workers' rights was on the political agenda before 2011, the adoption of C.189 gave further impulse to the national debate and has had a transformative effect outside the ratification route. In Sweden, on the other hand, ratification has had little added value because of pre-existing national and EU laws in place that provided for a similar level of protection – national actors have also not placed much significance on the Convention for national debates. In the UK, clear opposition to C.189 has left little space for local actors to draw on its provisions. Similarly, in Cyprus local actors' lack of interest meant that the Convention has had little, if any, impact on national debates. It is in the UK and Cyprus where ratifying C.189 would imply most changes to the national law and practice. Ironically, this is, I believe the reason why it is not on the agenda.

Conclusion

This book set out to examine the role of law in the construction of migrant domestic workers' vulnerability. I wished to find ways of framing and examining vulnerability that avoided an almost exclusive focus on the most severe forms of abuse and exploitation, such as 'modern' slavery and human trafficking. My approach on migrant domestic labour wished, instead, to shed light on the more widespread – almost mundane and normalised – vulnerabilities created by the normal day-to-day operations and framings at the intersection of migration and labour law regimes. To illustrate, for instance, how regimes regulating working time frame domestic workers' rights and protections. Or, how law contributes to domestic workers' notoriously low wages. Finally, to map how migration law, through the different migration statuses it creates, shapes migrant domestic workers' chances of accessing and enforcing any rights available to them.

To explore these issues, I turned to national European and EU legal regimes which I analysed through a comparative lens. Europe provided a useful regional case study not only because of the large volume of migrant domestic workers it attracts to manage its social reproduction crisis, but also because of the interplay between EU law and national legal regimes. By focusing on Europe, my analysis also wished to demonstrate how different regimes create vulnerabilities of different kinds and degrees when compared, for example, by state or by the different categories of migrant domestic worker. Hence, migrant domestic workers are differently legally vulnerable under rules that differentiate based on state of origin – such as the many different statuses created by EU migration law – and the rules in force in their state of destination at any given time.

In Chapter 1, I gave an overview of how several European national migration regimes regulate the admission and stay conditions of migrant domestic workers from outside the EU. By paying attention to both conditions of entry but also of lawful stay, I identified at least four different migration regime types: *Regulated Entry/Liberal Treatment*, *Open Entry/Restrictive Treatment*, *Employer-Led/Mixed Treatment* and *Restrictive*. The typology makes evident that, while all migration regimes contain elements that reinforce vulnerability, not all migration regimes are equally problematic. In those regimes where regulated entry is coupled with a relatively good set of rights post-entry – crucially the right to change employers and paths to permanent residence – migrant domestic workers are less legally vulnerable and have more opportunities to resist workplace exploitation. Open-entry and employer-led regimes, however, impose important restrictions on migrant domestic workers' right to stay – in such regimes, migrant domestic workers are likely to be almost as legally vulnerable as in restrictive regimes that grant no entry rights. While national contexts and debates of course matter, by juxtaposing the different migration regime choices European states make on migrant domestic workers we can create opportunities to challenge the necessity of restrictive regimes.

Chapter 2 turned to labour law regimes in four countries representing the four-fold typology developed in Chapter 1: the UK, Cyprus, Sweden and Spain. Apart from their different migration regimes, the four case studies yielded interesting insights on whether domestic work is a *sui generis* form of work and should thus be subject to its own labour law regime – the 'work like no other' approach – or whether it is similar to other forms of work and, as such, should be enfolded within existing labour rights and regulation – the 'work like any other' approach. Comparing four different national regimes demonstrated instead that the model has little impact on the construction of vulnerability. What does matter, though, is the substance of rights and protections each regime provides, as well as the enforcement mechanisms in place. The comparative analysis in this chapter illustrated similarities in how the migration/labour nexus constructs migrant domestic workers' vulnerability, but also important differences. While we can find elements of 'exceptionalism' on domestic work in all four labour law systems examined, in Spain, the legal instrument applying exclusively to domestic workers was adapted to deliver near-normal protection. Accessing justice and enforcing rights for domestic workers in Spain, while not necessarily straightforward, is at least not further hampered by migration status as in the other case studies.

Turning to the place of domestic work in EU migration law, Chapter 3 reveals, first of all, a highly fragmented landscape which creates a hierarchy of statuses. Within this framework, migrant domestic workers fall under different legal statuses depending on their state of origin. This is true not only for non-EU but also for EU citizens when caught under the EU transitional arrangements regime. The analysis of EU labour immigration directives tells us a story about the EU's lack of interest in regulating the entry and stay conditions of domestic workers despite the fact that this is a large and very relevant group of workers for the societies and economies of many EU Member States.

In 2014, social scientists Anna Triandafyllidou and Sabrina Marchetti proposed that the EU enacted a sectoral labour migration directive on domestic workers as a way to both meet the growing care demands of European societies and to create safe entry routes for migrants.[1] However, while it is important to create safe entry routes into the EU for non-EU domestic workers, pursuing a specific EU labour migration directive in this area is unlikely to reduce vulnerability to exploitation at work. As my analysis in Chapter 3 showed, when EU migration law rules allow the admission of migrant workers who are considered low-skilled, they are likely

---

[1] A Triandafyllidou and S Marchetti, 'Europe 2020: Addressing Low Skill Labour Migration at times of Fragile Recovery' Policy Paper 2014/05 (Robert Schuman Centre for Advanced Studies, Global Governance Programme, 2014).

to couple admission with substandard rights and protections while not effectively challenging the fact that Member States will potentially enact restrictive migration rules. An EU labour immigration directive on domestic work is, therefore, more likely to look like the Directive on Seasonal Workers. I believe that we need strategies that, while attentive to the specificities of migrants' vulnerability to exploitation, do not centre exclusively on migrants, but take an approach rooted in labour law and its institutions. It is important to think, in other words, about how to improve the conditions of all those working in and for private households, migrants and nationals alike.

In Chapter 4, I turned to EU labour law. Can EU labour law remedy aspects of the fragmentation we find in national regimes and in EU migration law shaping migrant domestic workers' vulnerability to exploitation? To some extent, yes. After arguing that paid domestic work falls within the personal scope of a range of EU labour law sources, I provided examples of mismatches with national law. As I show, the concrete implications of this finding are quite important and potentially deeply transformative, especially in the area of working time in view of the CJEU's jurisprudence concerning on-call.[2] Importantly, EU labour law sources – with the exception of those on the free movement of workers – apply to all migrant domestic workers regardless of immigration status; thus, even an illegally resident domestic worker can still derive protections from EU law.

Affirming the applicability of EU labour law to domestic workers is, however, only the first step towards more transformative responses to vulnerability. While EU labour law is not a panacea to all vulnerabilities at work, invoking compliance is, I believe, a useful strategy to extend protections especially in those countries where domestic workers have very little or no leverage to bring about any sustainable change. EU institutions, especially the European Commission, have an important role to play in challenging mismatches in national regimes and in monitoring Member States' compliance. It is equally important for local actors advocating for domestic workers' rights to raise the issue of compatibility with EU labour law. Instead of centring campaigns solely on promoting the ratification of ILO C.189, activists could place more emphasis on compliance with EU labour law. With this I do not mean to downplay the importance of ILO C.189. Rather, what I suggest is that it is useful to draw on the complementarity of EU labour law sources and of C.189 in advocating for legal frameworks that can effectively and holistically address migrant domestic workers' vulnerability.

In Chapter 5, by drawing on national debates in Sweden, Spain, Cyprus and the UK, I evaluated different strategies and avenues to challenge domestic

---

[2] My analysis focused on showing the mismatches between EU and national working time law in Spain, Cyprus, Sweden and the UK. Other scholars, building on my argument on the inclusion of domestic work in the personal scope of EU working time law, showed concrete implications for other EU states, such as Italy, Germany and Austria. See K Scheiwe, 'Domestic Workers, EU Working Time Law and Implementation Deficits in National Law – Change in Sight?' (EUI Law Working Paper 2021/03, 2021).

154 Conclusion

workers' vulnerability. The analysis made the critical observation that while a range of actors can usefully engage in the fight against domestic workers' vulnerability, where we are more likely to see transformative changes is in contexts with decisive trade union involvement and where the focus of engagement is placed on labour law and its institutions, rather than on migration. This is not to suggest that migration issues should not form part of the debate. Rather, what I suggest is that by approaching (migrant) domestic labour as primarily an issue of labour, we are more likely to find transformative responses to vulnerability.

Focusing on labour law and its institutions implies reforming national labour regimes so that rights and protections at work are effectively extended to those working in and for private households. However, it also implies promoting the collective organisation of domestic workers in membership-based organisations, ie trade unions. Traditionally, it is considered preferable for workers' collective organisations to emerge from below and autonomously of the state, in the sense that it should be the product of workers' own desire to come together and act collectively. Yet, for vulnerable workers who have been structurally excluded from collective labour institutions, such as collective bargaining, simply removing exclusions is not enough.[3] There are responsibilities for the state to promote and facilitate domestic workers' collective organisation. The best way for each state to meet these responsibilities will depend on national contexts. Promoting, for instance the change of domestic work's institutional setting away from direct recruitment by a private household and towards professionalisation, can help unionisation. Another, underutilised strategy would be turning immigration controls around. In those states where the entry of non-EU domestic workers is regulated by different visas, these could be used as contact points not only to allow the state to monitor working conditions, but also for trade unions to approach and unionise migrants.

For any strategies against domestic workers' vulnerability to be holistic and transformative, they must form part of broader political projects for addressing our social reproduction crisis in socially sustainable ways. Migration can be part of the solution but only if we create sustainable working conditions for migrant and national domestic workers alike. State involvement in funding accessible and high-quality care services is essential to guarantee good working conditions. Otherwise, we are perpetuating social dumping on both local and global levels.

---

[3] A Blackett and C Sheppard, 'Collective Bargaining and Equality: Making Connections' (2003) 142(4) *International Labour Review* 419–57.

BIBLIOGRAPHY

Acosta AD, *The Long-Term Residence Status as a Subsidiary Form of EU Citizenship. An Analysis of Directive 2003/109* (The Hague: Martinus Nijhoff Publishers, 2011).

Addati L and Cheong Lindsay, T *'Meeting the Needs of My Family Too': Maternity Protection and Work-family Measures for Domestic Workers* (Geneva: ILO, 2013).

Adinolfi A, 'Free Movement and Access to Work of Citizens of the New Member States: The Transitional Measures' (2005) 42 *Common Market Law Review* 469–98.

Albin E and Mantouvalou V, 'The ILO Convention on Domestic Workers: From the Shadows to the Light' (2012) 41(1) *Industrial Law Journal* 67–78.

Ales E (ed) *Health and Safety at Work. European and Comparative Perspective* (Alphen an den Rijn: Kluwer Law International, 2013).

Ally S, 'Caring about Care Workers: Organizing in the Female Shadow of Globalization' (2005) 38(1–2) *Labour, Capital and Society* 184–207.

Ambrosini M, *Irregular Migration and the Invisible Welfare* (Basingstoke: Palgrave Macmillan, 2013).

Andall J, *Gender, Migration and Domestic Service: The Politics of Black Women in Italy* (Farnham: Ashgate, 2000).

Andall J (ed), *Gender and Ethnicity in Contemporary Europe* (Oxford: Berg, 2003).

Anderson A, 'Europe's Care Regimes and the Role of Migrant Care Workers Within Them' (2012) 5(2) *Journal of Population Ageing* 135–46.

Anderson B, *Doing the Dirty Work? The Global Politics of Domestic Labour* (London: Zed Books, 2000).

Anderson B, 'Different Roots in Common Ground: Transnationalism and Migrant Domestic Workers in London' (2001) 27(4) *Journal of Ethnic and Migration Studies* 673–83.

Anderson B, 'Mobilising Migratnts, Making Citizens: Migrant Domestic Workers as Political Agents' (2010) 33(1) *Journal of Ethnic and Racial Studies* 60–74.

Anderson B, 'Migration, Immigration Controls and the Fashioning of Precarious Workers' (2010) 24(2) *Work Employment and Society* 300–17.

Anderson B, 'Who Needs Them? Care Work, Migration and Public Policy' (2012) 30(1) *Cuadernos de Relaciones Laborales* 45–61.

Anderson B, 'Migrant Domestic Workers: Good Workers, Poor Slaves, New Connections' (2015) 22(4) *Social Politics* 636–52.

Anderson B and Shutes I (eds) *Migration and Care Labour: Theory, Policy and Politics* (Baskingstoke: Palgrave Macmillan, 2014).

Anderson B, Ruhs M, Rogaly B and Spencer S, 'Fair Enough? Central and East European Migrants in Low-wage Employment in the UK' (York, Joseph Rowntree Foundation, 2006).

Andersson K and Kvist E, 'The Neoliberal Turn and the Marketization of Care: The Transformation of Eldercare in Sweden' (2015) 22(3) *European Journal of Women's Studies* 274–87.

Anthias F and Lazadiris G, *'Into the Margins: Migration and Exclusion in Southern Europe'* (Farnham: Ashgate, 1999).

Anving T and Eldén S, 'Precarious Care Labor: Contradictory Work Regulations and Practices for Au Pairs in Sweden' (2016) 6(4) *Nordic Journal of Working Life Studies* 29–48.

Apap J, *The Rights of Immigrant Workers in the European Union. An Evaluation of the EU Public Policy Process and the Legal Status of Labour Immigrants from the Maghreb Countries in the New Receiving States* (Hague: Kluwer Law International, 2002).

Ashiagbor D, Countouris N and Lianos I (eds), *The European Union after the Treaty of Lisbon* (Cambridge: Cambridge University Press 2012).

Askola H, '"Illegal Migrants", Gender and Vulnerability: The Case of the EU's Returns Directive' (2010) 18(2) *Feminist Legal Studies* 159-78.
Bakan A and Stasiulis DK, 'Making the Match: Domestic Placement Agencies and the Racialization of Women's Household Work' (1995) 20(2) *Signs: Journal of Women in Culture and Society* 303-35.
Baldaccini, A, Elspeth G and Toner H (eds), *Whose Freedom, Security and Justice? EU Immigration and Asylum Law and Policy* (Oxford/Portland: Hart, 2007).
Barnard C, *EU Employment Law* (Oxford: Oxford University Press, 2012).
Barone G and Mocetti S, 'With a Little Help from Abroad: The Effect of Low-skilled Immigration on the Female Labour Supply' (2011) 18(5) *Labour Economics* 664-75.
Baylos A and Pérez Rey J, *El despido o la violencia del poder privado* (Madrid: Trotta, 2009).
Beduschi A, 'An Empty Shell?' The Protection of Social Rights of TCN Workers in the EU after the Single Permit Directive (2015) 17(2-3) *European Journal of Migration and Law* 210-38.
Bell M, *Anti-Discrimination Law and the European Union* (Oxford: Oxford University Press, 2002).
Bellamy R and Warleigh A (eds) *Citizenship and Governance in the European Union* (London/New York: Continuum, 2001).
Benería L, 'The Crisis of Care, International Migration and Public Policy' (2008) 14(3) *Feminist Economics* 1-21.
Benería L, Deree CD and Kabeer N, 'Gender and International Migration: Globalization, Development and Governance' (2012) 18(2) *Feminist Economics* 1-33.
Berg L, *Migrant Rights at Work: Law's Precariousness at the Intersection of Migration and Labour* (Abingdon: Routledge, 2016).
Bettio F, Simonazzi A and Villa P, 'Change in Care Regimes and Female Migration: The "Care Drain" in the Mediterranean' 16(3) (2006) *Journal of European Social Policy* 271-85.
Blackett A, 'Making Domestic Work Visible: The Case for Specific Regulation' (Geneva: ILO, Labour Law and Labour Relations Programme Working Paper 2, 1998).
Blackett A, 'Introduction: Regulating Decent Work for Domestic Workers' (2011) 23(1) *Canadian Journal of Women and the Law* 1-45.
Blackett A, *Everyday Transgressions. Domestic Workers' Transnational Challenge to International Labor Law* (New York: Cornell University Press, 2019).
Blackett A and Sheppard C, 'Collective Bargaining and Equality: Making Connections' (2003) 142(4) *International Labour Review* 419-57.
Bogg, A 'Okedina v Chikale and Contract Illegality: New Dawn or False Dawn?' (2020) 49(2) *Industrial Law Journal*, 258-83.
Bogg A and Novitz T, 'Race Discrimination and the Doctrine of Illegality' (2013) 129 *Law Quarterly Review* 12-17.
Bogg A and Novitz T, *Voices at Work* (Oxford: Oxford University Press, 2014).
Bogusz B, Ski RC, Cygan, A and Szyszczak E (eds), *Irregular Migration and Human Rights: Theoretical, European and International Perspectives* (Leiden: Martinus Nijhoff Publishers, 2004).
Boris E and Nadasen P, 'Domestic Workers Organize!' (2008) 11 *The Journal of Labor and Society* 413-37.
Boris E and Fish JN, '"Slaves No More" Making Global Labor Standards for Domestic Workers' (2014) 40(2) *Feminist Studies* 411-43.
Borelli S, *Who Cares? Il lavoro nell ambitto ai servizi di cura alla persona* (Naples: Jovene Editore, 2020).
Busby N, *A Right to Care? Unpaid Work in European Employment Law* (Oxford: Oxford University Press, 2011).
Calleman C, 'Domestic Services in a "Land of Equality": The Case of Sweden' (2011) 23(1) *Canadian Journal of Women and the Law* 121-39.
Carlier JY and Guild E (eds), *The Future of Free Movement of Persons in the EU* (Brussels: Bruylant, 2006).
Carrera S and Wiesbrock A, 'Whose European Citizenship in the Stockholm Programme? The Enactment of Citizenship by Third-Country Nationals in the EU' (2010) 12 *European Journal of Migration and Law* 337-59.

Cerna L, 'Changes in Swedish Labour Immigration Policy: A Slight Revolution?' (Working Paper No 10, Stockholm: Stockholm University, 2009).
Cherubini D, Garofalo Geymonat G and Marchetti S, 'Global Rights and Local Struggles: The case of the ILO Convention N.189 on Domestic Work' (2018) 11(3) *The Open Journal of Sociopolitical Studies* 717–42.
Chuang J, 'The U.S. Au Pair Programme: Labor Exploitation and the Myth of Cultural Exchange' (2013) 36(2) *Harvard Journal of Law and Gender* 269–343.
Conaghan J and K Rittich (eds) *Labour Law, Work, and Family: Critical and Comparative Perspectives* (New York: Oxford University Press, 2005).
Costello C and Freedland M (eds) *Migrants at Work: Immigration and Vulnerability in Labour Law* (Oxford: Oxford University Press, 2014).
Cox R and Busch N, *Au Pairing after the Au Pair Scheme? New Migration Rules and Childcare in Private Homes in the UK* (London: Birbeck, University of London, 2014).
Cueva Puente MC, *La relación laboral de los empleados de hogar* (Valladolid: Lex Nova, 2005).
Dahlber KA, 'The EEC Commission and the Politics of Free Movement of Labour' (1968) 6 *Journal of Common Market Studies* 310–30.
Davies A, *EU Labour Law* (Cheltenham: Edward Elgar Publishing, 2012).
De Genova N, 'Migrant "Illegality" and Deportability in Everyday Life' (2003) 31 *Annual Review of Anthropology* 419–44.
Desdentado Daroca E, 'Las reformas de la regulación del trabajo doméstico por cuenta ajena en España' (2016) 7(1) *Revista de Investigaciones Feministas* 129–48.
Devetter FX and Rousseau S, 'The Impact of Industrialisation on Paid Domestic Work: The Case of France' (2009) 15(3) *European Journal of Industrial Relations* 297–316.
Düvell F, 'Paths into Irregularity: The Legal and Political Construction of Irregular Migration' (2011) 13 *European Journal of Migration and Law* 275–95.
Eisele K, *The External Dimension of the EU's Migration Policy. Different Legal Positions of Third-Country Nationals in the EU: A Comparative Perspective* (Leiden: Brill Nijhoff, 2014).
Esping-Andersen G, *Social Foundations of Post-Industrial Economies* (New York/Oxford, Oxford University Press, 1999).
Eurostat (2008) 'Ageing Characterizes the Demographic Perspectives of the European Societies', *Statistics in Focus* 72/2008.
European Network of Legal Experts in Gender Equality and Non-Discrimination. 'A Comparative Analysis of Gender Equality Law in Europe in 2019' (Luxembourg: Publications Office of the EU, 2020).
Ewing KD, 'The Function of Trade Unions' (2005) 34(1) *Industrial Law Journal* 1–22.
Fairwork 'The Gig Economy and Covid-19: Fairwork Report on Platform Policies' (Oxford, United Kingdom, 2020).
Fineman M, 'The Neutered Mother' (1992) 46(3) *University of Miami Law Review* 653.
Finkin M and Mundla G (eds), *Research Handbook in Comparative Labor Law* (Cheltenham, Northampton, MA: Edward Elgar Publishing, 2015).
Finotelli C and Arango J, 'Regularisation of Unauthorised Immigrants in Italy and Spain: Determinants and Effects' (2011) 57(3) *Documents d'Anàlisi Geogràfica* 495–515.
Fraser N, 'Contradictions of Capital and Care' (2016) 100 *New Left Review* 99–117.
Fredman S, 'Home from Home: Migrant Domestic Workers and the International Labour Organization Convention on Domestic Workers' in Costello C and Freedland M (eds) *Migrants at Work: Immigration and Vulnerability in Labour Law* (Oxford: Oxford University Press, 2014).
Freedland M and Kountouris N, *The Legal Construction of Personal Work Relations* (Oxford: Oxford University Press, 2011).
Fudge J, 'Global Care Chains, Employment Agencies and the Conundrum of Jurisdiction: Decent Work for Domestic Workers in Canada' (2011) 23(1) *Canadian Journal of Women and the Law* 235–64.
Fudge J, 'Precarious Migrant Status and Precarious Employment: The Paradox of International Rights for Migrant Workers' (2012) 34(1) *Comparative Labor Law and Policy Journal* 95–132.

Fudge J, 'Feminist Reflections on the Scope of Labour Law: Domestic Work, Social Reproduction and Jurisdiction' (2014) 22 *Feminist Legal Studies* 1–23.

Fudge J, 'Illegal Working, Migrants and Labour Exploitation in the UK' (2018) 38(3) *Oxford Journal of Legal Studies* 557–84.

Fudge J and Herzfeld Olsson P, 'The EU Seasonal Workers Directive: When Immigration Controls Meet Labour Rights' (2014) 16 *European Journal of Migration and Law* 439–66.

Fudge J and Hobden C, *Conceptualizing the Role of Intermediaries in Formalizing Domestic Work* (Geneva: International Labour Office, 2018).

Fudge J and Strauss K, 'Migrants, Unfree Labour and the Legal Construction of Domestic Servitude. Migrant Domestic Workers in the UK' in Costello C and Freedland M (eds), *Migrants at Work. Immigration and Vulnerability in Labour Law* (Oxford: OUP, 2014).

Fudge J, McCrystal S and Sankaran K (eds), *Challenging the Legal Boundaries of Work Regulation* (Oxford: Hart Oñati International Series in Law and Society, 2012).

Fundamental Rights Agency of the EU *Migrants in an Irregular Situation Employed in Domestic Work: Fundamental Rights Challenges for the European Union and its Member States* (Luxembourg: EU Publications Office, 2011).

Fundamental Rights Agency of the EU *Severe Labour Exploitation: Workers Moving Within or Into the European Union* (Luxembourg: Publications Office of the European Union, 2015).

Fundamental Rights Agency of the EU, Migrants in an Irregular Situation Employed in Domestic Work: Fundamental Rights Challenges for the European Union and its Member States (Luxembourg: EU Publications Office, 2011).

Gavanas A, 'Migrant Domestic Workers, Social Network Strategies and Informal Markets for Domestic Services in Sweden' (2013) 36 *Women's Studies International Forum* 54–62.

Gleeson S, 'Labor Rights for All? Undocumented Status and Worker Claims' (2010) 35(3) *Law and Social Inquiry* 561–602.

Gordon J, *Free Movement and Equal Rights for Low Wage Workers? What the United States Can Learn from the New EU Migration to Britain* (Fordham Law Legal Studies Research Paper, May 2011).

Goedings S, *Labor Migration in an Integrating Europe: National Migration Policies and the Free Movement of Workers, 1950–1968* (Hague: Sdu uitgevers, 2005).

Guild E and Harlow C (eds) *Implementing Amsterdam Immigration and Asylum Rights in EC Law* (Oxford: Hart Publishing, 2001).

Guild E, 'Equivocal Claims? Ambivalent Controls? Labour Migration Regimes in the European Union' (Nijmegen Migration Law Working Paper Series 2010/05, 2010).

Guild E, *The Legal Elements of European Identity: EU Citizenship and Migration Law* (Hague: Kluwer International, 2014).

Guild E and Minderhoud P (eds), *The First Decade of EU Migration and Asylum Law* (Leiden: Nijhoff Publishers, 2012).

Gumbrell-McCormick R, 'European Trade Unions and "Atypical" Workers' (2011) 42(3) *Industrial Relations Journal* 293–310.

Hadjigeorgiou N and Commissioner for the Administration and the Protection of Human Rights, 'Report on the Status of Foreign Domestic Workers in Cyprus' (Nicosia, 18 December 2020).

Halliday S and Morgan B, 'I Fought the Law and the Law Won? Legal Consciousness and the Critical Imagination' (2013) 66 *Current Legal Problems* 1–33.

Hayes LJB, *Stories of Care: A Labour of Law: Gender and Class at Work* (London: Palgrave, 2017).

Helbling M and Kriesi H, 'Why Citizens Prefer High- Over Low-Skilled Immigrants: Labor Market Competition, Welfare State, and Deservingness' (2014) 30(5) *European Sociological Review* 595–614.

Hoerder D, van Nederveen Meerkerk E and Neusinger S (eds) *Towards a Global History of Domestic and Caregiving Workers* (Leiden: Brill, 2015).

Howe J and Owens R (eds) *Temporary Labour Migration in the Global Era* (Oxford: Hart Publishing, 2016).

Hunt J 'Making the CAP Fit: Responding to the Exploitation of Migrant Agricultural Workers in the EU' (2014) 30 *International Journal of Comparative Labour Law and Industrial Relations* 131–52.

Hutton W and Giddens A (eds) *On the Edge: Living with Global Capitalism* (London: Jonathan Cape, 2000).
International Labour Organization, Preventing Discrimination, Exploitation and Abuse of Migrant Workers (Geneva, 2003).
International Labour Organization, Decent Work for Domestic Workers, Report no IV at the International Labour Conference, 99th Session, 2010 (Geneva, 2009).
International Labour Organization, Domestic Workers across the World: Global and Regional Statistics and the Extent of Legal Protection (Geneva, 2013).
International Labour Organization, ILO Global Estimates on Migrant Workers. Special Focus on Migrant Domestic Workers (Geneva, 2015).
Inghammar A, 'The Employment Contract Revisited. Undocumented Migrant Workers and the Intersection between International Standards, Immigration Policy and Employment Law' (2010) 12 *European Journal of Migration and the Law* 193-214.
Jiang Z and Korczynski M, 'When the "Unorganizable" Organize: The Collective Mobilization of Migrant Domestic Workers in London' (2016) 69(3) *Human Relations* 813-38.
Kierans D and Sumption M, 'Work Visas and Migrant Workers in the UK' Migration Observatory briefing (COMPAS, University of Oxford, 2020).
Klare K, 'The Public/Private Distinction in Labor Law' (1983) 130(6) *University of Pennsylvania Law Review* 1358-422.
Korczynski M, 'Communities of Coping: Collective Emotional Labour in Service Work' (2003) 10(1) *Organisation* 55-79.
Kubal A, 'Conceptualizing Semi-Legality in Migration Research' (2013) 47(3) *Law & Society Review* 555-87.
Kvist L (ed), *Global Care Work Gender and Migration in Nordic Societies* (Lund: Nordic Academic Press, 2010).
Kvist E and Peterson E, 'What Has Gender Equality Got to Do with It? An Analysis of Policy Debates Surrounding Domestic Services in the Welfare States of Spain and Sweden' (2010) 18(3) *Nordic Journal of Feminist and Gender Research* 185-203.
Lane L and Jordansson B, 'How Gender Equal is Sweden? An Analysis of the Shift in Focus under Neoliberalism' (2020) 50(1) *Social Change* 28-43.
León M, 'Migration and Care Work in Spain: The Domestic Sector Revisited' (2010) 9(3) *Social Policy and Society* 409-18.
León M, 'A Real Job? Regulating Household Work: The Case of Spain' (2013) 20(2) *European Journal of Women's Studies* 170-88.
Lewis S, Anderson D, Lyonette C, Payne N and Wood S (eds) *Work-life Balance in Times of Recession, Austerity and Beyond* (New York: Routledge, 2017).
López Gandía J and Toscani Giménez D, *El nuevo régimen laboral y de seguridad social de los trabajadores al servicio del hogar familiar* (Albacete: Editorial Bomarzo, 2012).
Lutz H, *The New Maids: Transnational Women and the Care Economy* (London, Zed Books, 2011).
Lutz H (ed), *Migration and Domestic Work: a European Perspective on a Global Theme* (Farnham: Ashgate, 2008).
Lyberaki A, 'Dea ex Machina: Migrant Women, Care Work and Women's Employment in Greece' (London School of Economics, Hellenic Observatory Papers, 2008).
Mantouvalou V, 'Servitude and Forced Labour in the 21st Century: The Human Rights of Domestic Workers' (2006) 35(4) *Industrial Law Journal* 395-414.
Mantouvalou V, 'Human Rights for Precarious Workers: The Legislative Precariousness of Domestic Labour' (2012) 34 *Comparative Labor Law & Policy Journal* 133-65.
Mantouvalou V, '"Am I Free Now?" Overseas Domestic Workers in Slavery' (2015) 42(3) *Journal of Law and Society* 329-57.
Mantouvalou V and Albin E, 'Active Industrial Citizenship of Domestic Workers: Lessons Learned from Unionising Attempts in Israel and the United Kingdom' (2016) 17(1) *Theoretical Inquiries in Law* 321-50.

Marchetti S, 'Dreaming Circularity?: Eastern European Women and Job-sharing in Paid Home Care' (2013) 11(4) *Journal of Immigrant and Refugee Studies* 347–63.

McCann D, 'New Frontiers of Regulation: Domestic Work, Working Conditions and the Holistic Assessment of Nonstandard Work Norms' (2012) 34 *Comparative Labor Law & Policy Journal* 167–84.

Medici G and Blackett A, 'Ratification as International Solidarity. Reflections on Switzerland and Decent Work for Domestic Work' (2015–2016) 31 *Connecticut Journal of International Law* 187–215.

Miñarro YM, 'La nueva regulación de la relación laboral de carácter especial del servicio de hogar familiar: una mejora mejorable I y II' (2012) 4 *Relaciones Laborales* 49–60.

Miñarro YM, *El trabajo al servicio del hogar familiar: análisis de su nueva regulación* (Madrid: Editorial Reus, 2013).

Misra J, Woodring J and Merz S, 'The Globalization of Care Work: Neoliberal Economic Restructuring and Migration Policy' (2006) 3(3) *Globalizations* 317–32.

Monereo Pérez JL (ed), *Protección jurídico-social de los trabajadores extranjeros* (Granada: Comares, 2010).

Morel N, *The Political Economy of Domestic Work in France and Sweden in a European Perspective* (LIEPP Working Paper, 2012).

Mullally S and Murphy C, 'Migrant Domestic Workers in the UK: Enacting Exemptions, Exclusions, and Rights' (2014) 36 *Human Rights Quarterly* 397–29.

Müller T and Vandele KWJ, *Collective Bargaining in Europe: Towards an Endgame* (Brussels: European Trade Union Institute, 2019).Mundlak G and Shamir H, 'Bringing Together or Drifting Apart? Targeting Domestic Work as "Work Like No Other"' (2011) 23 *Canadian Journal of Women and the Law* 289. Mundlak G and Shamir H, 'Organising Migrant Care Workers in Israel: Industrial Citizenship and the Trade Union Option' (2014) 153(1) *International Labour Review* 93–116.

Murphy C, 'The Enduring Vulnerability of Migrant Domestic Workers in Europe' (2013) 62 *International and Comparative Law Quarterly* 599–627.

Nando S, '"I Have Too Much Baggage": The Impacts of Legal Status on the Social Worlds of Irregular Migrants'' (2012) 20(1) *Social Anthropology* 50–65.

Naumann E, Stoetzer L and Pietrantuono G, 'Attitudes Towards Highly Skilled and Low-skilled Immigration in Europe: A Survey Experiment in 15 European Countries' (2018) 57 *European Journal of Political Research* 1009–30.

Novitz T and Syrpis P, 'The Place of Domestic Work in Europe: An Analysis of Current Policy in the Light of the Council Decision Authorising Member States to Ratify ILO Convention No 189' (2015) 6(2) *European Labour Law Journal* 104–27.

Nussbaum M, *Sex and Social Justice* (New York/Oxford: Oxford University Press, 1999).

OECD, *Recruiting Immigrant Workers: Sweden 2011* (OECD Publishing).

Oelz M, 'The ILO's Domestic Workers Convention and Recommendation: A Window of Opportunity for Social Justice' (2014) 153(1) *International Labour Review* 143–72.

Office of the Ombudsman, 'Report of the Ombudsman as Equality Body in relation to a Complaint on Restrictions of the Freedom of Association of Migrant Domestic Workers Complaint No 2/2005' (Nicosia, 2005).

Office of the Ombudsman, 'Report against Social Welfare Services in relation to the Handling of Public Fund Claims by Pregnant Migrant Women' (Nicosia: 29 December 2009).

Office of the Ombudsman, 'Report on the Procedure of Labour Dispute Settlement between Migrant Workers and their Employers' (Nicosia: 12 March 2010).

Office of the Ombudsman, 'Report of the Ombudsman as National Independent Human Rights Authority as Regards the Status of Domestic Workers in Cyprus' (Nicosia: 2 July 2013).

Palmer V, Mattar M and Koppel A (eds) *Mixed Legal Systems, East and West* (Farnham: Ashgate, 2015).

Parreñas R, *Children of Global Migration* (Stanford: Stanford University Press, 2005).

Pavlou V, 'Domestic Work in EU Law: The Relevance of EU Employment Law in Challenging Domestic Workers' Vulnerability' (2016) 41(3) *European Law Review* 379–98.

Pavlou V, 'Migrant Domestic Labour and Models of Immigration and Employment Law Regulation: A Comparative Perspective of Cyprus and Spain' (2016) 7(1) *Revista de Investigaciones Feministas* 149–68.

Pavlou V, 'Where to Look for Change? A Critique of the Use of Modern Slavery and Trafficking Frameworks in the Fight against Migrant Domestic Workers' Vulnerability' (2018) 20(1) *European Journal of Migration and Law* 83–107.
Pavlou V, 'Whose Equality? Paid Domestic Work and EU Gender Equality Law' (2020) 1 *European Equality Law Review* 36–46.
Peers S, 'Towards Equality: Actual and Potential Rights of Third-Country Nationals in the European Union' (1996) 33 *Common Market Law Review* 7–50.
Peers S, 'Legislative Update: EC Immigration and Asylum Law Attracting and Deterring Labour Migration: The Blue Card and Employer Sanctions Directive' (2009) 11 *European Journal of Migration and Law* 387–426.
Peers S, 'The Court of Justice Lays the Foundation for the Long-Term Residents Directive: Kambaraj, Commission v Netherlands, Mangat Singh' (2013) 50 *Common Market Law Review* 529–52.
Peers S and Rogers, N, *EU Immigration and Asylum Law* (Leiden: Nijhoff Publishers, 2012).
Queiroz BM, *Illegally Staying in the EU. An Analysis of Illegality in EU Migration Law* (Oxford: Hart Publishing, 2018).
Ragnhild AS (ed), *Transnational Migration, Gender and Rights* (Bradford: Emerald Publishing, 2012).
Ricci G, 'Tutela della salute e orario di lavoro' in Sciarra S (ed), *Manuale di Diritto Sociale Europeo* (Torino: G. Giappichelli Editore, 2010).
Riesenhuber K, *European Employment Law. A Systematic Exposition* (Cambridge: Intersentia, 2012).
Roberts DE, 'Spiritual and Menial Housework' (1997) 9 *Yale Journal of Law and Feminism* 51–80.
Robin-Olivier S, 'The Community Preference Principle in Labour Migration Policy in the European Union', *OECD Social, Employment and Migration Working Papers* No 182 (Paris: OECD Publishing, 2016).
Robinson MH, 'An Overview of Recent Legal Developments at Community Level in Relation to Third-Country Nationals Resident within the European Union, with particular reference to the Case Law of the European Court of Justice' (2001) 38 *Common Market Law Review* 525–86.
Rodríguez Fernández ML, 'Efectos de la crisis económica sobre el trabajo de las mujeres' (2014) 1 *Relaciones Laborales* 69–83.
Rönmar M, 'Sweden' in Freedland M and Jeremias P (eds) *Viking, Laval and Beyond* (Oxford: Hart Publishing, 2014) 241–61.
Ruhs M, *The Price of Rights: Regulating International Labour Migration* (Princeton, Princeton University Press, 2013).
Rubio Marín R (ed) *Human Rights and Immigration* (Oxford, Oxford University Press, 2014).
Ryan B, 'The Evolving Legal Regime on Unauthorized Work by Migrants in Britain' (2005–6) 27 *Comparative Labor Law & Policy* 27–58.
Scheiwe K, *Domestic Workers, EU Working Time Law and Implementation Deficits in National Law – Change in Sight?* (Florence, EUI Law Working Paper 2021/03, 2021).
Selberg N, 'The Laws of "Illegal" Work and Dilemmas in Interest Representation on Segmented Labor Markets: À Propos Irregular Migrants in Sweden' (2014) 35 *Comparative Labor Law & Policy Journal* 247–88.
Shamir H, 'What's the Border Got to Do With It? How Immigration Regimes affect Familial Care Provision – A Comparative Analysis' (2011) 19(2) *American University Journal of Gender Social Policy and Law* 601–69.
Simpson B, 'Implementing the National Minimum Wage: The 1999 Regulations' (1999) 28 *Industrial Law Journal* 171–82.
Sollund R, 'Regarding Au Pairs in the Norwegian Welfare State' (2010) 17(2) *European Journal of Women's Studies* 143–60.
Stein E (ed), *Regulating Transnational Labour in Europe: The Quandaries of Multilevel Governance* (Oslo, University of Oslo, 2014).
Stenum H, *Au Pairs in Denmark: Cheap Labour or Cultural Exchange* (Copenhagen: FOA- Trade and Labour, 2008).
Stenum H, *Abused Domestic Workers in Europe: The Case of Au Pairs* (Brussels: European Parliament, 2011).

Supiot A, *Beyond Employment. Changes in Work and the Future of Labour Law in Europe* (Oxford, Oxford University Press, 2001).
Theobald H, 'Care Workers with Migrant Backgrounds in Formal Care Services in Germany: A Multi-level Intersectional Analysis' (2017) 1(2) *International Journal of Care and Caring* 209–26.
Thym D and Zoeteweij-Turhan M (eds) *Right of Third-Country National under EU Association Agreements. Degrees of Free Movement and Citizenship* (Leiden/Boston: Brill, 2015).
Triandafyllidou A (ed), *Irregular Migrant Domestic Workers in Europe: Who Cares?* (Farnham: Ashgate, 2013).
Triandafyllidou A and Marchetti S, 'Europe 2020: Addressing Low Skill Labour Migration at times of Fragile Recovery' Policy Paper 2014/05 (Robert Schuman Centre for Advanced Studies, Global Governance Programme, 2014).
Triandafyllidou A and Marchetti S, *Employers, Agencies and Immigration: Paying for Care* (Abingdon: Routledge, 2015).
Trimikliniotis N and Demetriou C, 'Labour Integration of Migrant Workers in Cyprus: A Critical Appraisal' in Pajnik, M (ed), *Precarious Migrant Labour Across Europe* (Ljubljana: Mirovni Institut, 2011) 73–96.
Van Walsum S, 'Regulating Migrant Domestic Work in the Netherlands: Opportunities and Pitfalls' (2011) 23(1) *Canadian Journal of Women and the Law* 141–65.
Van Walsum S and Spijkerboer T (eds) *Women and Immigration Law New Variations on Classical Feminist Themes* (New York: Routledge, 2007).
Vosko L, *Precarious Employment: Understanding Labor Market Insecurity* (McGill-Queen's University Press, 2006).
Vosko L, 'Tenuously Unionised: Temporary Migrant Workers and the Limits of Formal Mechanisms Designed to Promote Collective Bargaining in British Columbia' (2014) 43(4) *Industrial Law Journal* 451–84.
Wall K and Nunes C, 'Immigration, Welfare and Care in Portugal: Mapping the New Plurality of Female Migration Trajectories' (2010) 9(3) *Social Policy and Society* 397–408.
Weicht B, 'Embodying the Ideal Carer: The Austrian Discourse on Migrant Carers' (2010) 5(2) *International Journal of Ageing and Later Life* 17–52.
Woodring J and Merz S, 'The Globalization of Care Work: Neoliberal Economic Restructuring and Migration Policy' (2006) 3(3) *Globalizations* 317–32.
Woolfson CA, Fudge J and Thornqvist C, 'Migrant Precarity and Future Challenges to Labour Standards in Sweden' (2013) 35(4) *Economic and Industrial Democracy* 1–21.
Zbyszewska A, *Gendering European Working Time Regimes: The Working Time Directive and the Case of Poland* (Cambridge: Cambridge University Press, 2016).

INDEX

atypical work
　EU labour law　113
au pair　29–30, 42–3

Barnard, C　111
Blackett, A　6, 7, 10, 57, 62, 130
blue card (EU)　88–9
Bot, Advocate General　97–8, 116

'care resource extraction'　2
change of employers, restrictions on　26–7
changing the institutional setting of domestic work　148–9, 154
　Spain　141
　Sweden　135–9
　　private companies offering domestic services　137, 138
　　tax reforms　135–6, 137, 138
　　trade unions　138, 139
collective organisation　132–5, 154
　civil society organisations　134, 135, 141, 142, 150
　community-based associations　134, 135, 148
　non-governmental organisations　134, 145, 150
　trade unions　133, 134, 135, 149, 150, 154
　workers' rights centres　134, 141, 148
　see also **Cyprus; United Kingdom**
'communities of coping'　135
criminal liability
　illegal migrant working　65–7
Cyprus
　collective organisation, lack of　142, 143, 144, 145
　　nationality-based associations　144
　　non-governmental organisations　145
　　reduction of wages　144–5
　　trade unions' indifference　144
　complaints from migrant workers　55, 56
　family reunification　99
　highly skilled migrants　94
　illegal migrant working
　　criminal liability　66
　　workers' rights under labour law　70–71

　information on terms and conditions of work　125
　labour law regime　52–7
　long-term residence　98
　migration law regime　34–6, 47
　model contract of employment　52, 53, 54
　Ombudsman, role of　145–6
　public debate　142
　'very special vulnerability'　52–7, 75–6
　wages　56–7
　working time　54–5, 127–8

Davies, A　109
Denmark
　au pair migration　43
dismissal
　Spain　63–4

employer-led / mixed treatment migration regime　30, 36–9, 44
employer's insolvency
　EU labour law　112–13
EU labour law　105, 106, 130, 153
　compliance with EU labour law　153
　personal scope of EU labour law
　　sources　107, 117, 153
　　atypical work　113
　　employer's insolvency　112–13
　　free movement of workers　107, 108
　　gender equality law　107, 108
　　health and safety　109–11
　　illegal migrant working　115–17
　　pregnant workers　111
　　transparent and predictable working conditions　114–15
　　work / life balance　115
　　working time　111, 112
　substance of protections and entitlements　117
　　information on terms and conditions of work　117–18
　　national labour law regimes, and　124–30, 153
　　pregnancy and maternity rights　118–21
　　working time　121–4

EU migration law 77, 152–3
  association and cooperation agreements
    EFTA countries 84–5
    Maghreb nationals 86
    Turkish workers 85–6
  family reunification
    non-EU nationals 99–100
  fragmentation 92, 93, 94, 103–4, 152
  freedom of movement for workers 80–82
  hierarchy of migrant statuses 92, 93, 94, 103–4, 152
  illegal migrant working 100–103
    complaints against employers 102, 103
    legal proceedings against employers 102, 103
    wages 102
  legal sources
    association and cooperation agreements 78
    free movement of workers 77–8, 80–84
    treatment of non-EU workers 78–9, 86–92
  long-term residence 95–9
  non-EU workers
    harmonisation, attempts at 86–7
    highly skilled workers 88–9
    intra-corporate transferees 89
    seasonal workers 89–91
    sectoral approach 87, 88
    single permit for TCN workers 91–2
  sectoral labour migration directive on domestic workers
    proposal for 152–153
  transitional citizenship 78, 82–4

familialism 31–32
family reunification 99–100
feminisation of migration 1
  global inequalities 4
freedom of movement for workers 77–8, 80–82, 107, 108

gender and human rights scholars 7
gender equality law 107–108
global and regional statistics on domestic workers 13–14
'global care chains' 2

Hayes, L 5
health and safety at work
  EU labour law 109–11
  'dignitarian understanding' (of health and safety) 109

National labour law regimes
  Spain 64
  UK 48
Herzfeld Olsson, P. 87
hierarchy of migrant statuses
  EU migration law 92–4, 103–4, 152
highly skilled workers
  non-EU nationals 88–9

illegal migrant working
  criminal liability, and 65–7
  EU labour law 115–17
  EU migration law 100–103
    complaints against employers 102–103
    legal proceedings against employers 102, 103
    wages 102
  migrant illegality and deportability 24–6
  workers' rights under labour law 65, 67–8
    Cyprus 70–71
    Spain 69–70
    Sweden 68–9
    UK 71–5
ILO
  Convention 189 (decent work for domestic workers) 9–12
    combination of a sectoral approach with equality of treatment 10, 11
    impact of 150
    ratification of 12, 13, 48, 139, 148
    worker-enabling approach 11–12
  domestic workers' inclusion in the scope of most ILO Conventions 10
  Recommendation 201 9
  resolutions on the conditions of employment in domestic work 9–10
information on terms and conditions of work 117–18, 124–5
intermediaries, reliance on 27–8
intra-corporate transferees
  non-EU nationals 89

Justice for Domestic Workers (J4DW) 135, 148

Kalayaan 148
Kommunal 138–9, 149–50

labour law regimes 46, 47
  'work like any other' approach 10, 47, 76, 152
  'work like no other' approach 10, 47, 76, 152
  see also Cyprus; EU labour law; illegal migrant working; Spain; Sweden; United Kingdom

Index

labour market participation
  women 3
'law of the household workplace' 6–7
live-in employment 28–9
long-term residence 95–9

Marchetti, S. 12, 152
marketisation of care 3
McCann, D 111
'menial work' 6
migration law regimes 23, 31, 43, 45, 151–152
  au pair schemes 29–30
  contributing to vulnerability to exploitation 6, 22, 24, 45, 151–2
  employer-led / mixed treatment regime 30, 36–9, 44
  live-in employment 28–9
  migrant illegality and deportability 24–6
  open entry / restrictive treatment regime 30, 34–6, 44
  regulated entry / liberal treatment regime 30, 31–3, 43–4
  reliance on intermediaries 27–8
  restrictions on sectoral mobility 27
  restrictions on the right to change employers 26–7
  restrictive regime 30–31, 39, 44–5
    au pair scheme as the only available lawful entry route 42–3
    facilitated labour market access for transitional EU citizens 41–2
    selective migration policies 39–41
  see also EU migration law
modern slavery and human trafficking 7–8, 147–148
Mundlak, G 133, 134

nationality-based associations 144
Netherlands
  migration law regime 41, 42
non-governmental organisations (NGOs) 134, 145, 150
normalisation of migrant domestic workers' exploitation 9
Norway
  au pair 42–3
Novitz, T 121
numbers of migrant domestic workers
  demand and supply factors 2–4
Nussbaum, M 5

on-call time see working time
open entry / restrictive treatment migration regime 30, 34–6, 44

personal autonomy
  labour law regimes
    Spain 63
pregnancy and maternity rights 111, 118–21, 125–7

regulated entry / liberal treatment migration regime 30, 31–3, 43–4
restrictive regime 30–31, 39, 44–5
  au pair scheme as the only available lawful entry route 42–3
  facilitated labour market access for transitional EU citizens 41–2
  selective migration policies 39–41

seasonal workers
  non-EU nationals 89–91
sectoral mobility, restrictions on 27
selective migration policies 39–41
Shamir, H. 133, 134
social context 143
social dumping 154
'social location' 143
social reproduction crisis 3–4, 6, 154
'social stigma' 5
societal and economic role of migrant domestic workers 1
Spain
  EU labour law, and
    information on terms and conditions of work 125
    working time 129
  family reunification 99
  illegal migrant working
    criminal liability 67
    workers' rights under labour law 69–70
  labour law regime 47
  migrant domestic workers 17
  migration law regime 47
  reforming labour legislation on domestic work 139–42
    civil society organisations, participation of 141, 142
    institutional setting of domestic work 141
    integration of domestic workers into the social security system 139, 140
    trade unions, cooperation of 140, 141, 142

substance of labour law protections and entitlements
  dismissal 63-4
  health and safety 64
  personal autonomy 63
  separate regime, but near-normal protection 60-64, 76
  wages 61-2
  working time 62-3
'spiritual work' 6
Supiot, A 62
sustainable working conditions 154
Sweden
  change of institutional setting of domestic work 135-9
    private companies offering domestic services 137, 138
    tax reforms 135-6, 137, 138
    trade unions 138, 139
  EU labour law, and
    information on terms and conditions of work 124-5
    working time 128-9
  family reunification 99
  illegal migrant working
    criminal liability 67
    workers' rights under labour law 68-9
  labour law regime 47
  migrant domestic workers 17-18
  migration law regime 36-9, 47
  ratification of ILO C.189 139
  substance of labour law protections and entitlements
    collective agreements and trade unions 58-9, 60
    'double exclusion' 57-60, 76
    working time 57-8

trade unions 133-135, 138-142, 144, 149-150, 154
transitional citizenship 78, 82-4
transparent and predictable working conditions (EU Directive) 114-15

United Kingdom (UK)
collective organisation
  barriers to 146-7
  community-based associations 148
  workers' rights centres 148
EU labour law, and
  information on terms and conditions of work 125
  working time 127
'fight against modern slavery' 147-148
illegal migrant working 103
  criminal liability 65-6
  workers' rights under labour law 71-5
labour law regime 47, 48
migrant domestic workers 18
migration law regime 40, 41, 47
substance of labour law protections and entitlements
  formally normal protection but with key exceptions 48-52, 75, 76
  health and safety at work 48
  minimum wage 49-51
  working time 48-9

Vosko, L 143
vulnerability to exploitation 4-6

wages
illegal migrant working
  EU migration law 102
labour law regimes
  Cyprus 56-7
  Spain 61-2
  UK 49-51
work / life balance
  EU labour law 115
workers' rights centres 134, 141, 148
working time
  EU labour law, and 111, 112, 121-4, 127-30
  national labour law regimes
    Cyprus 54-5
    Spain 62-3
    Sweden 57-8
    UK 48-9

Printed in the USA
CPSIA information can be obtained
at www.ICGtesting.com
LVHW021534191023
761572LV00005B/302